ILLEGAL

AMONG

US

A STATELESS WOMAN'S QUEST FOR CITIZENSHIP

MARTINE M. KALAW

SUNBURY
PRESS

Mechanicsburg, PA USA

Published by Sunbury Press, Inc.
Mechanicsburg, Pennsylvania

www.sunburypress.com

For information about special discounts for bulk purchases, please contact Sunbury Press Orders Dept. at (855) 338-8359 or orders@sunburypress.com.

To request one of our authors for speaking engagements or book signings, please contact Sunbury Press Publicity Dept. at publicity@sunburypress.com.

ISBN: 978-1-62006-088-9 (Trade paperback)

Library of Congress Control Number: 2018962530

FIRST SUNBURY PRESS EDITION: November 2018

Product of the United States of America
0 1 1 2 3 5 8 13 21 34 55

Set in Bookman Old Style
Designed by Crystal Devine
Cover by Riaan Wilmans
Edited by Janice Rhayem

Continue the Enlightenment!

This memoir is a work of nonfiction. The experiences, dialogues, locations, and timeline are factual. All names of characters have been altered, except for the names of public figures, my mother, and biological father, in order to protect individuals' privacy.

To Mutoto, who made this journey possible.

CONTENTS

ACKNOWLEDGMENTS

My journey to citizenship and reaching home has presented itself as a complex jigsaw puzzle that I could not have completed on my own. Saint Anne's-Belfield, Hamilton College, and the Maxwell School community played pivotal roles in connecting the pieces. "Noor" and "Celeste," thank you for your sisterhood. "Celeste," you traipsed to all ends of the earth for me and acted as my backbone. "Noor," you have consistently cheered me on and believed in me since we were roommates in boarding school. Thank you, Josh, Calin, and Obio, for joining me early in my journey and staying the course. "Judge Wells" and "Tiffany Wells," I am greatly indebted to you for seeing my potential before I saw it in myself. Marva Redmond, wherever you are, I owe you my life. "Señora Castillo" and Sallie, thank you for nurturing each step of this process. Javed Rezayee, the hours you spent editing my book from a stream of consciousness to a real page-turner are much appreciated. James D. O'Connor, how can I forget the many months you spent editing my very first manuscript, before the entire story had unfolded? Thank you, Manal, for your wisdom, creative input, and for our lengthy chats.

I would be remiss not to thank Janice Rhayem for caring so much about the quality of this story. Denise, thank you for all the hours you put into my project. Thank you to Lawrence Knorr for recognizing the potential of this story. A special thanks to my dad, Joseph Kayembe Kanga Moy, for his unconditional love . . .

Thank you to the individuals who believed in my book before it was published. Please see a list of your names in the final pages of the book.

demons and highest highs can present themselves casually before the waiter even drops menus.

"I want to go to Zambia and meet my father," Martine says.

Cool. I'm coming with you, I said to myself while eyeing the platter of moules y frites between us. My darling, fashionable, super-intelligent friend had limited travel experience as a result of her questionable immigration status. She had a taste for the finer things. It only made sense for me to accompany her journey as a sounding board and guide if anything got gritty.

The conversation continued. It twisted and turned from life dramas to jobs, from love interests to news of mutual friends and old teachers while I sat distracted, daydreaming of Martine reconnecting with her long-lost father. We had just barely had time to soak in her news of receiving her green card after an arduous and tortuous road. Martine's immigration battle was a beast. Her experience with the immigration courts and their treatment of her status was terribly complicated and layered. It was exhausting to even try to understand the intricacies of her case as a friend, and I couldn't imagine what she felt going through that. Her mother brought her to the States as a young child from Zambia. At fifteen, Martine was an orphan in a country that didn't claim her and sent to live with an extended family that was far from pleasant. Per policy since her status was "complicated" she was at risk of being deported, which seemed so radical, considering she only knew the United States to be home. Due to life's circumstances, and distance across the continent from her, I felt far away and less involved with supporting her during her immigration struggles. That could not happen with her search for her father.

And that's how we came to be two "American" girls, many shades of brown between us, carefully stepping over a questionable trickle glimmering between makeshift structures in a market on the non-touristy side of Lusaka. One of us feeling comfortable navigating through the unfamiliar smells and clamor, while the other winces at the acrid air, still woozy from the previous week's events of incredible discovery. Where is home when you feel foreign in your country of birth and at home in a place you (until recently) didn't "belong"? What if you fought forever to fend for yourself because you were all you had, only to realize there was a greater story, a greater journey to behold? What if you were an orphan, an only child one day, and the next surrounded by twenty-one siblings and a plethora of aunties, nieces, nephews, and a father whom you thought had not existed until one fateful ping in your inbox?

Martine's account of her spectacular struggle with the United States immigration courts as a youth into adulthood and her journey back to her country of birth thirty years later is a tale that highlights multiple layers of luck, misfortune, surprising humanity, love, humiliation, discrimination, and (baby powdery) celebration. I applaud her courage and tenacity as she searches for her identity and worth. She chronicles her family's love and abuse, a lengthy immigration battle, inspiring, helpful outsiders, and unexpected discoveries. Her story is a great lesson in not making judgment calls on others, no matter what you imagine their ethnicity, backstory, or experience to be.

We all come from somewhere and carry our own stories along with our families' stories. We are here now in this experience learning from and living with each other. Were each color a musical note, it would be a rather boring song to keep playing the same note on repeat. Rather, lets mix up the tempo and make something worth dancing to together.

— Celeste

PROLOGUE

I was subhuman. The grime you carry under your shoes after trudging through streets. At least, that's what *they* meant when they referred to me as an illegal alien. *They* being the immigration court and the judge who loathed me and I him. And *she* referred to me as a nobody. My mother. She was my lifeline and verification that I was a person. When she died, so did my identity—and all I was left with were unanswered questions amplified in a courtroom. Was my name really Martine? Where did I come from? Who were my mother and father?

Eleven years undocumented. Seven years in deportation procedures. My legal nightmare was cunning; while I thought I was battling the judge, I was also pitted against my mother, and sometimes my own attorney would attack me.

Life had become a twisted game of Russian Roulette. Oftentimes, it wasn't me but my opponent who'd place the muzzle against my head. *Click.* No bang. Every time that trigger was pulled, I was sure that was it. Life was over. But again, *click!* No bang. *Click!* No bang. I kept waiting for the trigger to go off, and at one point, I wished the damned thing went off already. *Sssss! Ssss!* of the cylinder spinning went on for years, replacing self-love with self-defense and cold laughter to drown out that whirring noise.

But one day LinkedIn delivered a countershock to my misery, reviving the connection between my dead father and me like a defibrillator awakening a nonbeating heart. He sought me while I searched for my identity, which plunged me into the depths of Africa. He gave me access to a part of my mother I needed to become complete. Rather than an expedition, this was an exorcism of the past, conjuring up the ghosts of my parents from their youth.

What I would encounter in this reunion in Africa would be unimaginable, leaving me changed, but silencing the trigger. This time forever. The heaviness of my history no longer defined me or outweighed the serendipities sprinkled throughout my life, making it easier to go back home, to America.

CHAPTER 1

MOULES ET FRITES AND THE B WORD

His voice was the texture of velvet.
It wasn't just any velvet; it was black velvet.

I. BETRAYAL

When I buried my mother, I had also buried my memories of her mistreatment to honor her. But one day in a law office in the once-famous Statler Towers in Buffalo, New York, I was asked by my attorney to betray her in order to win my freedom in the Land of the Free.

How audacious of him to even suggest.

This immigration hearing needed to be the final because I was running out of stamina and coping mechanisms. Just how long could I maintain the charade of being a normal American girl? John James, my pro-bono lawyer, had assured me that everything would go smoothly, as the August 9, 2004, date approached. Today's appointment was an actual hearing, rather than a Master Calendar appointment. It meant that I would be able to testify and present witnesses on my behalf.

"Why don't you come into my office for a second," John James commanded the morning of my hearing, interrupting my reverie.

"What's wrong?"

"In my office."

I went.

I knew John well enough by now to distinguish between his condescension and concern. He had a plane face, which offered him little distinction. The kind of face that you could look at for hours but you wouldn't be able to confirm in a police lineup. His baldness was the only thing that stood out. I could imagine running into this man, who had control over my life, ten years later in the street and trying to figure out where I knew him from.

"Listen," he said, sitting at the edge of his desk almost hovering over me as my sweaty palms clasped each corner of my chair. "Nothing is wrong. You alluded to the fact that your mom was abusive to you. Did she ever hit you?"

My eyes widened, and a sudden panic rushed over me. Please don't let this conversation go where I think it was headed. He may have asked a follow-up question but my mind was elsewhere. I noticed how plain John's office was for a lawyer, and I wondered if it was because he didn't make enough money as a pro-bono attorney. Shouldn't he have had photos of Supreme Court judges on his wall or something? He had a scattering of law books, but I expected to see more of them. At least his desk was covered in paperwork like all the lawyers I had seen on television. The carpeting should have been nicer but instead it was dingy.

I couldn't lie to my lawyer, so I confessed. "Yeah," I said with my head hung low and tears streaming down my face as if I had just plead guilty, awaiting my sentencing. Ya Marie didn't just hit me, she used to beat the shit out of me, but I wanted to remain mild in my accusation so I wouldn't share any more detail. If John dug further, should I also talk about my mother's verbal assault that pushed me to the brink of death? No, I couldn't. This wasn't how today was supposed to play out, this entire case was supposed to be built against my Aunty Amelie, and not my mom.

My mom's real name was Marie-Louise, which sounds better in French, my mom's native language. Most Americans just called her Louise. The "Ya" is like a prefix that means "Sister." It is used as a sign of respect when speaking to an older sister. I must have heard her sisters referring to her as Ya Marie when I was a toddler and started to do the same. I never referred to her as mom in all the years that she was alive.

Before this hearing, John had submitted a petition to adjust my status based on two statutes: 1. *Nunc Pro Tunc*, translated from Latin as *Now for Then*, which means a ruling is made based on an earlier law and has retroactive legal effect. Unbeknownst to me, I had a window of time where I was eligible to petition for permanent resident status (green card) after Ya Marie had died. Since the government failed to inform me of my rights, we argued that the government was at fault. Also, since immigration laws changed after 9/11, John argued that I should be treated under the old law—hence, *Nunc Pro Tunc*—and given a path to citizenship. 2. *The Battered Child Statute*, which says that an abused minor is guaranteed permanent residency (green card) if the abusive parent or guardian is a legal US resident or in the process of becoming a resident. We were building the case against Aunty Amelie because she was my legal guardian and violently abusive.

"We need to tell the court," my attorney posited. "This is our strongest argument in your case." He was sitting so close to me at this point and spoke with so much fervor that I could smell the milk and cereal that he had for breakfast on his breath.

"But John, I can't. I just can't." I shuddered and shook my head profusely as once-buried memories of the abuse resurfaced into my mind. My esophagus tightened into a rope so that I could barely get air through my windpipe.

John's stupid and messy office was getting louder to the point where I couldn't hear myself think. Suddenly, the honking and beeping from the cars outside blasted through his office window, and the *click-clack* of his assistant's heels outside his door became overbearing. John's desk creaked as he shifted his weight on it, and I couldn't stand the sound. To John, I must have looked like a mouse who had just stepped on a trap.

"Look," he said with a no-nonsense and get-yourself-together tone, "this is the strongest evidence we have to support our argument of battery. All you need to do is be honest and tell the truth to the judge and the court. We could really win your case with this evidence."

All I need to do? He wanted me to expel my deepest and darkest secrets about my mother who was not alive to defend herself, and that was his way of convincing me? Exposing my mom also meant reliving the tormenting words and the beatings, and I just couldn't. I wasn't ready. But John said that if I did this one thing, then we would win the case. Then I could finally have a normal life as an American, and I wanted that more than anything. I couldn't bear living this immigration nightmare any longer. Why did it have to be at the expense of digging up this other tragedy? Ya Marie's abuse would live in those legal transcripts for anyone to access and read and make judgments about. What kind of daughter would even consider doing such a thing? I couldn't bare the idea of my first time breaking the silence of my mother's lack of love for me to a courtroom full of white men who didn't know me.

John's little, round eyes bulged out as he stared at me, and all I could hear was the *tic-tic-tic* of the second hand of the clock. Time was running out before we had to return to the courtroom and continue with my testimony. I had exactly ten minutes to make a decision about a secret that I buried for almost a decade that would determine my fate. Regardless of the decision, there would be consequences.

II. TO AFRICA WE GO

Here we were. A plate of mussels and frites and a rainbow coalition of women—one brown, one white, and one black—in a Harlem bistro one fine evening. It wasn't just any mussels and frites. This one involved a tango between white wine and yellow butter that created a thick, creamy soup with a hint of black pepper. Yet the best part was soaking the truffle-coated French fries into the soup. We had it down to a science; you let the fries soak just long enough in the sauce, about twenty seconds. This would produce a slightly soggy frite that still maintained a slight crunch.

The Harlem sun was unforgiving in May. It blazed on the freshly black tar that covered Malcom X Boulevard—alternatively called Lenox Avenue—bouncing the heat from the ground onto the swanky cars that whizzed by, pumping base so hard it reverberated down into the ground and up the residential buildings. Even my bedroom window on the seventh floor cascaded to the beat. Harlem was electric.

While it was nice of Celeste and Priti to visit me in Harlem, I was nervous having them in my part of town. Harlem was up-and-coming, but would my friends feel comfortable and safe in a sea of blackness? After all, we grew up in Charlottesville, Virginia, attending Saint Anne's-Belfied, the exact opposite of what Harlem represented. Sure, the neighborhood was changing and gentrifying, but one couldn't overlook the occasional black bum who loitered the corner. I observed white people having a greater aversion to black homeless persons than white homeless persons. It even took me time to become accustomed to walking past a swarm of young black men in puffy jackets hanging outside of the neighboring bodega. You would never encounter this kind of scene in whitewashed Charlottesville. Well at least the part of Charlottesville where Celeste and Priti lived. I was less concerned about Priti, who had lived in New York City long enough and had adequate melanin in her skin to not feel threatened by her surroundings. But it was Celeste who I was most worried about. Although she was half-Filipino, I considered her to be whiter. She lived in Tahoe and went hiking, snowboarding, and skiing. What would she think of Harlem?

At least my residence was in a high-rise building with a doorman; one of the nicest on the block. Every time we passed by a white person in the neighborhood, I wanted to point it out to my two friends to reassure them there were tons of other white people in Harlem and, therefore, they were safe.

The year had been off to an incredible start. I was convinced that I had materialized a gorgeous apartment in the heart of Harlem. I overlooked one major detail when I envisioned my dream apartment. It came with a twenty-two-year-old roommate, making me skeptical at first. How would a thirty-three-year-old share a common space with a twentysomething? I dreaded our apartment turning like a revolving door hosting endless parties. What if they pre-gamed excessively, ending up puking in the living room?

But my roommate Raquel was mature, beyond her years. She had a steady, long-term boyfriend, a medical school resident, who had created a sense of stability and routine in her life. The apartment was always quiet and clean, boasting high ceilings, state-of-the-art appliances, and freshly polished wooden floors.

We carried on nicely. Raquel became the little sister I didn't have, mainly because she indulged in my advice. I could have told her to wear purple socks every day and stand on her head each morning to guarantee success in life, and she would have done it. Not because she was simple—Raquel was the epitome of brilliance, and I was convinced that she possessed a much higher IQ than me—but because she looked up to me. I was always dumbfounded when her eyes widened and her voice went up five octaves as she exclaimed, "Thanks, Tini!"

A new job had followed two months after the new apartment. So when Celeste and Priti brought me a housewarming gift of a Jade plant, which I actually named Jade, I couldn't wait to see what other good luck would come from that.

The bistro was like a college dorm room masked as a French restaurant for the evening. Somehow the uniformed waitstaff didn't match the unframed posters on the wall or the miniature plastic flags that hung in the ceiling to represent some of the best club teams in soccer. The jazz music in the background illustrated the character of the restaurant, as random, clashing, yet soothing and cozy.

"We should ask for bread so that we can soak up the soup," Celeste said.

"Oh my goodness!" I exclaimed. "That's a great idea."

I loved confirming Celeste's brilliant ideas. She always had them.

"So tell us about your dad and when you're going to meet him," Celeste asked.

Priti's eyes lit up like display lights, showcasing the beauty of her entire face.

"I can't wait to meet him," I said while playing Ping-Pong with eye contact. Celeste sat to my left in the booth, and Priti sat across the table. "He seems like such a cool dude. I originally wanted to bring him to the US, but it's risky. If something were to happen to him while he was visiting, the US government could sue me if I incurred medical expenses. I also thought about meeting him in Canada, but I would need to get him a visa and it would be twice as costly. So I've decided that I'm going in November."

I had become accustomed to sounding like a voice recorder because I always felt like my life was on display and I had to give pageant-like responses to win the favor of others. I didn't believe everything I was saying to my buddies because I was scared to death to travel oversees alone to meet my father. What if I got kidnapped by a family member and they stole my passport? I'd heard such stories before. What if I was not allowed to reenter the US? What if my father turned out to be a horrible person whom I couldn't stand the sight of? It was May 2014, and I hadn't even started to look at tickets for this supposed November trip. I originally planned to meet my father the week after Priti's wedding, but September was ambitious.

Two weeks later, I was on the phone with Celeste discussing her next visit to New York City. In pure Celeste fashion, she casually mentioned something that warranted much more of a buildup. She had been doing that since the first time that I met her. Celeste's white father was the stereotypical successful, white, American patriarch—a handsome, tall businessowner. So why was Celeste always juggling two or three waitressing jobs? I simply couldn't understand that part.

When we were at St. Anne's-Belfield in Charlottesville, also referred to as STAB, I assumed that everyone was rich except for me, because what non-posh school would have something called a "Headmaster"?

"I hate my parents. They suck," she would casually mention during our childhood conversations as if asking someone to pass the salt. She only resented her parents because they were in the middle of an ugly divorce, and poor Celeste was trying to cope. "So yeah, dude, guess what? I'm coming with you to meet your dad in Zambia. I'm not letting you go alone." Celeste wasn't one to change her mind; her decisions stood firm and unmovable.

"Wow, Celeste, I don't even know what to say." I let out a breath of air from my diaphragm; this air was waiting to be released for quite some time. "Are you sure though? I mean, I can't let you do that. That's a big trip." I wanted her to fight me on this and insist on coming because I couldn't bear to go alone. Would I be okay going by myself? I had been secretly wishing someone would accompany me but was unsure who would be willing to traipse across the world for me.

"No, dude, I'm coming and that's final. This is so exciting. I know that you were thinking of going in November but what date? I feel like we should buy our tickets soon and then sit and plan everything out when we're in Charlottesville for Priti's wedding." Celeste maintained the pace of a sprinter when she spoke. If I was Winnie The Pooh, then Celeste was Tigger, who did backflips and jumped hurdles in her speech.

It was a surreal moment. A few days ago, the idea of meeting my dad evaded me and now it was going to happen. Celeste and I agreed to travel from November 11 through November 20. "I'll buy both of our tickets and then you can pay me back," Celeste had offered. "Don't worry, I have enough money saved." I had been meaning to ask her to give me a financial planning tutorial. She was as good with finance as she was with ideas. Celeste was the only person that I knew who could buy a house by saving her waitressing earnings. Her methods were as radical as Suze Orman's and involved sharing meals with friends, ordering appetizers instead of entrees, and having two backup saving accounts. Not only was she offering to go with me across the world to meet my father, but now she was up-fronting the money for the trip because I couldn't afford it. I wasn't surprised by her gesture though.

This was the same woman who sent me a $100 bill in the mail during college without a return address. It was spring of 2003, senior year at Hamilton College, and I needed money to submit my grad school application. After forking up the $75 application fee to Columbia University, I could only hope for a miracle to cover the $80 similar payment to the Maxwell School at Syracuse University. My life depended on my getting into grad school; I had no alternate plan. But even if I got into a program, I wasn't exactly sure how I was going to afford it. Since I was technically illegal, I wasn't qualified for a student loan. I hadn't fully thought through my next steps, but all I knew was I at least needed an offer in hand; which meant that I needed to apply to multiple institutions. The $100 bill was wrapped in a piece of paper that read "surprise!" Our campus mail center was unable to help me trace back the origins of the envelope.

"I bet it was you!" I would excitedly call out every person listed in my makeshift address book. "Martini," she would refer to me, "I wish that I had the creativity and the money to do something that special for you. But honestly it wasn't me," a college friend commented. Then who was it? I needed to know because while I loved the surprise element, the control freak in me needed to know. "Martina," another friend remarked, "maybe the person who sent you the money never intended for you to know. Can you accept that?"

It was only a year later while I was still in grad school when I considered Celeste might have sent that invaluable gift. How could I have missed the hints? She was the one person who would absolutely do something like that. The exclamation mark was a clear giveaway. She was the only person I knew that excitable. "Yeah, it was her. She doesn't want you to know. You can never tell her that you know that it was her," Priti confessed over the phone. How Dickensian of her; it was straight out of *Great Expectations*. I had to thank her for her random act of kindness, which was the reason that I was where I was. "No," Priti said. "She can never know that you know that it was her."

Why was Celeste so nice to me? We had been friends since high school, but I thought it superficial. Even when I shared my most personal stories with her, it was from a place of survival and only meant to warrant sympathy. We had met through Priti, who was in the same advisory class as I was when I entered STAB. "Dude," my sentences always started off with when I was about to go into a soliloquy about my pain. The mere prefix of "dude" seemed to disqualify the depth of my pain, making me less vulnerable. That's how Celeste and I knew each other.

"Dude, you're like a coconut and I'm a papaya," I once said as I tried to change the subject after a conversation about our families that left both of us feeling raw and exposed. That's how I defined Celeste: someone who had pain but delivered it with such nonchalance and humor that one couldn't help but laugh it off.

It was a miracle that I found a safe haven and friends after the journey that I had been on. After Ya Marie died, I was tossed from three different homes within the course of three years. If STAB hadn't showed up when it did, I don't know how I would have survived my aunt's wrath.

III. KKK

It was not more than two years after burying Ya Marie that I was standing in what felt like a prison. It was a 3,000-square-foot cavity in the shape of an L, cold, infested with mildew, and its only source of light being the glass doors and windows that sat at the store's front.

"Let's call it Kibibi Kalaw's Kollections . . . Kollections with a K!" Aunty Amelie exclaimed as we stood in the center of the room, hoping that the sunlight would blaze its way past the windows and warm us up.

"You mean KKK?" my twelve-year-old cousin, Sidney, asked rhetorically, trying to disseminate our facial expressions. It wouldn't be the least bit ironic if Aunty Amelie's store ended up taking on the name of the KKK, as her persona embodied fear and terror alike.

"Maybe we could drop the last K and just call it Kibibi Kalaw's," she regrouped. "It's going to be a family business, and it's going to make us very rich. It will be run by us and maintained by us. One day when you girls are all grown up, you'll be able to take over and manage this whole thing."

None of us looked particularly excited. To us three teenage girls, this was just a store full of old, used clothes and knick-knacks. How would this make us rich? She got so excited that her nose began to itch like it usually did when she was on the brink of a new discovery. Her sniffles, which were light and graceful but not any less annoying than anyone else's sniffles, always accompanied the itch. It was all because of that nose. Shakespeare could have written an entire sonnet on Aunty Amelie's nose. By 1997, her perfectly pinched nose was about twenty years old. She must have gotten it after arriving to the United States from Spain back in the early seventies. All the children in the family were supposed to think that it was her real nose, but who couldn't help but wonder what was wrong with her nose when it was runny 365 days out of the year?

"That's what happens when you get a fake nose," Ya Marie used to say, taking a jab at Aunty Amelie when she was not around to defend herself, "it drips until it falls off." As a little girl, I believed everything that Ya Marie said, so I waited eagerly, hoping not to miss the moment when a slight pat would send Aunty Amelie's nose tumbling off her face like a Mr. Potato Head. Aunty Amelie had these schemes to further the Kalaw clan, but what ultimately happened was she created a well-oiled Kalaw machine where everyone scurried about, appealing to her every demand. Shortly after signing the lease to Kibibi Kalaw's Kollections, which was the final name for the Georgia Avenue residence that sat in Washington DC, she put her entire family to work with set up.

"Martine, Cassie, and Sydney, look at how I'm hanging the clothes. You need to place the clothes on the hanger and then hang them like so, therefore, allowing for the question mark side to show." Aunty Amelie used pretentious language such as "like so" and "one ought to" in her everyday speech; something I grew to admire and try to mimic. As a fifteen-year-old who had just lost her mother and was looking for a role model, it didn't seem pretentious at first. Aunty Amelie's accent, which was a perfect cosmopolitan, transitioned to French and then to the Queen's English midsentence.

Being around Aunty Amelie exuded two sentiments: complete awe or complete terror, which could shift as fast as the second hand ticks on a watch. "I speak nine languages," she would brag to us, to encourage her nieces to excel and dominate. All her claims proved to be accurate as I heard her transition from

French to the most eloquent Castilian Spanish, to Portuguese, then Swahili, and so forth—it was so exotic and romantic, and I wanted to sound just like her.

Like a slave master, it was her hard-earned money that brought the entire Kalaw family, nine siblings and some of their kids, to the United States between the early 1970s to the late 1990s. She owned us. Maybe that's how she got away with forcing me to drink a glass of spoiled milk when I was six years old as a punishment for forgetting to put the gallon of milk back in the refrigerator. Then there were the times when she would banish me to her basement and I had to kneel on my knees with my arms raised up, holding a stack of books for what seemed like hours. The basement was dark, and I was scared of the Boogey monsters coming to get me. Aunty Amelie got away with treating me this way because Ya Marie was in the hospital with tuberculosis.

When Aunty Amelie commanded us to help her with the consignment store, no one could refuse, as we all felt indebted to her. Without having a mom or a dad to protect me from her wrath, I became the primary target.

Before moving in with Aunty Amelie, Aunt Frances broke her promise to her now-deceased sister, my mom, and kicked me out of her home in Andover, Massachusetts. She cried when she did it and swore that it was causing her more pain than it would me. "We're trying to have a baby and it has become increasingly difficult. I need to alleviate the stress in my life." In addition to being Cassie and Sydney's mom, she had two older sons and was now trying to have her fifth child. I could understand her not being able to take care of another person's child, but she shouldn't have made the promise to be my guardian to my mom on her deathbed. Under no circumstances was she supposed to get rid of me unless I became a problem-child. If refusing food until being forced to eat was my only issue, considering the circumstances, then I wasn't a problem. It was she who undid the progress once my therapy sessions were over with her interrogations as she drove us home.

"Martine, I still don't understand how you couldn't have seen the signs. How couldn't you have known that your mother was dying?" Did she think that my answer would magically change one day? The truth was, I honestly didn't know that Ya Marie was dying, and no amount of questioning would alter the response.

Aunt Frances confiscated all my books, including Edgar Allan Poe and Sylvia Plath's *The Bell Jar*, suspicious that I may get ideas on killing myself. What she didn't know was that those reading assignments from English literature class were more potent than any amount of counseling because the pain and anguish in the writing validated my own. After futile attempts to have me live with her youngest sister in the spotty town of Lawrence, Massachusetts, she finally decided to send me to Maryland right before the Christmas Holidays. "You're gonna go live with your Aunty Dominique, who has always wanted a daughter."

Aunty Dominique, the younger sister, lived in Germantown, Maryland. I guess the plus side was that she recently upgraded from living in a trailer park community to a two-story house. I already began to miss Andover, Massachusetts, before I left.

The arrangement lasted two weeks before Aunty Dominique's batty episodes crept in. There were so many instances where I could remember Aunty Dominique laughing, dancing, and drinking in the living room with my mom and other relatives and then suddenly begin to cry about being the black sheep of the family. She felt that everyone in the family secretly thought she was pathetic. All of a sudden, the celebration stopped and everyone was consoling Aunty Dominique. I was only eight or nine when Aunty Dominique let me watch *Hellrazor* and *Friday the 13th*. But letting a child watch horror movies certainly wasn't what made her strange. What was odd was when she made me close my eyes during the sex scenes but was perfectly fine with me watching knives being rammed through people's orifices. Not much had changed since then, so I wasn't surprised when two weeks after moving in with her, she kicked me out of her house to go live with Aunty Amelie.

Aunty Dominique allowed me one phone call to have someone come pick me up. In a state of frenzy I could only think of one person in the Maryland area whom I knew would save me. Claude was Ya Marie's half-brother on my grandfather's side. Since he was only six years older than me and resembled an older brother, I seldom called him Uncle Claude. I never knew Claude to become angry and seemed to see the best in people. As a young adult in his early twenties, he was still figuring out his life or else I would have asked to live with him. "But Claude, I didn't do anything wrong. I don't understand why she hates me," I said in between sobs.

"Don't cry, baby girl. It's going to be okay, I promise," Claude reassured as he sat in the driver's seat containing his disgust of the situation.

"Aunty Amelie, what's a consignment store?" I asked in my naiveté in the first few hours of moving in with her and her son, Emanuel.

"It is like a high-end pawn shop for expensive garments. Rich people bring in high-end items of clothing, books, and furniture that they want to get rid of for whatever reason, and they sign a contract with us. If we sell it, then they get a certain percentage of the earnings. If the item doesn't sell after a set period time, they must come to retrieve their belongings or they become property of the store. We will also accept donations, tax deductible."

Her description was opposite to the run-down junkyard that contained a mix of worn-out polyester suits coupled with Burberry jackets from five seasons ago. The store was partitioned into various subsections: a library section in the far back, a kitchen section, and an apparel section in the front.

"Hello, welcome to Kibibi Kalaw's Kollections," was my coined phrase in my initial job as the foot traffic greeter as well as the telephone operator. It got boring after a while and sometimes to amuse myself I imagined saying: "Welcome to KKK." Aunty Amelie led me to believe that being an unpaid cashier, salesperson, and manager at seventeen years old would ultimately lead to my success in the business world.

"Martine, you are learning how to run your own business. This is what people go to school for, and you are fortunate that you get to learn from experience." Because it was still winter break and she had yet to enroll me in school, I worked alone from 8:00 a.m. to 10:00 p.m. for seven days a week, in one of the most dangerous parts of DC. Apparently, a murder had taken place directly across the street from our store on Georgia Avenue.

When Aunty Amelie returned from her day job as a Spanish translator at Howard University Hospital, she would come to the store and begin to rearrange new merchandise that we received that day. In a Cinderella-like fashion, I had no choice but to continue working until she was done, which was somewhere between midnight and 1:00 a.m.

"Martine and Emanuel, we have a lot to do this evening before we can go home and eat dinner," she chimed in at 11:30 p.m. on a weeknight. "I need you to fold, sweep, create piles of expensive clothes that we received versus tattered ones, and put price tags on merchandise." The store grew particularly cold at night, and while Emanuel and I shivered from the cold, Aunty Amelie simply sniffled and continued to go through the assortment until finally she suspected that we must have been hungry.

IV. PAIN RELIEF

Her home was nearly impossible to describe because it was packed with expensive junk. Aunty Amelie was a hoarder, which was evident by a mere glimpse through her living room windows. Sitting on an end table were porcelain dishes piled high.

"Martine, this is the rarest of all china. It is Wedgewood china. You must know the quality of the plate that you are eating off of." Everything was a collectable according to Aunty Amelie so we didn't have the opportunity to enjoy it. All three bedrooms had closets filled with her high-end clothes, many of which still had their Neiman Marcus tags on them. The intensity of her Chanel No. 5 wafting through her closets, coupled with the mounds of extortionate crap and the files of papers spilled on the floor just made the house stuffy. She had stashes of medication she collected throughout the years that she couldn't part with. She hoarded files of immigration paperwork and death and birth certificates of all her family members, including her parents. Even the kitchen counters were buried with quality silverware and Waterford crystal, ultimately making everything appear cheap. If Emanuel or I attempted to move anything, she would have a conniption.

"Do you know how expensive this is?" she ranted. "This is what will give you money to survive when I die. You need to learn how to appreciate this. Imbecile!" It made it nearly impossible for anyone to live comfortably in the house.

Though I was charged with the task of making sure that Emanuel completed his homework, it was pointless because his lack of proper sleep kept him from functioning coherently in class. By the time we arrived home at 1:00 a.m. from the shop, Aunty Amelie forced us to have a "civilized" meal. At 1:30 a.m. she screamed, "Martine, Emanuel, set the table!" In the dead of the night, Emanuel and I fumbled with the dinner fork and the salad fork, struggling to remember which went on the outside. I cringed as she made us set both the water glasses and the wine glasses because that just meant more dishes for me to wash while everyone else was in bed. We didn't taste the food; we were so starved that cardboard would suffice. The sooner we could eat, the sooner we could get to bed because sunrise was at 6:00 a.m.

When the dragon had retreated to her bedroom for the night, Emanuel and I celebrated our momentary freedom: "Quick, let's get some ice cream! Hurry up!" Emanuel rushed me as I hesitated, considering the likelihood of getting caught. This nine-year-old wasn't scared of his mom; not like I was. "Martine, hurry up!" He quickened me as we dug two soup spoons into the tub of ice cream and enjoyed the cool sweetness of heaven, making us oblivious to Aunty Amelie's charge into the kitchen. Her softly coiffed hair stood up on her head like a porcupine as she scolded us: "Is this what I taught you? Did I teach you to eat ice cream with these spoons? If you guys want to be barbarians, then get out of my house. Do you realize how stupid and ignorant you both look?" Even in her rage, she had an ability to articulate her words with such precision.

Aunty Amelie was cruel, and I became the subject of that cruelty one fateful evening. Avoiding eye contact and feigning exhaustion was the only way to maneuver out of the stronghold she had, especially when she became increasingly agitated.

"Is that where the plate goes?" she asked while she hovered over me in the kitchen. It was a sizeable kitchen with granite countertops. The cabinets were a dark wood, and the floors were an ashen-grey linoleum, which dated the house. The kitchen light always seemed to be flickering, as if the wattage of the bulb was too high for the circuit. Honestly, her question didn't matter. It was a trick question, and I was supposed to get it wrong. With her back turned to her, I shrugged my shoulders. "Martine, answer me!" Why couldn't she just let me be just for once and go bother her son, who should have bated the brunt of all this abuse just by being her son. "What's wrong with you? It's like you're retarded or something. You act like an idiot and you don't speak." As the malice encroached her voice, those almond-shaped, brown eyes turned beady. Her pinched nose began to itch as she rubbed it with her hand. "Answer me, Martine!"

"I don't know, Aunty Amelie!" I groaned. "Why are you always picking on me? What did I do wrong? I didn't do anything; I'm just trying to wash the dishes." My moxie came out of sheer exhaustion. It must have been momentary amnesia that caused me to forget that this woman could finish me. According to her, she had the power to send me back to Africa.

Aunty Amelie could always detect when I was at my lowest and would breech the topic of my dead mother as a final jab. It was my job to protect my mother's integrity, especially from her hateful sister. How dare she question my love for my mother? Was my aunt even capable of love? Aunty Amelie abused her only child, terrorized her siblings, kicked her blind mother into the street, and neglected her father—how dare she question my love for *my* mother? I may not have known how to love my mother during the first thirteen years of my life, but I learned to love her in her final days.

"I loved my mother!" I screamed with rage bursting from lungs, ready to shatter Aunty Amelie's fine china into a million and one pieces.

"If you loved your mother, you would not have let her die!" she shouted into eternity.

My heart stopped momentarily, trying to absorb the shock of her words. Where was the floor? I couldn't feel it under me, and suddenly my feet started to sink into a cesspool of my own sadness and self-pity. The room was spinning uncontrollably, and the stupid kitchen light seemed to flicker incessantly as if it, too, were mocking me. It was the only sound I could hear—that annoying sound of the lightbulb dimming in and out. Aunty Amelie was fighting off her grin so hard that the side of her mouth started to twitch so that the light bounced off one of her gold molars. She robbed me of my dignity and won the battle. My mother's death was my Achilles's heel. No matter how much my therapist tried to convince me that I couldn't have saved my mother's life, I knew that I probably could have if I had been smart enough to figure things out. I couldn't come back from such a low blow. Her work was done, and she left the kitchen to get a good night's rest, leaving me in misery.

The only solution was to end my life and make the pain and the accusations go away. I tried to kill myself once before, almost a year ago when my mom took a turn for the worse with her health. If one more person complimented me on being so strong in the face of my mother's illness, I would scream. Someone did, and instead of screaming, I opted for a more dramatic approach. I chose to swallow a bottle of aspirin and end my life. Although I failed suicide once, here I was making my second attempt. The poison label on the bottle of the Clorox bleach reassured me that it would be a successful attempt. It was only a sip, which I nearly gagged on before forcing it to slide down my throat. Bloody vomit immediately followed, but unfortunately, I was still alive. I couldn't handle the sensation of salty burning liquid going down my throat, so I opted for alternate methods. This experience was followed by suicide attempt number three, where I shuffled through Aunty Amelie's outdated prescriptions to find the most lethal one. I imagined myself as Sylvia Plath. Tomorrow night, I would take a nice, warm shower, put on my beautiful cream dress, and swallow all twenty pills in the bottle if I could, surely ending my life.

Emanuel and I were woken up every morning to the shrill cry of Aunty Amelie's voice: "Martine and Emanuel, get up!" Like two little mice being chased by a broomstick, she would follow us around the house, asking us to move faster: "I have to get to work. You need to hurry up Martine. Emanuel, find my other shoe! Where is my shoe? Martine, did you finish making lunch for you and your cousin? I don't need you both complaining that I'm not feeding you. There is plenty of food in that refrigerator." The statement was true, except for the fact that ninety percent of the food in her refrigerator was spoiled. Since she was into starving herself to maintain her size-four frame, she barely noticed. "You should stop stuffing your face, Martine, or you will become fat." It was from Aunty Amelie that I learned about fad diets and her latest one where she only consumed a salad with no dressing, just vinegar and a dash of black pepper. Her face became bony after she ate like that for a week, and I grew envious.

"Martine, where are the deposit slips? Don't act like an idiot; you know that this is common practice every morning!" As Aunty Amelie shuffled through her jewelry box for her gold rings and her pearls, I found a small, open space at the dining room table. My hands shook as I dared not make a mistake to prepare deposit slips for the bank, so we could submit our daily earnings from the store. Any shortcomings from her list of demands led to name calling: "dumb," "imbecile," "retarded," "stupid." I couldn't wait for her to drop me off at the store in the mornings, anything to get away from her. The worst were the car rides from her house to the store. That was where this dainty little woman, dressed like the First Lady, would unleash the cruelest of intentions. Aunty Amelie was the real-life Joan Crawford in the film *Mommy Dearest*.

"You know, your mother did a terrible job with you. You are too naïve, and you are not quick. You have to think quick to get far in this world. Now I have to undo all the damage myself by brainwashing you." Who used terms like *brainwashing* except for diabolical tyrants? I didn't dare talk back. Any backtalk I gave would bring on more hateful words along with a backslap. Her words were cunning and powerful and full of poison—poison I wished killed me rather than keeping me in a worse state of eternal torment.

V. LOST AND FOUND

The springtime's sunny skies had little effect on my spirit. The agony of my recent breakup just after my thirty-first birthday wouldn't let up. I curled up on my Moroccan red love seat and cried out in heartache. My living room was womblike with red walls and mounds of books on my bookshelf that cascaded onto the floor, making the room look more cozy than messy. I wouldn't leave my Upper East Side nest if I didn't have to. For the past few days, I assumed three positions: sitting on my couch with my laptop on my lap, lying in my bed while crying myself to sleep, or staring blankly in the fridge, hoping for food to magically appear. Today, I chose the former and sifted through social media and my emails.

"Hey, my grand-uncle asked me to look up his long-lost daughter by the name of Martine Kalaw, alias Mwanji Kayembe, whose mother's name was Tshilombo Marie Louise Cooper Ekanga. Are you by any chance that person? I live in Chicago, please respond," the LinkedIn message read. It was enough to get me to read it twice more just to make sure that my eyes were not playing tricks on me. Was this a joke? This person referred to me as Mwanji Kayembe and not Mwanj. Mwanji was the original spelling of my middle name. At some point during my childhood someone must have decided to drop the "i" as if that would make it easier to pronounce. I answered to both Mwanj or Mwanji though. Kayembe was my biological father's surname that I hadn't heard in years. Wasn't my father dead? I had no recollection of him because the last time I saw him I was a toddler in Zambia. I only spoke to him once in my life, and that was through a letter when I was thirteen.

Ya Marie reluctantly gave me a letter from my dad: "Here. This is from your father." I made sure not to seem too excited to reassure my mom that I was loyal to her. The letter was generic and full of religious context and formalities. It didn't require any translation because it was written in English. "Write him back and tell him to help your sister Zalika by bringing her from Zaire [DR Congo] to Zambia and letting her stay with him. You know that your sister is suffering." I knew not to question anything that Ya Marie said and to simply obey.

"Dear, Dad," I wrote, but I didn't mean it; he wasn't dear to me, and he certainly didn't earn the name Dad. I might as well have been writing a letter to Santa Claus or to the Tooth Fairy. The letter was short and sweet, and by the time I reached my last sentence, I was just happy that I had fulfilled my obligation. If this man was everything that my mom said he was, then he was a waste of my time. I didn't expect nor want him to ever respond to my letter. I guess that's why I wasn't fazed a year later when, in a state of her usual tirades, my mom said in her native Swahili, "I wish you would die like your father." Never mind that my mother wished me dead; I was used to her lethal words. Like a detective, I was trying to encrypt her message; she must have been telling me that my father was dead.

Perhaps the LinkedIn message was a hoax to get me to send money to Africa. Sitting on my couch, I replied, "My middle name is Mwanji but my father is dead." Why did I even write that? What if this person was hacking into my bank account? I couldn't wait to catch this imposter in his or her lie. This jerk was too stupid to research that my father was dead. I didn't have time to further investigate this person; I was preoccupied with my citizenship application that I was eligible to apply for now that I'd had my green card for five years.

"This is not a joke," the woman on the other end of the email replied. "Your father has been looking for you, and if you are interested in getting in touch with him, please call me at this number. I am his niece." I got this message within twenty-four hours. Was this possible? I started to think back to what Ya Marie said so many years ago. Is it possible that she was implying that he was dead to her but not actually dead? Or did she mean that she wished that both he and I were dead? Questioning her when she was on her verbal tirades warranted a beating or a shoe flying across my face.

"Hello, dear," a chipper but mature woman's voice answered when I called. She was the mother of the woman who sent me the message. "My name is Hope! I'm so happy to be speaking with you. When we told Uncle that we found you, he started to cry on the telephone. He cannot wait to hear from you, dear. Let me give you his telephone number and his email."

It was two days later when I decided that maybe this whole conversation about my father was not a joke after all and I decided to pursue it. How ironic that her name was Hope; it made the story that much more unbelievable. She had a heavy Central African accent mixed with American slang; while it was odd, it was also endearing. Hope was technically my cousin. I wonder if that made her daughter, who originally contacted me, my second cousin?

"Hope, I have so many questions to ask. What is he like? How old is he? Where is he?"

"My dear uncle has been looking for you for a long time. He almost gave up. But I promised him that we would find you. He didn't even know if you were alive or if you were in America or anything. He is in Lusaka with his wife, who is my auntie. My daughter is the one who messaged you on LinkedIn. Uncle is an old man, but he is very young in spirit. I hope that you will get to meet him soon. It is important that you meet him soon."

The idea that I would be meeting my father in a month's time was surreal. The journey of reconnecting with my father began with my ex-boyfriend, Barrington. By New Year's Day, 2012, the sinking sensation seeped in as if someone took a shovel and dug a hole in the pit of my stomach. My life with Barrington flashed before my eyes. The image of mediocrity scared me, and I could no longer pretend that it was okay. I insisted on more, and he objected. Then why was I so scared to live without him?

I wasn't still in love with him, but I was like a wounded soldier from a battle. I hadn't healed; it was difficult to make sense of anything. Barrington said that we weren't compatible but maybe he was wrong. While I felt immediate relief after the breakup, I also felt a deep despair and loneliness. I couldn't live without him. Only two weeks after my thirty-first birthday and looking for engagement rings, it was over and I was alone.

There were three breakup conversations. The official one was when he called me to tell me that he couldn't do it anymore and didn't want to try couple's counseling. The second was when he dropped off my duffle bag of clothes at my apartment and gave me a look of disappointment. He was so quick to discard me from his life, that he stuffed every memory of me into the bag, even my tiny, lime-green bikini that would hardly occupy space in his condo for at least a few more weeks. The final communication was when I sent him a pathetic email asking if he would take me back.

". . . All those things are just secondary indicators of the main issue . . . which is that we aren't right for each other. No matter what you may think of me right now, trust me when I say that I believe this was the best for both of us. There is someone out there who can make you happy. But it isn't me," Barrington wrote in a final email. My ego was bruised and concerned about being single with a bald head; how would I find a new man? I shaved my hair off to embrace my natural hair. I did it for him under the assumption that he was the man that I would spend my life with, and therefore, I didn't need to impress anyone else. When I was bald and dating him, I felt sexy. After the breakup, people just thought I pulled a Britney Spears; I was a joke.

I sent my first email to my father in March 2012. While I was relieved to know that he was alive, I was angry. Why now? What took him so long? How dare he leave me with my mother who hated both he and I so much? I needed to confront him about all this. He needed to know how much I suffered as an orphan after she died, and it was all his fault because he was my father and didn't protect me or save me. I purposely called him Joseph to remind him that he meant nothing to me and that he was only my father by name. His response was gentle and full of broken English. There was so much he said that he wanted to tell me, but we would speak in person one day, he hoped. He loved me so much, he said. When Father's Day came around, I was excited by the ritual of sending a card to my father. My words fell flat because he was a stranger to me. I had never even heard his voice.

I sat on my bed and practiced what I would say when the phone rang. "Hi, Dad?" Would I say it sort of apprehensively? "Hi, Dad!" Somehow the enthusiasm and excitement seemed inauthentic because I was scared and guarded. After all, this would be the very first time I would speak to this man. I imagined his voice to be deep and commanding. "Hi, Joseph," I decided. Yes, that's how I would refer to him to signify that he would have to earn my trust and love. My heart raced as I counted down the minutes before his call. What do you say to a man, your father, whom you have no recollection of? What if we had nothing to talk about? Then this whole buildup would have been for naught and what hope did I have with my life if I couldn't look forward to reuniting with my long-lost father?

"My Doh'ta, Mwanji!" the voice on the other end of the line rang. His voice was the texture of velvet. It wasn't just any velvet; it was black velvet. His tone was somewhat animated but not overly exaggerated. His English sounded just like his English in his email; it had a British influence like most Zambians' English with a sprinkle of Africa. I found it endearing that he referred to me as his daughter but offered his unique pronunciation. I could see him smile right through the telephone. He turned what could have been an awkward conversation into a stand-up comedy special. "How are you, my Doh'ta?" He tended to echo what I said and then laugh joyfully. "Oh, you are fine?" Laughter.

I took myself by surprise when I revealed to him that I missed him. "No, my Doh'ta. You cannot know what it is to miss. I held you in my arms when you were a baby and then I have not seen you for twenty-nine years. It is I who misses you." His words were so heartfelt and seemed so sincere that I quickly began to make comparisons between him and my mom. Whereas she was a closed book and was reluctant to share her emotions with me, Joseph was just like me. Or was it that I was more like him?

"My Doh'ta, I have been looking for you for many years. You can even ask your uncle or your sister Mimi. I ask them if they can tell me if you were alive. I sent your sister Mimi letters and photographs of your late mum to give to you. Did she ever share this with you?"

"No, Dad. No one ever mentioned you," I said. "And I speak to Mimi a few times a year and she has never mentioned you. I don't understand. Why?" I surprised myself again by calling him Dad. I couldn't figure out where that came from, and I also couldn't guarantee that it would happen again. My loyalty remained with my mom, and loving him was equivalent to cheating on my mom.

"I do not know myself. My Doh'ta, do you go to church?" This initial conversation was indication of what would be the dynamic between my dad and me. He had a playful personality and didn't allow himself to dwell on things. He was also deeply religious. I heard of Seventh Day Adventists because I think that's what Michael Jackson's family was but that was the extent of my knowledge.

"Dad, church is in my heart."

"What you say?" he chimed.

Our conversation was a comedy.

"Dad, I said that church is in my heart."

"That is good, my Doh'ta. You must go to church."

The more questions that I asked my dad, the more confused I became. He shared as much as he could, considering the barriers in communication that we had. He said that I spoke very American and that it was "quite fast."

No amounts of phone conversations, emails, or letters were a sufficient introduction to my father. Who was this man? He had already given my number to a handful of strangers all insisting on being my brothers and sisters. Based on my recollection about Africans, they claimed everyone as family. Even your next-door neighbor could be considered a cousin, an aunt, or a brother depending on the occasion. Not only did I have a dad, but his kids also came as a package deal. I just had no idea who they were; nor was I sure if I cared to know.

He sent me photographs of his thirteen children and his two wives. Great, so my dad was not only a deadbeat but also a polygamist! I couldn't believe what he was revealing to me as if it was normal. He, my mom, his second wife, and all their children shared one roof in Lusaka, Zambia. I made a mental note to keep this information to myself. No one could ever know that poised and sophisticated me was a product of a polygamous family. It was so lowly and backwards and fed into every possible stereotype I could think about regarding Africans.

Being one of thirteen children overshadowed the next layer of detail, that he and my mother were married for almost ten years. These years I thought that I was a bastard; that my father and mother had a one-night stand and then she got pregnant with me a few months later. How come my mom never mentioned any of this? The portrait of the woman my father painted was opposite of the shell of the mother that I knew. It was almost as if she lived a double life.

"My Doh'ta, you would have been the third child between your mother and I. She did not tell you that? We had two boys before you were born, and they died when they were babies."

I read that statement repeatedly as if the sentence would disappear from the page. Two babies? Two brothers? I couldn't sit peacefully with the idea that there were once two people on Earth that I was genetically matched with from both parents and they were gone. I mourned their loss in that moment. How did Ya Marie keep this bottled inside for so many years? For the fifteen years that I knew my mother, she never shared any of this. It must have been gut-wrenching to have to bury two children. But still, why did she keep my own past from me? Did I even know the real her? My memory of my mom was tainted by her being ill for much of our time together. Who was the person before the illness? Clearly, she was a product of a polygamous relationship, a woman who had seven kids by four different men and a woman who lost all her children except for one. None of it made sense, and the more my dad shared, the less I understood my mom.

VI. PRITI'S WEDDING

"You can't wear heels with the saree," one of Priti's aunties said as she began to fold the delicate fabric around my waist. *What do you mean?* I thought to myself. I waited fifteen years to wear a saree and not being able to throw on a pair of stilettos made the experience lackluster. The first and last time I wore a saree was at an event at STAB where we had to celebrate global diversity. Other than Halloween, this was my sole opportunity to wear whatever I wanted and get away with it. Priti lent me her saree after I begged her each day for about a week. I felt like the Congolese chanteuse, Mbilia Bel, in the video where she wore a green, Indian-inspired, saree-like dress and a *bindi*. She looked like an exotic princess, something that I desperately wanted to be.

Okay, so I couldn't wear heels; that was fine. I was still wearing six yards of purple and gold silk around my body. In that moment, a wave of panic came over me. How would I use the bathroom? Celeste and I took turns running upstairs to Priti's room to get a peak of her getting ready. The bathroom was lit with the sunlight that blazed through the large windows. Beyond the windows, you could see the rolling hills of the farm. Green grass was set in the backdrop, and the wooden fence ran across the center of the window. Charlottesville, Virginia, was many things, but ugly was not one of them. I opened the door to a waft of an Aoud-like perfume that was thickened by the heat of the multiple bodies in the bathroom. She was sitting on a throne-like chair in front of a vanity mirror with more lights that shone on her face and illuminated her *café con leche* skin. Her hair was a mass of jet-black, silk threads that were being carefully curled and pinned on her head.

"Hi, Martine." Her elaborate makeup made her look like a goddess, but her voice was still sweet and innocent. All you had to do was take one look into Priti's big, deep-set eyes and you could see her soul. I couldn't believe that she was getting married.

The last couple of days were like a whirlwind. Celeste and I had been in communication leading up to Priti's wedding, frantically planning our Zambia trip. While she had already secured our flights, I made reservations at the Radisson Blu, which was rated five stars, so it couldn't be that bad. "Dude, we're gonna be living in luxury." The least I could do was find Western accommodations to reassure Celeste's family that their precious white cargo wouldn't get eaten by lions or killed in a tribal war.

"Umm, I have an important question to ask you about Priti's wedding. Will you be my date?" Like a perfect date would, she picked me up from the Charlottesville train station. I stood with my luggage and army fatigue jacket while a tall and leggy Polynesian-looking model with long, straight, brown hair came running to me in short shorts and a T-shirt. To her, she was slumming it, but I just couldn't believe how gorgeous my friend was and she seemed to get more beautiful with age. "Hey, date! Are we ready to party?" As soon as we got in her dad's Volkswagen, she started to blast "Groove Me" by Salt-n-Pepa. I had never heard the song before but after that car ride, I will never forget it because she played it nonstop.

There was a break between the ceremony and the dinner party, which allowed Celeste and I to cool off. The procession was straight out of a Bollywood film with Priti's prince coming on a horse—a substitute for an elephant since PITA probably would have objected—with a posse of family and friends and drums accompanied. There was no shade to be found, and that's when I felt the first bead of sweat trickle from my head and dance all the way down my tailbone. This carried on for almost two hours as I partly watched the couple walk around a fire seven times, while fanning myself with the program.

"Dude, this heat is for real," Celeste said as we made an exit from the crowd. We were unsure of whether to change out of our traditional Indian attire. This would probably be the first and last time that I would get to wear a saree for a period of eight hours so I had no plans of changing. Sure, I now felt the sweat trickling down my inner thigh—or was it pee—but I imagined living in the sweltering heat of India and having to wear this daily. So what was I complaining about?

I sat across from Celeste in the Italian restaurant where we reflected on the day while cooling off. If anyone didn't know any better, they would have thought that we were a random black and white duo coming from an Indian costume party. After all, we were in Charlottesville, Virginia. "We just came from a really crazy Indian wedding that is decked out in glamour and cool-ness," Celeste would tell passersby when they would look at us questioningly.

"Priti looks so happy. I can't believe she's married. I wonder when she will get pregnant," I thought aloud.

"Dude, who knows, but guess who is pregnant?" Celeste interrupted.

That was where Celeste and I were like carbon copies of one another. We had a way of delivering big news in a matter-of-fact and blasé way. A friend once told me, "Martine, when you ask most people how they're doing they usually say 'fine.' But with you it's like 'I'm fine. My father who was dead came back to life and reached out to me.'" While somewhat of an exaggeration, it was mostly true. Celeste was the only person that I knew who did that, too.

"Oh my goodness!" My heart skipped a beat.

"Dude, Ethan and I didn't plan this. Can you believe that I'm knocked up? It's so weird, dude. I have like this alien baby liv-ing inside of me, so weird. But don't worry. We're still going to Zambia. I'll be like five months pregnant, and I spoke to a doctor. It's perfectly safe for me to travel."

It would have been perfectly safe to travel to Chicago, maybe, but not across the world to a developing country! How could I jeopardize her and the baby's health by making them come with me to Africa to meet a man that claimed to be my father? Deep down, I knew that he was my father, but I never got him to send me a vile of blood so I could take a paternity test, as a paranoid friend once suggested. Just when I was close to meeting this man and verifying what he claimed to be, it seemed like it might not happen. How could I explain my frustration to my friend when the reason it was not happening was because of something wonderful and miraculous that was happening for her? The right thing to do would be to call the entire thing off, right?

VII. STAB

It quickly became evident that Aunty Amelie had no intention of enrolling me in school by mid-January 1998. My prison was the consignment shop, so I had to learn to make peace with it. Ben, who started out as a creepy, old man, became my only friend. Ben was as tall as he was wrinkled and white, probably in his midsixties, but he only had two teeth in his mouth, which made him look even more ancient. Though frail and gaunt, he was sharp as a whistle. He may have been homeless, but he turned up at the store each day with a fresh blazer and a large, brown paper bag with clothes under his right arm. And there was not a day that went by where he didn't carry a fat wad of money in his back pocket.

That must have been what caught Aunty Amelie's attention that Saturday when Ben first walked into the store. While I paid him very little attention, Ben winked at me, giving me the creeps. Aunty Amelie, clearly amused by the situation, went over to Ben.

"Can I help you?" She flashed her pearly whites so hard that you could see all her gold molars.

In a loud whisper, he said, "I fancy your daughter there. She's mighty swell." I was even more repulsed when Aunty Amelie said that she would send me right over, like a pimp making her last deal of the day.

She came over to me and whispered, "Never underestimate the spending power of anyone. Just because he looks poor doesn't mean that he doesn't have money. If he is attracted to you, then persuade him to buy stuff in the store. You can get him to spend hundreds of dollars if you want. He has a lot of money, trust me." Everything was about her, and it didn't matter if it meant selling her seventeen-year-old niece or taking advantage of a stranger. "Just go over there and talk to him and smile." Aunty Amelie's glare followed me as I obeyed and walked over to Ben. His eyes glazed over my body.

"You should purchase this blazer here. It's Calvin Klein, see?" I pointed to the faded-out label. Ben was motivated by lust, and

I was motivated by obedience to Aunty Amelie, so I sold him the most expensive suits in the store, and he just bought them. I even made up prices on the items that didn't have price tags. Did I feel bad about it? No, because if I didn't make the sale, I knew that Aunty Amelie would somehow punish me.

As I began to walk Ben over to the register to complete his purchase, Aunty Amelie interrupted: "Martine, did you show Ben the ties that would go well with that jacket?" My total worth must have been about $500 that day because that was as much as Ben was willing to pay for me. I felt cheap and dirty, but I despised Aunty Amelie more than Ben for taking advantage me. After that first sale, I refused to exploit Ben again—what if that wad of cash was all that he had? Ben and I came to an unspoken under-standing—we were both being manipulated by Aunty Amelie so the least we could do was to not exploit each other. I'd like to think that Ben came to understand that I was practically a little girl, and that his lascivious thoughts about me were improper. Regardless, he stopped by everyday while I was alone at the store to see if I wanted any food, in which case I always responded, "No thank you, Ben," with a sincere smile. But one day, not know-ing when my first and last meal of the day would finally arrive, I devoured the fistful of donuts that Ben brought wrapped in nap-kins. I should not have been so trusting of a complete stranger, but I was desperate for a friend and I was hungry.

It was well into January 1998, and although Aunty Amelie kept hinting at registering me at the local public high school, I prepared myself with the idea of being a high school dropout. I would have given anything to be a student again, but Aunty Amelie preferred having me as free labor. My life flashed before my eyes, and the reality was that I would be stuck in this consignment shop for the rest of my life, and I better start getting used to it.

"Good day," the solid woman with auburn locks waived as she walked into Kibibi Kalaw's Kollections on a frigid Saturday afternoon. After fifteen minutes of aimlessly wandering around the store, she picked up a few trinkets and walked to the register to speak to me.

"Hi," she said, and I replied with a weak smile. I loved her soft tone and her rhythmic Jamaican accent. She had a bronze com-plexion, and her dress was simple, but what she lacked in dress, she made up for in her voice. There was something comforting about it, so I hung onto her every word and allowed her to speak.

"Do you work here alone?" she asked.

"No," I said, because on this day, Aunty Amelie was in the stock room, organizing.

"You look about my son's age. Do you go to high school around here?"

"No, I'm not in school," I admitted, not realizing how odd that sounded. Maybe it was my dismissive nature or my lack of eye contact that made her more curious. Fearing that I had said too much, I wanted to change the subject and talk about the store. What questions might she have about our hours? Maybe she wanted to hear more about the consignment process. This woman, who eventually told me that her name was Pauline, amused me for a bit, but she quickly jumped back to our prior topic.

"Would you ever consider going to boarding school?"

Was this crazy woman trying to get me into trouble? Somehow this would get back to Aunty Amelie and she would kill me. "No. No, thank you," I responded abruptly, hoping the conversation would end.

Aunty Amelie walked over at that point and greeted our client with her accent, a see-saw between American English and British English. As I watched Pauline hit it off with Aunty Amelie, I realized that I could not trust her. The two of them stood in the back section of the store having a soul session.

Three hours passed when Aunty Amelie walked up to me with Pauline trailing behind with a mischievous smile. "Martine, Pauline is affiliated with boarding schools, and she is going to see if we can get Emanuel in a boarding school because I told her about how awful this public school is treating him. She will see if she can get you in, too." Completely unconvinced that my life would change, I smiled blankly.

About two days later Aunty Amelie, Emanuel, and I were knocking at Pamela Smith's door in a lovely neighborhood in Silver Spring, Maryland. Pauline was friends with Pamela Smith and Janet Washington, who were affiliated with the United Black Episcopalian (UBE) Black Episcopal schools and churches. Their mission, among many, was to get qualified black students into private Episcopal boarding schools. The first thing that I noticed about Pamela's townhouse was her large, expensive-looking mural, which was a depiction of an Indian woman wearing a green sari, a red *bindi*, and a necklace that hung from one ear to her nostril. The living room was immaculate with antique furniture and nice framed photos. At the far end of the door, past the dining room, were a kitchen and a dinette. It was in the dinette where the five of us sat to discuss boarding school. The conversation was supposed to be geared to Emanuel, but midway through the conversation, the focus shifted to me. I knew that Aunty Amelie would scold me later, so I tried my best to dumb myself down to get the attention back on my cousin.

After looking at our school transcripts, Pamela commented, "Emanuel, my main man, what happened here?" That was her polite way of saying "*D*s and *F*s will not get you into a top-notch boarding school." Mrs. Smith was a very pale yellow with cropped, jet-black hair that had natural waves, suggesting a racial mixture within one of her generations. She was Aunty Amelie's height, about 5'2", slim, and casually dressed, but it was evident that she came from class.

"It's the schools that Emanuel has attended. They don't know how to respond to him because he is gifted and talented. I have had evaluations conducted on him, and Emanuel has one of the highest IQs." She sat at the edge of her seat and pleaded her son's case.

"Well, let's see if he can get his grades up by the end of the semester. But a lot of these prep schools also give tests to measure aptitude, so that would be an opportunity for Emanuel to strengthen his application," Mrs. Smith said with a slight Southern drawl.

I remained silent when the conversation about me came up. If there was anything I was good at, it was being a student. I prided myself in getting straight *A*s in middle school, and despite all the moves from one school to another, I maintained an *A* average.

"Martine's grades should be enough to get her in the door. She'll probably be interviewed at some point, so we'll just have to prepare her for those." Aunty Amelie was still stuck on getting Emanuel into a prestigious prep school—she could care less if I was eligible to go to Mars. "Okay, so Janet and I will get crackin' on applications and scholarship searches. Then we'll be in touch with you after we've located some schools that we can visit with Emanuel and Martine." If Emanuel didn't get accepted into school, then there was no chance in hell that Aunty Amelie would let me go.

Without warning, Pamela Smith walked into the consignment shop the following day to speak to me. Aunty Amelie was working at Howard University Hospital, and Emanuel was in school. Business at the shop was slow in the mornings, and I had not seen Ben all week so the company was welcomed. She had a maternal presence—comforting and unassuming.

"Oh really?" she raised her brow when she learned that I was working at the shop alone. "We had conversations with UBE, and they're interested in getting you into a boarding school. I have two schools that I'm looking at for you. One is St. Catherine's in Richmond, Virginia, and the other is Saint Anne's-Belfield in Charlottesville, Virginia. I'd like to take you to visit each school and to have an interview with both headmasters. Then we can go from there. Would you like that?" For the first time in a long time, someone wanted my opinion. People were trying to help me. Maybe there was a way out but how would we get past Aunty Amelie? Pangs of guilt shot through my body; this was something that Aunty Amelie wanted for Emanuel. "Call me tomorrow evening so that we can begin to make plans."

"Um . . . I'm not allowed to use the telephone in the store, so I can't call you. I'm really sorry," I said.

"Well why not?"

"Because Aunty Amelie says I can't use the telephone because it costs a lot of money," I replied while lowering my eyes from shame; I had just outed my aunt, which would result in serious repercussions.

Mrs. Smith took out a few quarters from her purse and handed them to me. "You can go to a nearby pay phone and call me during your lunch breaks." I couldn't find it in my heart to tell her that I didn't get lunch breaks.

While I worked closely with Janet Washington, who was also part of the UBE organization, it was Mrs. Smith whom I connected with the best. When I was not on the telephone with Mrs. Smith, I was surely talking to Janet Washington. Mrs. Washington was a pistol who could give Aunty Amelie a run for her money in the intelligence department. She didn't take no for an answer, and she was so knowledgeable about everything. She was a darker complexion, like me, and she wore big, round glasses that pressed into the bridge of her nose, leaving a dent. I depended on her and Mrs. Smith alike, and I indirectly put pressure on them to save me as I began to reveal more about the abuse that I endured. When they were around, I felt a sense of freedom like I hadn't felt in years.

The closer I got to the potential of going to boarding school, I tried to imagine it in my head. My only knowledge of boarding school came from the films I watched—they were for rich, white kids. How would I ever fit in, in my raggedness? Aunty Amelie allowed me to go on school visits with Mrs. Smith and Mrs. Washington because she was still under the pretense that Emanuel would also get accepted into boarding school. But the truth was, St. Christopher's and the Church Farm School in Pennsylvania would not take him with such a poor academic record. It was after my interview at St. Catherine's that Mrs. Smith and I exchanged notes on the experience on our way to lunch.

"You never had chicken and waffles? You never heard of Roscoe's Chicken and Waffles? Girlfriend, we used to have those all over California. You don't know what you're missing," Mrs. Smith commented as she pulled up to a pancake house near Richmond, Virginia. While St. Catherine's was a lovely campus, it didn't feel right, we both agreed. Besides, it was an all-girls school. That's how we decided on St. Anne's.

While filling out my scholarship application with Aunty Amelie present, Mrs. Smith and Mrs. Washington came across paperwork, which lead them to question my status. "Does Martine have any issues with her status? Is there anything that we need to do to adjust her status?" they asked Aunty Amelie with suspicion.

"Martine's status is fine. She is legal here, and she has no immigration issues," Aunty Amelie retorted.

Later that evening, Aunty Amelie began her rants: "Who do they think they are? These black Americans seem to think that they know everything. I don't trust them. You better not forget and start trusting them, do you hear me?" With Aunty Amelie's assurance, Mrs. Washington and Mrs. Smith focused on generating more donations through UBE to cover the $27,000 annual tuition at St. Anne's-Belfield.

Pauline and Mrs. Smith both accompanied me to St. Anne's-Belfield in Charlottesville in the spring of 1998. It looked like a monastery sitting on top of a hill. From Ivy Road all you could see was the silhouette of white stucco buildings that sat against the backdrop of powder-blue skies. The trees were lush, and even the birds seemed to be singing like in one of those fairy tales. There was a parking lot to the right as you drove up the hill, and all I could see were fancy cars—Audis, Mercedes Benzes, BMWs, Range Rovers, you name it. Students lounged on the grass and sat on the various benches under the walkway of the main building, which was connected to the dorms. Although the cafeteria and the dorm rooms were not as nice as St. Catherine's, it felt real and welcoming. Sitting in Harriett Johnson's office for my interview, who was the Dean of Admissions, I looked out her palatial windows and noticed the leaves on the trees sway in the cool breeze. It had been such a long time since I was at such peace to notice something so delicate.

"I have always loved school, and one of the last promises that I made to my mother before she died was that I would excel in school. Coming to a place like Saint Anne's-Belfield will allow me to do well," I spoke with all the determination that my body had left. I needed to get accepted into the program. I needed them to like me. Mrs. Johnson sat tall and erect in the chair across from me, and her gray hair sat around her face in a prominent fashion. She was sturdy and strong and had a handsome face. I imagined her playing tennis throughout her youth and into her adulthood. She probably came from Southern stalk that paid for private tennis lessons. I watched in the window behind her as students walked across the yard; they looked so happy and free. Maybe I could be like that one day. I had found my new home, and unbeknownst to me, the school also found me.

"Let's get Martine up and running and then let's focus all our attention on Emanuel. Meanwhile, Emanuel can work on improving his grades for the second semester," was how Mrs. Smith and Mrs. Washington massaged the news to Aunty Amelie, and she bought it. As the three of them sat together to fill out the final application for St. Anne's, the question of my status came up once again, and Aunty Amelie reassured them: "Martine is fine. She has permanent resident status." So that was the box that we checked off and submitted the application.

The days leading up to my departure were filled with resentment coming both from Aunty Amelie and Emanuel. "You see how you are leaving us?" I never knew how to respond to this. Was this a rhetorical question? Was it even a question, or a statement? I could reassure her and say that I didn't want to go, but we would both know that I was lying. The truth was that I couldn't wait to get out. I felt bad for leaving Emanuel, but I was leaving him with his mother; it was no longer my problem. *Aaah!* The prospect of being back in school and living in a school, away from the insanity! Just in case I had gotten carried away by the idea of going to boarding school, Aunty Amelie reminded me of the nobody and nothing that I would always be.

"I bet that's what Martine will bring home from boarding school," she mocked as we drove past a lowly, black bum. Emanuel laughed because he thought that it was funny. "Martine, if I ever catch you associating yourself with someone like that, a black American, I will disown you, you hear me?" I was shocked by her prejudice and her own self-hatred. Weren't we all black at the end of the day?

"Yes, Aunty Amelie," I replied, hating harder.

The day before my departure to St. Anne's, Stone, Aunty Amelie's beau, snuck me some money to take with me. "I know that your aunt doesn't give you much so take this and let's keep it our little secret." It was a hundred dollars, which might as well have been a million dollars to me. I know that I shouldn't have been accepting money from a grown man that I barely knew, but I desperately needed some spending money. I accepted the hundred dollars and thanked him, and he wished me luck. It must have killed Aunty Amelie to drive me down to St. Anne's to drop me off.

"You are there to study so that you can go to a good college," she declared. "You don't have time to make friends or boyfriends. Is that clear?" Funny that suddenly she was concerned about my education.

"Yes, Aunty Amelie," I obeyed. I told myself that there was no point in forging relationships; at this point, it was just about my education.

It was my first week in the dorms and in a boarding school. The air in Charlottesville had a perfume-like sweetness; when you breathed it in you could taste the honey suckle at the tip of your tongue. Saint Anne's was a complete contrast to Columbus, Ohio, and Andover, Massachusetts, where I lived after Ya Marie died. It wasn't the first time that I heard people use the phrase "y'all," but at STAB it came with a certain aristocratic charm. These kids reeked of money. Most the girls talked just the way they did in those movies I watched about rich plantation owners in the ante-bellum South. I wondered if they were all debutantes. The men all had cool names where their first names sounded like last names. So many of the kids were tall and blonde. While I was mesmerized by what I saw, I was grateful to be in the dorms with whom everyone called "the boarders."

In contrast to the rest of STAB, we were a sea of shades and languages that almost seemed out of place in the establishment.

Unlike the exterior of the building, the dorms were geriatric with creaking, wooden steps that led to our dorm mother's apartment. The walls were thick from the many coats of paint they endured. The dorms were one of the few places where I felt normal being black.

The other was Señora Castillo's advisory. She was the very first Peruvian person I had knowingly ever met. Moreover, how could a Peruvian be a Jew? Señora Castillo stood about five feet and no more than one hundred pounds soaking wet. She had the most commanding presence. It wasn't just due to her exquisite beauty. She had a dark-olive complexion, indicative of her Incan Indian ancestry; that sat against her high cheekbones and shoulder-length, very-straight and very-black, silk hair.

I looked forward to starting the school day in her advisory just so I could listen to her sophisticated accent and partly for her fashion shows. Señora donned a gorgeous scarf of a different color or pattern each day. I imagined her to have a walk-in closet decorated with thousands of scarves of every color and pattern. In my mind, she never wore the same scarf more than once. She was generous about sharing her scarf with young girls who decided to show their bra strap or cleavage that day. I loved how she stood in the hallway and would greet each young man and woman as Mr. This or Miss That. She was both a drill sergeant and a dainty ballerina.

Priti and I immediately hit it off in Señora's advisory. She was a pretty Indian girl who maneuvered through French and Spanish without effort. She also danced hip-hop and knew all the latest rap songs. The Indian girls I knew of my past were very traditional and didn't listen to DMX, Naughty By Nature, and Salt-N-Pepa. That and the fact that she liked one of the three black guys on campus gave her street credibility. When Priti introduced me to Celeste, I was further intrigued. Celeste had a very Bohemian flare, and if you didn't know her well enough, you would think that she parented herself. She wore sarongs made of batik, a tank top, and flip-flops. She was the most independent fourteen-year-old I had ever met. Celeste was the same person who came up with the idea of having an all-star retirement team.

"I have a rad idea! We should all grow old together and, like, take care of each other. So we should buy houses near each other and start what I'm calling an All-Star Retirement Team. Martini, are you in? It's exclusive, and I'm only inviting a few people." Celeste was always full of ideas, great ideas.

CHAPTER 2

EBOLA

I will hurt you so bad.
Your real father didn't even want you, you makaka.

I. READY TO TAKE OFF

"Your friend is five months pregnant and she's going to Zambia with you?" my doctor who gave me my travel vaccines asked. "I would advise against that."

We were leaving in a month, and all signs screamed, *don't go.* Cautiously, I wanted to call everything off as the tinge of fear crept in. First, I had to stop telling people that I was going to Africa; and second, I had to refrain from telling them that my pregnant friend was going with me. God forbid they knew she was white.

The nurse administered my yellow fever, hepatitis B shot, and a rabies vaccine. While I wasn't expecting any wild animals to bite me, one could never be too safe. Celeste and I had gone back and forth about malaria pills, and she recommended one for me.

"You don't want the one that will give you daymares. It's the worst. I got a prescription that pregnant women can take. We should get some snacks for the trip because this baby loves to eat." She wasn't concerned by the fact that she was pregnant. "I'm more worried about you and your stomach. I've travelled so much that I've built up bacteria but you haven't, so you need to get some serious antibiotics for diarrhea. Ask for Cipro. One time, Ethan and I had some gnarly diarrhea in South America. I hope that you don't get it, but let's just be safe." She was like the Wikipedia of third-world travelling.

She insisted on staying at a hostel for three nights while we travelled to Livingstone with my dad. I wanted to stay at the Zambezi Sun but Celeste made a good point: "Your dad is of modest means," she said, "so like he actually might feel uncomfortable if we go to a place like that, you know?" I wanted to impress my dad and show him that I was moderately successful without his help, but maybe she was right.

"Fine, but please can we stay at Latitude 15 afterwards?" I countered. "It looks really cool and Sacha says that it's super upscale. Just for two nights."

The truth was I was terrified of staying in a hostel, even though the ostentatious photos on the website made it seem more like a motel than a hostel. Quite honestly, I didn't see myself staying in a motel either. I wanted my lodging to be like an *Out of Africa* scene. But I had to keep up with the pregnant lady, so I obliged. Sacha, who was Priti's friend's friend, was in Lusaka for a stint for work. How ironic that I was getting advice about travelling to Zambia by an Indian woman from Seattle, Washington. She had been there for a few months and seemed to be culturally sensitive and street smart.

"Martine, I don't think that you should be going to Africa right now with the Ebola outbreak and all," my coworker said. As soon as I heard about the Ebola outbreak in West Africa, I knew that this would happen. Why did people clump Africa into a monolith? If it wasn't the stereotype of it being backwards with jungles for streets, then it was war torn and riddled with AIDS. The last thing we needed was another story about being wrought with the Ebola epidemic. I wondered how people felt so comfortable alluding to prejudices in front of my face. White people did the same thing to me when they talked about ignorant black Americans, as if to elevate me and remind me that I was not a black American. It also happened during the many years that I was illegal. People excused me for also being illegal by pointing out that I was an exception to all those illegal border-crossing Mexicans. It was a waste of time to explain that while there was an outbreak of Ebola in some parts of West Africa, an American was more likely to contract it in North America than someone in Zambia.

Another bizarre concern I had was that my stepmother would poison me. This was the result of a conversation that I had with my dad's eldest daughter months prior. "Don't tell Papa but our stepmom tried poisoning Mama Marie (Ya Marie, my mom) many years ago. She became very ill." I guessed that she was threatened by my mom. Sure, it sounded like a Nollywood rendition of *Snow White*, but I wasn't willing to take the risk. "Make sure that you don't eat any food that she offers you. Only eat from the same plate that everyone else is eating."

My imagination ran wild. What if she insisted on my eating her cooking? Maybe I could just tell my dad upfront that my doctor had advised eating at home because the water might be contaminated. But would I offend him? "Don't tell your dad right away because he'll tell your stepmom, and she might find another way to poison you," a college friend said. I couldn't believe that anyone else besides me was entertaining such nonsense, but I appreciated it. I needed a plan and a backup to that plan.

"Dude, we'll just not eat in your dad's house, and you can use me as an excuse," Celeste said. I loved how nonjudgmental she was and somehow nothing seemed farfetched to her. The last few weeks before our departure were full of questions from all my friends who cared about me so much that their paranoia as well as their prejudices had surfaced. How was I sure that he was my father? What if he tried to kidnap me? Why didn't I just have my father meet me on neutral territory instead of going to Africa? What if Celeste had complications with her pregnancy while in Zambia? That one haunted me endlessly. What if I contracted Ebola on the flight?

I didn't have any real answers for these questions. I leaned on Celeste, who reassured me that everything would be fine. She maintained her enthusiasm in every email and every call. "We're going to Zambia! If I wasn't pregnant, I would head to Tanzania after Zambia, but the baby is slowing me down a little," her text message read. Was she crazy?

We were leaving on November 11, 2014, in just two weeks, after Celeste flew in from Tahoe by way of Phoenix. She was attending her sister-in-law's wedding.

Then came the rare news that the Zambian president had died. Just when it felt like the inquisition was coming to a halt, we got more bad news. "What the fuck?" There would be an interim president who would hold the presidential seat until a new president was announced. This interim president was Scottish, the first white president since Zambia's independence. There was alleged rioting in the capitol of Lusaka.

"No, my Doh'ta, do not worry," my dad said over the phone. "You and Celeste will be fine. Do not worry, my Doh'ta." I wanted to trust my father, but I wondered if his response was colored by his eagerness to meet me. He was very knowledgeable about world events and local politics. I took him seriously for the most part, except when I didn't. There was that one time where he advised me not to be a lush because it wasn't ladylike. Then he backtracked and said in a broken, British English, "You can drink a little bit in America because it is very cold and you must keep warm." I burst out laughing after processing his statement, and he joined me with a guffaw when he realized how ridiculous he sounded. He also said that there were parts of Russia where our native language, Swahili, was spoken. I doubted that, but I was never able to verify it. Maybe my dad was an occasional bull-shitter but there was no harm in it. I just hoped that he was right about our safety with the riots.

In less than twenty-four hours we would be on our flight to Africa. I had been hoping for this day for so long that I never took the time to imagine it. What did one do before a life-changing event? Noor, my best friend since STAB, assured me, "Martine, this journey is going to change your life." What did she mean? She sounded like a prophet sometimes. "I don't know exactly but all I know is that it'll change your life," she elaborated. "Just be open." Right, be open, but what did Noor mean?

Celeste looked very pregnant with her belly the size of an in-flated soccer ball. Was I doing the right thing by having her tag along? I didn't know the answer to that until her husband asked to speak to me a few hours before our takeoff.

"Martine, she's going to be okay, right?" It was the vulnerabil-ity in which he delivered the question that confirmed that I would make sure that we would be okay. "Just look out for each other." It was honorable and deeply touching that he would selflessly let me take his wife and unborn child on a trip across the world with me just so I could meet my father. Celeste, Ethan, and the unborn baby were putting themselves at great risk for me. For me! Even though we took every precaution possible, fate would make the final determination.

"I can't listen to any more people freaking out about us going on this trip," Celeste said after hanging up the phone with her mom. "We need to have a dance party," she said as she turned on some music on her iPhone and began bouncing to the beat. In the morning, we packed some leftover chicken wings, because as Celeste put it, "I'm sooo pregnant!"

Was this happening or was I being pranked? They called our gate number to board the plane, and I suddenly felt like I was going into another dimension. I imagined that this was the same feeling as being on a psychedelic. Everything was at arm's reach, the plane seats, the airline stewardesses, but nothing seemed really there. If I went to reach for it, would it vanish into the air? Whereas Celeste was excited for her next adventure, I was unsure. My stomach tightened, and I felt a sensation to cry uncontrollably or maybe it was just to vomit, the feeling I always got before an anxiety attack. I was in a fight between the adrenalin in my body and my brain trying to talk me out of going through with the trip. My stupid breathing exercise was useless. I couldn't let Celeste know that I was scared, because I promised her husband that I would take care of us. I feigned a smile until I calmed myself down enough to remain inconspicuous to Celeste.

I waited for the flash mob to sing *The Lion King* theme song. I heard about this happening on South African Airways. Besides that one trip to Paris in 2010, I had never flown outside of the United States, let alone on such a long flight.

The many old couples on the flight must have been rich, white South Africans. I wondered if they were once guilty of perpetuating apartheid. Gosh, how come there were so many white people travelling to Africa? There were three South African black guys who sat in the far-right isle, each in a different row. Were they part of the Lion King show? Were they visiting New York City? Did they find South Africa to be accepting of their black skin? I wondered if they spoke Zulu or Xhosa, both sounded awesome. They seemed cool and full of swag and laughed a lot. One of them was cute and, under normal circumstances, I would have made a mediocre attempt to flirt with him—not flirt-flirt but maybe cough uncontrollably so that he would turn and notice me. Not today, though; I was just trying to mentally prepare for the journey. Was there a certain way that a girl who is about to go to her home country and reunite with her father is supposed to feel?

After Celeste finished wiping down her seat and my seat with disinfectant and making me put Neosporin in my nose, she advised me to write my thoughts. "I saw it on the news. The Neosporin traps the germs that permeates the plane." Celeste was giddy and glowing the entire time I was subdued and unsure. That often happened when I became overwhelmed or scared. I would either break out into uncontrollable laughter or I would go into a catatonic-like state. She helped me come out of it with her schemes and brilliant ideas.

Somehow, she finagled it so that we got an entire isle to ourselves.

By the time dinner came around, Celeste was excited that we got served first since she put me down for gluten-free meals and her for vegetarian; except on the rare occasion when she asked for a second meal with chicken. "Dude, this baby loves to eat!" She was a solo comedy act. Meanwhile, I was ogling all the non-gluten free meals and wondered if it would be weird to also ask for the pasta.

"This is it," I muttered under my breath. I was on a flight going back to my birth country to meet my birth father. I repeated that statement like a primer to diffuse the shock. I tried to remember that initial experience I had all those years ago back in 1985 when I took my first airplane to come to America. I barely remembered that I had to give away my favorite mahogany sandals that hugged my brown feet until the day we departed for the United States, or "Etats Unis" as my mom used to call it when using her native French.

"Shesheme," my mom said, looking down at my stubby, four-year-old body that somehow found itself in a blue blazer with gold buttons with anchors designed on them. Shesheme (pronounced Shay-shay-may) was the nickname that my mom gave me, which I loved exponentially. Aunty Amelie had sent the blazer for me to wear for my trip to America. It would only be a few hours later that the flight attendant would accent my blazer with little wings. Ya Marie and I both looked down at my feet secured to a sole by crisscross mahogany straps; both my feet and the sandals were ashen from walking on the dirt road. "You need to give those sandals to someone else. We are going to *Bulaya*, where you can have all the sandals you want," she said in Swahili. *Bulaya*, our native Swahili term for America, means paradise. With such high expectations for America, it's no wonder she grew bitter and depressed during her eleven years here.

The air was static and cold with a hint of that airplane smell; you know, that mix of room spray and sanitizer. The pressure in my ears was very real and so was the dimmed mood lighting and the snoring from three rows behind me.

I looked at Celeste who was sprawled out at the other end of our isle, listening to the Nigerian music station, I was sure, and bopping her head. Her smile was reassuring as if she could read my mind and wanted me to know that I was doing the right thing. The many movies that I watched were not a divergent from the reality of what was about to happen. My jaw clenched when I thought about how scared I was, and then it softened when I also thought about everything that transpired to bring me to this point. No one could argue that all that was a dream. Surely, this wasn't either and, hopefully, it would be unforgettable in a good way. I was going to meet my dad!

What if I didn't like him? Again, the same fears kept coming up. What if we have nothing in common and nothing to talk about? Didn't he already tell me everything there was to know about my past? It was Celeste's suggestion that the three of us take a seven-hour bus ride from Lusaka, the capitol, to Livingstone so that I had time to catch up with my dad without the distraction of other family members. Suddenly, I was overwhelmed by the idea. What if I couldn't stand the guy?

My brother, whom we called Maxwell, was also recently reunited with our dad when our dad went to visit Maxwell in South Africa. "Yo, man, dad is a funny guy," he told me. "He loves nature so the bus ride will be cool for him to get inspiration for his paintings, man." I had never met my twenty-six-year-old brother, but in the two years that we started speaking, we had already gotten into three brother-and-sister arguments, and he had already made fun of me a few times.

"Welcome to having a younger brother. They get mad at you for no reason," Priti remarked as if this was some sort of initiation into becoming an older sister. The truth was, the idea of meeting my biological dad reminded me of the absence of my true father, Uncle Dan, who died when I was thirteen.

As a photographer by trade, he had a way of capturing Ya Marie's beauty and my youth through his 35-millimeter lens.

Uncle Dan brought sanity to what would have otherwise been an insane relationship between Ya Marie and me; he was my buffer.

"Stay away from black Americans, especially the men; they're all hoodlums and they're uneducated," Aunty Amelie warned my mom when she and I arrived in America. That was her African immigrant mentality that she attempted to infiltrate Ya Marie with. It is only safe to assume that Ya Marie took immense satisfaction in marrying Uncle Dan, an African American, in November 1988. Dan Cooper stood six feet with copper skin, black freckles sprinkled about his round face, and a fade cut. Although he was husky, his fat was well proportioned to his body. Uncle Dan's obsession with playing tennis kept his belly from bulging, so he never appeared overweight, except for when he wore his Hawaiian shirts with white boat pants. With a big, bright smile and a high-pitched laugh that sent others into a cacophony of laughing fits, it was difficult to see him as anything less than perfect. The only time that I witnessed Ya Marie smile or laugh, was when Uncle Dan was around. I realize now that it was weird to refer to your stepfather as uncle. I must have called him Uncle Dan because all of my cousins referred to him as such and the name sort of stuck.

Uncle Dan and I bonded through Michael Jackson videos after I moved in with them when Mama, my maternal grandmother, passed. "Martine, come watch this Michael Jackson video with your mom and me," Uncle Dan would invite me to the living room where he and my mom sat on the 70s-inspired tweed loveseat. While he wanted to cuddle with my mom on the couch, she kept a respectable distance, as she felt that any display of affection in front of me was inappropriate. He would watch our faces for excitement and then turn up the volume when Michael hit the perfect note or when he did his moonwalk dance. "Look at that! Haha," Uncle Dan blurted out making it nearly impossible for my mom and I to be mere spectators.

My voice sang the lyrics to "Bad." This was the ideal way to perfect my English.

Ya Marie chimed in the remainder of the lyrics: *Who's bad?* This seemingly insignificant encounter brought the three of us closer. I was only seven or eight then.

When it wasn't Michael Jackson that facilitated our nuclear family, it was the Smithsonian, the Lincoln Memorial, the Jefferson Memorial, and the Air and Space Museum. We practically frequented downtown Washington DC every weekend, but

Uncle Dan never grew tired. Being a history buff and the son of a former soldier, these trips were sacred, and Uncle Dan wanted to convert me into a lover of history.

"Hey, did you check out the giant elephant statue?" he asked me every time we visited the Smithsonian.

Oh gosh, here we go again, I thought to myself while appreciating the attention deep down.

"Louise and Martine, get in front of the elephant statue so I can get a photo. Martine, why don't you pretend that you're listening to the message and pick up the receiver," Uncle Dan commanded in less of an authoritative tone; sounding more like a child who was on his way to meet a childhood superhero. He waved passersby out of the way of our picture, eager to chronicle our lives through his lens. "Louise," Uncle Dan sang my mom's name. "Give me a big smile." My mom stood out in an odd way as she wore her African garb in public. We suddenly became the quirky television family with the overenthusiastic and slightly corny dad who embarrassed his family just a bit. This was the luxury of normalcy.

When it was time for checking and reviewing my schoolwork, Uncle Dan was serious. The two of us sat at our kitchen table, with a gaping window in front of us. From our third-floor Silver Spring apartment in Maryland, one could see my elementary school, Greencastle, which wasn't green and didn't resemble a castle. Long division was awfully confusing. How was anyone supposed to know where to place the decimal point, and did it really matter where the decimal ended up?

"Martine, are you guessing or are you focused on your homework?" Uncle Dan asked as he reviewed my homework and marked all ten problem sets incorrect. "Do you understand the homework?" he asked searching for my face, which was bent down facing the paper. When he noticed big tears spill onto my homework assignment, he grew aggravated. When he got angry, his nose would flare, and he would bite his tongue. "Martine, do you even want to do your homework?"

"No, no I don't." My head shook from left to right. Crying was risky, because if Ya Marie caught site of it, she would attempt to intervene by beating me.

"Fine," he said, beginning to chew his tongue harder, "if you don't want to do your homework, then don't do it. Tomorrow, when your teacher asks you why you didn't complete your homework, make sure you tell her that you didn't want to do it. Eat your dinner and then go to your room." He was so gentle even when punishing me that it only caused me to feel more guilt.

When he went to join Ya Marie in the adjoining living room to watch Jeopardy and Wheel of Fortune, I caught her glare. The intensity in her look matched with her words: "I will beat the right answers out of you," her stare said.

"She doesn't want to do her homework, Louise. Leave her alone. This is the only way she will learn," he calmly said to my mom, who wanted to make sure that her daughter hadn't disrespected this gentleman. About thirty minutes later, Ya Marie caught me walking down the hallway on my way to my room.

"Shesheme," she spoke sternly yet softly in Swahili so Uncle Dan wouldn't understand, "do you realize that he's not your real dad, so you can't afford to act so stupid around him, huh? What's wrong with you? He's trying to help you, and this is how you show him your appreciation? I will hurt you so bad. Your real father didn't even want you, you *makaka*," (a derogatory word in Swahili that means monkey). When she began her verbal assaults, she couldn't be stopped.

She continued, "He [your father] was a liar and ugly just like you. And here you are acting like you're so high and mighty. Be careful. Be very, very careful with me. Don't forget who I am and what I can do to you." I wasn't sure what was more tortuous: Ya Marie's words or the fact that she wouldn't shut up.

"You remember how I beat your sister Zalika? I'm not afraid to do it to you, too. You are not American, so stop acting like an entitled American. You better not give any more attitude unless you want me to beat that attitude out of you." My only comfort was in knowing that as long as Uncle Dan was at home, he would not let Ya Marie lay a finger on me.

It would have been better if Uncle Dan was my real dad and Ya Marie wasn't my real mom. She grew unnecessarily angry when this wasn't even her business. I wished that Uncle Dan would walk by in that moment and catch her bullying me. She seemed to not want to upset him, maybe for fear of him walking out on us. I wasn't allowed to show any kind of expression at the risk of her perceiving it as insolence. My mom was good at reserving her beatings for later when no one was around. The longer she held her assaults, the worse they were.

Uncle Dan acted the same way my friends' parents acted—normal. He didn't seem like the beating type. He seemed like the kind of dad you could have a healthy argument with. It was still very foreign to me, because I had grown accustomed to being beaten.

While Ya Marie preferred to inflict pain through beatings, Uncle Dan's punishments were sophisticated. Whenever the chores didn't get done or my homework wasn't complete, Uncle Dan took charge. "I'm giving you two weeks to read *Alice in Wonderland* and then by next, next Saturday night, I expect you to write a two-page book report and present it to your mom and me." The punishment seemed egregious; perhaps Ya Marie would speak up for me for once and point out that reading a three-hundred-page book in two weeks was cruel and humanly impossible for a kid. As painful as the punishment was, I always walked away from its completion feeling proud of my achievements.

It was excruciating to overhear them watching *The Cosby Show* from the living room—my favorite show. It would not come as a complete shock if they laughed harder just to further antagonize me. If there was any chance of even watching the last five minutes of Bill Cosby's show, then quick action had to be taken.

After getting dressed for bed, I walked into the living room and announced, "Excuse me, Uncle Dan. I'm ready to finish my homework now, please." Thankfully, he softened up, and a smile appeared on his face. The rest of the evening resulted in us working diligently to help me understand where to carry the decimal. When it was my bedtime, my homework was complete, and I was ready for an in-class pop quiz. Even more delicious was learning that Uncle Dan recorded the episode of *The Cosby Show* so that I got a chance to see it.

It was Ya Marie's yelling in the next room that woke me from my slumber and sent chills down my spine at midnight.

II. AN ENIGMA

"Dan, I will kill you! Do not do this to me!" Then I would hear her begin to cry. What exactly was he doing to her that brought on her spells? How could she speak to Uncle Dan that way? He never yelled back, he just mumbled words that were inaudible through the walls and cried.

It was during these fights or when eavesdropping on Ya Marie's phone conversations with one of her sisters that Uncle Dan's past was unveiled. It was hard to believe that this Ohio State graduate who spoke a perfect cosmopolitan English could have had a sordid past. Before he was with Ya Marie, and lived the life of a bachelor, he was involved in the possession of drugs and abused drugs. While it wasn't clear if he had ever served time in jail, his two brothers had been incarcerated. As far as I knew, Uncle Dan had cleaned up his act by the time Ya Marie and I came into his life.

I blamed my mom once again for these arguments. She always had a way of bullying others, and now she was doing it to poor Uncle Dan. She didn't deserve such a kindhearted man. It hurt me to hear her bring him to tears. What kind of mean person did this to their spouse? I didn't care what awful things he had done in the past; he loved me, treated me well, and protected me. As far as I was concerned, he was a saint.

During the weekends when Ya Marie was preoccupied with selling her African clothing designs at the flea market, Uncle Dan and I would go to the local Blockbuster video store to rent my favorite movies: *Pippi Longstocking, Ramona Quimby,* and *Anne of Green Gables.* Before getting home, we took a detour to Dominos to pick up a large pizza. The bubbling, hot cheese and meaty disks of pepperoni that sat on a thin crust went hand in hand with the movie. The movie was so much better when Uncle Dan added his personal commentary: "Pippi is nuts and so is that crazy monkey of hers!" he exclaimed, which followed by me laughing. To keep Uncle Dan from dozing off, I would ask him a question or comment when his eyes started to close during the movie: "Uncle Dan, isn't Pippi crazy?" These were some of the fondest moments of my childhood.

It seemed like Uncle Dan grew ill overnight. His belly became bloated, making him appear eight months pregnant, his eyes were sunken in, his skin was the color of a yellow Crayola crayon, and he seemed exasperated and cold all the time. "I'm fine. We'll just need to review your homework after dinner from now on because I need to go to the hospital for chemotherapy." That word—chemotherapy—seemed so big and ominous.

"He'll be okay. You worry too much, Shesheme," Ya Marie actually showed me compassion during these times. Things were not okay, and they became more apparent by the time of my elementary school graduation when Uncle Dan was in the hospital and couldn't attend. "Your Uncle Claude will take you," Ya Marie said as she picked out white stockings, white shoes, and a pink, rayon wrap dress that Aunty Dominique bought for me. Ya Marie would also have to miss my graduation because she needed to be in the hospital with Uncle Dan. It was fine if she couldn't come, but it was heartbreaking to not have the man whom I owed my educational success not watch me receive my diploma. I no longer cared about the stupid graduation. It had little meaning without Uncle Dan there. Who would shout my name and laugh uncontrollably when it was my turn to retrieve my diploma? Who would take incessant photos of me walking to the podium, shaking hands with the principal and smiling with my diploma in hand? Nobody. And there wouldn't be a party afterwards at our apartment like I played out in my head.

"Martine M. Kalaw," the principle of my school called out through the microphone, creating an echo inside the oversized gym room, which housed about one thousand adults and children. The parents were sitting in the bleachers, and all the students sat in rows of seating around the stage. My heart skipped a beat as I walked to the stage to accept my diploma. I looked around to see familiar faces in the crowd, but everyone seemed unrecognizable, even my classmates. I had allowed my imagination to run wild just minutes ago: *Maybe Uncle Dan will surprise me and actually be in the audience when they call my name.* But I accepted my diploma and sat back down and there was no Uncle Dan. In fact, I even went home and went to bed and woke up the next morning and Uncle Dan was still in the hospital.

I hoped that meeting my dad wouldn't overshadow the memory that I had of Uncle Dan, who was the best father I could have imagined. I didn't talk about him much to my friends because the final memories of my childhood with him and my mom and his passing were incredibly painful and confusing. How do you describe a man who you once thought was your knight but then seemed to betray you in the end? Was he responsible for my mom's death? Until I was sure he wasn't, I could no longer hold him in such great light. Talking about him forced me to talk about the painful latter part of his life, which left me raw with emotion.

It was enough hurting to write a four-hundred-page book about it. But two years ago, those dimwit editors seemed to disagree.

"My memoir is about a self-made immigrant girl who—" before I could complete my statement, the author who had organized this workshop with prime-time book editors interrupted: "Martine, that's boring. The news is full of stories about immigrants. Everyone's tired of that story."

What did this bitch say?

Absolutely warranted profanity thinking. Reducing my circumstance to a story merely for entertainment and then disqualifying it angered me. I suffered as an illegal immigrant and that was real. I sat in the author's chaise lounge chair that had a recliner but opted to sit at the edge of the chair to illustrate my discomfort. I didn't care how many bestsellers she had written, she had no right to comment. I was sick of these New York City big-shot writers thinking they had the authority to rewrite everyone's lives. The workshop organizer was dumb, her house was stupid, and all the books she had shelved in her perfectly laid out library were even more stupid!

"And might I add that you're way too young to be writing a memoir?"

I told the workshop owner to eff off, mentally, which brought me great satisfaction. The only thing that would have been better was if I had stormed out of there like a madwoman.

Little did they know that I had been through enough in my thirty plus years to qualify for a memoir. The pains I had experienced would have produced enough pages for two memoirs, is what I thought. My body seemed to dwarf in the sofa as I clung to the far-right corner and begged for them to approve of me: "So much has happened in my life," I reassured them. "For instance, my dad found me through LinkedIn and lives in Africa."

It was an incoherent thought that formulated into the statement that I blurted out. But suddenly my gusto was gone, and I was desperate for their approval. "And he's a polygamist. I just found out." It was like throwing out bread crumbs for pigeons to lure them in.

"Now, that's fascinating!" the Asian editor confirmed his approval with a slight leaning in and a half smile.

"What would be even better is if you meet your father, and you can't stand him. That'll be worth putting in the book. It's about conflict among people," the workshop owner said as she turned towards the other students in the room. To which everyone smiled and nodded their heads like they were in some sort of trance.

I felt the tears well up and the back of my throat tighten. For someone with such an expressive face, I could not afford to feel angry because it would show from ear to ear. Perhaps if I remained stoic and didn't move or say anything, I could conceal my disapproval. In that moment, I hated every single person in that room. How dare they wish for me to dislike my father to further their own interests in reading a good book? I hoped they would all get hit by a garbage truck.

"Woah, dude, the baby just kicked for the very first time." Celeste's face was beaming, and she put my palm to her belly. What a miracle to witness the formation of life, so I patiently waited for Baby Fischer to kick again. That's what we were calling it for the time being. "Man, it was totally kicking a minute ago," Celeste confirmed. I wondered what that must have felt like. "Kind of like someone elbowing you but a little softer. It feels a little bit like gas." It didn't matter that Baby Fischer didn't want to kick for me. I was just grateful that it was up to travelling all the way to Africa at a tender five months. "Baby Fischer, we're going to Africa," I spoke to him or her telepathically.

III. GOOD-BYE PARIS

I was going home, home. I breathed a sigh of relief, finally able to be honest with myself. It was only five years ago that I had denied my African heritage. "I'm an American, it's all I have ever known myself to be," I recalled telling the reporter. Deep down, I was a liar. I knew that I was just as much African as I was American but how could I explain that so that people could understand? It seemed to me that the only way to gain sympathy from Americans was to reject anything that was not.

It was the year 2000 and the dean of Hamilton College Admissions offered to "clear up" my immigration problem by reaching out to his trusted friend Sarah Davis, an immigration attorney from Brooklyn, New York. I was nineteen, so what did I care? I didn't fully understand my immigration problem, nor did I see it as a problem. It was more like a lingering cough. I conceded without question and was relatively unconcerned because there were no real visible issues.

Throughout freshmen year, Sarah was on a mission to establish my identity and therefore confirm my immigration status. Her Freedom of Information Act (FOIA) request revealed extensive documentation related to my mom and me that Sarah began to dissect. She was able to validate that my mother and I came to the US legally in 1985. How suspicious it would look to anyone that didn't know me that my name was different on every official document, making it virtually impossible to validate that I was in fact the same person. Sarah could establish that my mom was a permanent resident—a green card holder—at the time of her death. But that still didn't seem to answer the question of my status.

During the summer of my sophomore year I secured a fellowship to study US foreign policy at The American University in Washington DC. Sarah continued to point out the roadblocks.

"As you correctly observed, travel abroad in your current state is unwise." Meaning that any realistic aspiration for my junior year to be spent studying abroad in Paris was impossible. How unfair! If these countless hours of wracking my brain in French class didn't amount to noshing on quiche lorraine in a Parisian café, then what was it all for? I'd been ogling at paintings by Henri Matisse and Toulouse Lautrec since middle school art class, dreaming of days visiting the Louvre Museum and eating croissants while conversing in the most romantic language imaginable. Cliché? Yes, but that's the experience I yearned for.

"It will be nearly impossible to travel outside the United States and then gain reentrance," I read the statement and tried to imagine the voice and the face of the woman behind such biting words. I imagined her to look as doughty and plain as her emails. Apparently, I lacked the necessary status with which to apply for a passport or visa. But the more daunting question: if I needed status to gain status, where did that leave me? My first pangs of fear related to my immigration status crept in. Damn my denial all these years, but there could be no denying all the doors that were closed to me now. In my email correspondence to Sarah, I begged for her to save me: "I don't know what to do next. I'm frightened because I don't want to get deported and because I want to get permanent resident status before I graduate from college. . . . I need your help because I don't have money, parents, a family, a job, a stable home, or an income." My pleas were pathetic but necessary.

When Hamilton College's President's Office realized that there had been little progress made to my status, the college's president put his assistant, Heather Lewis, on the case. She was assigned to reach out to the office of the local congressman, Sherwood Boehlert, due to the school's close affiliation with him. Boehlert's office had to assist in expediting my immigration inquiries so that I would have proper status by the time I graduated, only a year and a half left. After she connected the dots and realized that my battle would be long and difficult, Sarah bailed. "The needs of your case require a different level of understanding of immigration law, which I cannot provide," she wrote in her final correspondence.

Stupid bitch!

So much precious time lost; I got the run around from Sarah Davis and somehow had to make up for three years of lost time.

I needed someone to blame for everything that followed. I needed something to justify the tragedy that was before me. What was to come was like the fifteen-year civil war in the Congo; it just kept going and going leaving me more lifeless after each shot.

IV. A WITCH HUNT

The September 11, 2001, attacks created a heightened police state, which paralyzed my life due to lack of national identity; I was considered a threat under the Department of Homeland Security. My life became a secret, or a lie. Mrs. Smith and Mrs. Washington warned me about traveling alone: "And when you do travel, don't even consider flying. Only take the bus and train. As a matter of fact, just take the Greyhound bus," they ordered. The goal was to remain as invisible as possible and not draw attention to myself. I stayed on campus during every holiday and never left my dorm room. At almost twenty-one years of age, I was practically a fugitive; my anxiety and paranoia about "getting caught" multiplied.

I had a persistent nightmare, where the INS would perform a sweep on the Hamilton campus and every finger, student and teacher alike, would point to me, the leper, to be reprimanded like the Salem Witch Trials or McCarthyism. My status made it impossible for me to be a good student, which was all I had known until that point. The blows kept getting rougher to handle.

To apply for an identification document, I needed some level of identification—a genuine Catch-22. Forget about voting; basic pleasures in life, like going to a local bar once I turned twenty-one, was out of reach. I wore my student ID like a badge of honor because it was the only identifier that legitimately affirmed me. I dared not risk confiding in anyone, fearing they would out me to the authorities. I maintained friendships, but my "situation" was hard to explain, and I was too ashamed to speak about it, so I remained somewhat elusive within my circles. Simply stated, they would never fully understand my incomprehensible dilemma.

Since I couldn't study abroad in Paris, I settled on doing a semester in the second-most amazing city in the world—New York City. While it was the precipice for a national catastrophe, it still had a rhythmic magic. I lived in a luxury high-rise building in Battery Park City. "My bedroom overlooks the statue of liberty," I told friends who remained back on campus. The ceiling of the lobby looked like what I imagined the Sistine Chapel's ceilings to resemble. It was rumored that Mike Tyson and Lenny Kravitz lived in the building.

"The UN needs some form of ID to allow you to enter the building. It needs to be government issued so your college ID won't be sufficient," Professor Azar informed me while avoiding eye contact. Another blow. For those brief hours, my classmates visited the United Nations as part of our coursework, it occurred to me that this is what Hell must be like: watching everyone enjoy the life that you've been denied.

Twenty-one years old and technically I should've been able to waltz right into a New York City club, but instead I plotted with Ashanah to obtain a fake ID. "A friend of mine told me about a sex shop in the West Village where you pay about $60 to get a fake driver's license. But they look real, and it's guaranteed to work." She was only nineteen and insisted that we go. If only I had noticed that the hologram on my Connecticut "license" was backwards. To further the ID irony, my fake identity was denied, blocking access to a world that I desperately sought after—the party world—where I could escape the realities of my life. I just watched my coevals enjoy life.

The following summer, I got accepted into the Ronald E. McNair Research Program at the University of Rochester (U of R). What a relief to secure a home for the summer where I didn't have to worry about being polite and walking on eggshells, in an effort for people to like me and want to help me. In the dorms, I could be myself without scrutiny. Maybe I could impress the administrators of the program into giving me a post-graduate fellowship. Sure, getting accepted into the program was prestigious but my motive was having free food and a bed to sleep in. I was honest in my application and wrote "in process" wherever it asked about my citizenship.

Getting accepted into the McNair Program seemed like another small miracle. Only two weeks into the program, I received a call from the U of R attorney. I was in my friend's dorm room diagonal from mine. Roxana was a cute Polish girl from New York City with the tiniest frame I had ever seen on an adult woman. She cared about three things: boys, becoming a doctor, and learning to drive. It was in that order, and that's all we talked about. She wanted to talk about her ex-boyfriend and what her psychic said about him. I was slightly curious but not looking forward to the drawn-out story that she liked to retell about how they broke up. I was grateful when I heard the phone ring in my room and told Roxana to hold her thought and that I would be right back.

"I'm Jim Crumble, and I represent the U of R's legal compliance department. Martine, we're reviewing your paperwork, and we're not sure that you'll be able to remain in the program. We can't find any records in our files that prove that you're a permanent resident. And because the McNair Program is federally funded, I'm not so sure how we can let you remain in the program." His words were jarring. If I got kicked out of the program, where would I go? Where would I live? I was virtually homeless until the last week of August when Resident Advisor (RA) training started. I calculated every move to secure a roof over my head.

"I'm probably going to get kicked out of the McNair Program," I warned my friend Ashanah later that evening when she stopped by my room. Ashanah was my confidant because we were both from Hamilton College and were now in the McNair program together.

"Why?" she asked.

That looming question, which I dreaded, always prompted the same ambiguous, ambivalent, surface response that I hated to give but only had the energy and the faculty to give.

"Because of my immigration situation."

"Oh, man," she responded but was more preoccupied with talking about her latest crush. Sometimes I appreciated her ambivalence. It was better than being interrogated with questions about my immigration status.

I began to pack my room, preparing for my fate. I didn't own that much stuff to begin with, but still, where would I put all this stuff? Maybe I could offer to house sit for a professor again for the summer until school reopened. No way would I ask to stay with Señora Castillo or Mrs. Smith. I didn't want to overstay my welcome with either. I felt the throbbing of my temples as if my blood vessels would burst. I had no solutions. I was going to be homeless this time around.

After what seemed like days, I got a call from the attorney. I already prepared myself for the worst. Would they consider what I did as perjury or fraud? I wasn't equipped to go to jail. Technically, I didn't lie on my McNair application. If they kicked me out that same day, how would I face my classmates, Roxana? Why wouldn't life just give me a break? I was just trying to survive.

I held my breath and picked up the receiver and resigned to the next wave of bad news that my luckless life warranted. "Martine, we've been able to figure out a way to allow you to remain in the McNair program. The university will subsidize the cost of the program for you so that we're complying with the federal guidelines of the program as well." I could never understand all the work that it took for him to make this possible, but I sure was grateful. I felt a sense of relief and sighed as the butterflies in my stomach settled.

By November 2001, the US Department of Justice responded to Congressman Boehlert's office about the inquiries of my status: "There is no record that would establish her lawful presence in the United States. Additionally, there is no relief." Why did they have to make it seem so final? No relief? My life was over then, I would always remain the nobody that I was. A staffer in Boehlert's office recommended that I obtain a lawyer and consider applying for the Diversity Visa Lottery program. I had heard of this lottery program by word of mouth, but I also heard rumors that the authorities falsely advertised this to capture illegal aliens.

Myth or not, I was afraid to risk it. A month later the college received a letter from the Albany Office of Immigration dated December 18, 2001: "At the present time, service priorities are such that there is little likelihood any action would be taken to place her [Martine Kalaw] in proceedings or enforce her departure."

Heather Lewis and I both breathed a sigh of relief. Immigration services was too preoccupied with actual threats to the safety of the US to worry about little old me. This correspondence reassured me that it would be years before authorities would come looking for me, and by then, I would have already become naturalized. By being a good student and always filing my taxes, I was an asset to the US economy, and ultimately, I was convinced that I could become a US citizen overnight. Since I sounded American, acted American, officials would grant me citizenship. Becoming a citizen seemed like a mere formality. My misconception was a mix of impatience and naïveté.

With reassurance from Immigration and Naturalization Service (INS) that I was not a threat and would be overlooked by authorities, Heather offered to drive me to Albany; the president's office encouraged that I obtain a social security card to maintain my work status. I had a social security card at one point but the last time I saw it, it was at Aunty Amelie's house, and I wasn't back there to retrieve it. Although I hadn't gotten far in my last attempt at the Social Security Administration three years ago while attending STAB, I felt that my luck had changed and things were about to improve. Hamilton administrators were fully aware of my nonworking social security status, but they also wanted to maintain proper records; thus, my part-time job in the Dean of Faculty's Office was funded through scholarship money instead of federal funding.

The work was menial—answering phones, mail and package currier to various buildings on campus—and it provided additional income. Many slow days in the office afforded me the time to do my homework. I didn't consider the reasons for the visit to Albany and the Social Security Administration, except that we were directed to go there.

During the car ride, I fought off sleep to impress the president's "right-hand person" with all my acquired knowledge since coming to Hamilton. But Heather insisted that we were beyond formalities and that there was no need to recite my resume every time I saw her.

"Martine," she laughed, "you can relax around me. I'm not going to quiz you."

At this point, she knew of my dedication to being an active citizen on campus: RA, a member of the Hamiltones (the coed a cappella group on campus), and co-chair of the Adler Conference, a campus-wide event created to align the community with common goals and initiatives.

We arrived at the Social Security Administration in Albany, New York—a washed-out room with outdated orange-brown carpeting, dirty, white walls that needed a fresh coat, and jaunty, faux-leather chairs. Unlike my encounters with Pauline and Señora Castillo, I was about to meet another woman who would play a heavy and unfortunate hand in my fate.

V. US vs. THEM

We were seen by a sarcastic woman with thinning, brown hair and a shapeless skirt to hide the rolls on her legs and buttocks. The social security lady pointed her attention to Heather and failed to look in my direction. Instead of being frustrated, I experienced immense gratitude that she was at least willing to take my spokesperson seriously. Heather presented a very corporate look with her oval face, milky-white skin, and blue eyes; she was dressed like Murphy Brown. I couldn't wait to fill out all necessary paperwork so that we could finally obtain a new card issued to me. The faster we accomplished this, the sooner I could return to my burgeoning school homework; my biggest priority was a ten-page essay for sociology class, critiquing J. M. Coetzee's book on South African race relations and apartheid versus Brazil's racial tensions. There was also that horrid economics assignment that I hadn't even begun to review.

"I'm sorry, but we can't issue a new social security card for her at this time." The social security agent spoke to Heather and I as we sat motionless and crestfallen in her cubicle.

I shifted my attention onto her for mere acknowledgement that I existed.

"The status on her card is outdated at this point, and she'll need to clarify this with INS," the woman continued.

Every syllable that exited the fat woman's mouth sounded foreign to me. How could my card be outdated?

"I'm sorry, I'm afraid that I don't understand," Heather said with a tone of irritation and confusion. Breathe. Pause. Then she continued, "We just want to see if we can get a copy of Martine's existing social security card." She said this as she turned towards me in acknowledgement that I was in fact the Martine under discussion.

Heather always had a way of including everyone in the conversation, just by a slight shift of her shoulders or a subtle glance your way.

"I'll make note of that in the system. But she'll have to go to immigration services to get her status cleared," she said as her fleshy fingers took notes.

The agent cut Heather off before she could put in her final request. "I'm sorry, but this is the best that I can do. You'll have to meet with an immigration judge in court to adjust your status. Then we can issue you a new social security card."

The way she said it made it sound simple enough. "Can you please verify your name and mailing address?" the woman continued.

"My name is Martine Mwanj Kalaw," I said in the most clear and calm voice possible. This was just a mild hiccup, and if I remained calm, everything would work out.

"Wow," the fat lady looked up from her paper, "you don't sound like the rest of them."

What exactly did she mean by "them"? Her comment caught me off guard and infuriated me. "Them" suggested that there was also an "us," which in my mind alluded to superiority.

From that simple statement, I could complete the picture of this insignificant peon: she probably hated her job and her life; the sole outlet available to her was to exact authority over individuals that she believed were weaker than herself. If she perceived me as a "them" then in her thinking I was lowly, which explained why she acted as if I was invisible during the entire appointment.

I thought of Ya Marie, who worked diligently to master the English language, yet her thick francophone accent prevented her escape from the reality of "them." She would never live the life of the "us" crowd. "Them" inferred my best friend from my short middle school stint in Columbus, Ohio, whose family were first-generation Vietnamese immigrants. Their ten-person family lived in a three-bedroom house, within which the only language spoken was Vietnamese. But when they walked outdoors, they consistently tried their best to assimilate to avoid being seen as one of "them."

Another example of this outsider syndrome was my childhood babysitter from El Salvador. She watched *telenovelas* during the daytime and fed me beans and rice when I came home from school. All these years I thought that I was different from "them" because I spoke proper English and attended the right schools. But harsh reality set in that day: it didn't matter what I did or how I acted, the world saw me as one of "them." My head guided my eyes as my attention shifted down to the carpet. My skeleton failed me in that moment and could no longer hold me up in that erect sitting position that Aunty Amelie taught me to convey authority. In that moment, I felt ashamed, subhuman, and lowly just as fat woman intended.

"You should be receiving something in the mail," she said. "We're going to direct your case to the closest immigration court, which is in Buffalo, New York. They will most likely get in touch with you."

By February 2002, the President's Office, led by Heather's efforts, began to inquire within the community for a reputable immigration attorney who could guide us. After experiencing the run-around by another immigration lawyer from New York City, we were able to identify a decent attorney six months later, but time was running out.

The only avenue I had to obtain status was from a direct relative, of which I had none. Many laws that would have remedied my case were no longer enforced. I was considered unlawful because I overstayed my visa. I came to the US when I was four as a visitor on my mother's visa and was granted to remain in the US only for a certain number of years. I stayed here past that expiration date and did not take the necessary actions to adjust my status, relegating me as an unlawful nonresident; I went against the law. As a result, I was not eligible to apply for resident status.

But I was a child, so how could I have known all of this? It finally occurred to me that I was one of them—an illegal alien. I was Quasimodo from *The Hunchback of Notre Dame*. I already felt the fingers pointing at me, waiving to me in disapproval because I was a bad person. From that moment, I was overtaken with shame.

My heart became a yo-yo: some days I felt hopeful, and I believed this was mere protocol and would soon end; other days I feared the unknown. Days turned into hours, hours into minutes, and that's when the nightmare began. What would happen in a year when I graduated from Hamilton? I was grateful for all the assistance the college provided, but I also feigned gratitude for people like Sarah Davis, who were supposed to help me but only created more damage. I had to smile and act appreciative because I was desperate for help. By senior year, I had experienced enough setbacks regarding my immigration saga that I could no longer deny its looming reality.

"The college will support you in whatever way that we can in paying for your legal fees. John James was referred to us because he practices out of Buffalo, New York. Considering that your case is directed to the Buffalo Courts, it would make most sense to have representation from someone who is familiar with that jurisdiction," Heather commented.

"So I was thinking," she continued, "that we arrange this conference call with Mr. James to see what advice he can offer." The call was scheduled for that following day, after my last class of the day, which was an Eastern Versus Western Feminism course taught on the north side of campus, which Hamiltonians also called "The Light Side."

Heather and I sat in the air-conditioned room with its large, oval, oak table and leather, reclining office chairs, with a three-sided speakerphone in the center of the table. The telephone rang and Leslie Vidal, John's assistant, transferred us to him.

"Helllooo," a gentle and perky male's voice echoed from the other end of the telephone. I tried to imagine this man's face, but nothing clearly came to mind. I did get a slightly blurred vision of John James's stature; he sounded like a very small man. His voice lacked base.

Heather jumped in, "Mr. James, we spoke briefly about Martine Kalaw's case. She's sitting right here next to me. We want to know about the next steps and how we should prepare. It's not clear to us what the issue is and whether or not we need to go to Buffalo for a trial or if we need to fill out an application for anything."

"Okay, here is the issue. Martine, are you there?" John James asked.

"Hi, um, Mr. James," I spoke in my most monotone and professional voice. I couldn't afford to have my attorney see me as one of "them."

"Okay, Martine, you're required to appear in court . . .," John continued.

The rest of what he said was muffled by the voice in my head. It had all come down to this: I was being summoned to appear in court like some sort of criminal, someone who offended the system. According to legal standards, I was an "illegal alien." "Alien" because I came from another country and was not a citizen of my host country. "Illegal" because I was in violation of immigration laws. The oxymoronic phrase of "illegal immigrant" didn't make sense because an immigrant is someone who has applied for residency or is a citizen of their host country. Therefore, an immigrant can't technically be illegal. Nevertheless, it sounded better than the cringe-worthy idiom "alien," so I used it most often. (The euphemistic term of "undocumented immigrant" was birthed almost a decade after my immigration journey.) My label was intended to evoke a sense of inferiority, and it worked.

For the last five years, all I had been doing was surviving, certainly how was that an offense? I felt my tonsils get hot and the back of my throat burn, the sensation I had when I was fighting back tears. But I wouldn't cry. Not in the president's Oval Office. Not in front of Heather. I didn't want to annoy these people who were trying to help me.

"Martine, listen to me carefully," he annunciated each syllable. "Right now, you are a non-immigrant late overstay. You have been placed in removal proceedings because you have yet to establish your lawful status in the US. Your Master Calendar Hearing in Buffalo will be presided by one of three IJs, or immigration judges: Judge Wood, Judge Colucci, or Judge Minor."

Interestingly, hearing this level of detail gave me a sense of comfort; finally, there was an actual person from the immigration apparatus—having a name validated my existence, or so I thought.

"You will receive a form in the mail, which will notify you of your court date and time."

It was a very scattered conversation, but he seemed to know what he was talking about.

"Why don't you speak to my assistant, Leslie Vidal, to schedule an appointment? Are you there? In the meantime, I need Martine to put together a timeline detailing every major event that occurred in her life from the time that she was born until now. Also, I would like for Martine to write a testimonial about her life."

Should I have been taking notes? Heather, who was sitting on my right with her body facing me was scribbling on fancy paper. Her blonde bob stayed perfectly intact and never once interfered with her ability to see what she was writing. Was it hairspray that caused that effect? I noticed her eyes this time. They were a baby blue but painted over with a gloss always making it look like she was teary eyed.

"Explain your life and put as much relevant information about your immigration as possible." Mr. James added. "Can you have that for me by the next time we meet?"

"Yes." My response was quickly followed by a reassuring "yes" from Heather.

John continued his rant. What was he saying? Was I that foreign that the English language no longer made sense to me? I grabbed onto the beginning of each sentence like life support but quickly gave up midsentence. Everything he said seemed to have a qualifier, "but," "if," and "however." It was dreadful. John's locution was so matter-of-fact, devoid of emotion. Heather kept reminding me that as an attorney, his job was to not sugarcoat anything and to view the case from its worst scenario. How could this stranger on the other end of the line, who was spouting his learned expertise from case studies and law books, ever understand my burden?

"As a backup," he concluded, "we need to start lobbying congressional staffers to see if they can motivate their representatives to create a rider to a bill for Martine. I must remind you that getting a private bill is an exception to the common law."

Finally, something promising!

I saw myself as a black Reese Witherspoon in *Legally Blonde*, with a Martine Bill being approved by the Senate and the House, then signed into law by our president. I would be famous and change the state of immigration. If that was where all this was leading, then perhaps it was worth the sacrifice. The congressional bill could take years, but if we exercised all other avenues, then it would be our last resort. I would stay the course this time, no more trying to quit. I wanted this.

Heather and I proceeded to request from all who knew me to submit a letter, attesting to my good moral character and verification as an asset to the United States. I begged and implored my friends in a general email, which began: "I've missed numerous opportunities for fellowships and scholarships and I'm afraid that this is just the beginning . . ." I was no longer in hiding. I could finally share with my close circle of friends that I had an immigration problem. I was careful not to reveal too much, though, for fear of their judgments.

Professor Azar, eccentric and full of knowledge about US foreign policy, was perplexed by my situation. "It's just unbelievable," he would say with a slight lisp as he raised his arms fifty degrees and shake his head in disbelief. A handsome forty-something-year-old-man of Lebanese decent, he often reminded me of Jeffrey Goldbloom. I had a little crush on Professor Azar, but who didn't? I'm sure that even the straight guys had a "bromance" with Azar.

It was how he crossed his legs when he spoke and prepared to say something intellectual. Azar was also incredibly sarcastic and carried a boyish grin whenever he said anything. Students referred to him as just Azar, as if he had been initiated into the cool college students club. He used the word "provocative" often when describing his commentary of foreign policy.

He and Elizabeth Giles, a graduate of the college who also taught study skills classes on campus, offered to edit my testimony. Elizabeth lived on the college campus, a bit further uphill near another faculty. She had always taken a liking to me, and I attributed it to my taking her class seriously, unlike seemingly most students. I was also serious about the mouth-watering marinara sauce that she abundantly poured on her spaghetti. There wasn't much planning or outlining involved in writing my testimony, just stream of consciousness—except for one bit of detail. There was absolutely no chance in hell that I would reveal my mom's abuse.

It was difficult enough to write about the torment administered by Aunty Amelie. I was ashamed of my past and felt that I had somehow deserved it. If I shared my abuse, would it reinforce the stereotypes that white people had about blacks? Wouldn't my experiences just prove that, once again, black people were terrible at raising their kids and took provincial methods to discipline them? I was asked to appear at the Buffalo Immigration Court on January 15, 2003, for a Master Calendar Hearing at 9:00 a.m. As John explained via the speakerphone, it was mere protocol.

"You're presented with a Notice to Appear on January 15," he said. "The goal of this hearing is for us to buy time with the court. The judge will ask you if you have a lawyer, and you will say that you need more time and that you just recently hired an attorney, me."

Like a nervous tick, my head bobbed up and down uncontrollably. I bumbled "uh huh" every five seconds. My arms held onto the armrests for dear life. I crossed my legs with a double knot, hearing Aunt Frances's disapproval: "Only crazy people in mental institutions cross their legs like that. You look like you have a mental disorder." I uncrossed them and persisted to bite the inside of my cheek, which was comforting.

"My role is to make it clear to the court that I'm unfamiliar with this case as it currently stands and I need more time for review," John spoke with such self-assuredness, as if he had done this a million times in his sleep. "This will lengthen the case and a new court date will be appointed to us."

"Lengthen the hearing?" I asked in complete shock. The cheek biting stopped, and my face drooped as I tried to quantify the statement. There was not a patient bone in my body; the thought of not knowing results for an indefinite period was excruciating.

Annoyed by the line of questioning, John retorted: "Sometimes it goes on for years."

As if the situation would change if I could just get John to say what I wanted to hear, I pleaded: "Do you think it will take that long?" I could not imagine spending years of my life in limbo; the idea was agonizing.

"Let's focus on getting ready for the hearing," he responded impatiently.

After extensive research, we determined that I was not a recognized citizen of either Zambia or DRC. I was, in fact, stateless.

VI. STATELESSNESS

"This is good!" John James shared various sentiments. Even when he was excited, he maintained the same monotone. "Do you know why this is good? This is good because now you don't have a country to be deported to. It will be difficult for the court to deport you if no one will take you."

It was a difficult argument to make; that I didn't exist and, therefore, I needed relief. My psychological disrepair was deepening: in documents and conversation I was being told that I'm a nobody; now I may have to claim it as my truth. Regardless of the laws of the Democratic Republic of the Congo, the US Immigration Court simply wanted to get rid of me and would try to deport me there.

A life in the Congo terrified me; it's a country that had been in a state of war for over a decade, where over half of the population was destitute. Rape is still a common act of torture in certain parts of DRC. Although I took French classes, I wasn't exactly fluent in French, Lingala or Swahili, another native language in DR Congo, so I would have no way to communicate. I had maternal siblings in the Congo, like my sister Mimi—albeit, I didn't know them personally at that time nor was I certain that they were all alive. The living circumstances there were deplorable. I was sure that Mimi, a pediatrician in DRC, could not afford another mouth to feed. Zambia was not that much safer for a young, single woman in my circumstances. Based on what I read and heard about both countries, I wasn't confident that I would survive either.

Then the most daunting reality hit me: If a third country couldn't offer to take me in, then I would end up in a detention facility. After all the years of fighting and anguish, this is how my life would end? In my Google search, I learned all the bad things that happened to people in detention facilities and as a deportee being held in a detention facility, what legal recourse or power would I really have? Detention facilities were, simply put, jails. What if they raped me in the facility or beat me? What if I remained in there until my case was finalized, which meant that I could be in there forever. It hit me like a ton of bricks; I was stuck in this nightmare.

On the day of the hearing, John commented, "Look, this hearing is formality."

All my hearings including my visits to John James's office were in Buffalo, New York, which was a three-hour car ride each way from Hamilton College. I was too busy emotionally preparing myself for every visit to Buffalo that I didn't consider what would happen if Heather or Elizabeth Giles no longer offered to drive me there. Taking the train and bus was still risky because of the raids that immigration authorities were conducting, especially being so close to the Canadian border.

"The judge's name is Colucci. He just wants to know that you understand the charges being brought against you and that you have a lawyer. I will do most of the talking. He will most likely ask you if your address is updated with the court so that the court can always reach you. Then he will schedule the next calendar hearing."

How appalling to be accused of "charges" by the court! It was the other way around; I felt violated by the weight of potential deportation, when I was clearly a victim of circumstances.

The courthouse sat one block away from Statler Towers, the location of John's office. Heather and I braved the cold with John walking ahead of us, resembling a child playing dress up in an oversized coat and duck boots. After going through a pair of revolving doors, we were greeted—more of a grunt than a greeting— by INS security guards, who worked under the Department of Homeland Security (DHS). In case anyone forgot, there were DHS posters plastered to every wall in the foyer as a reminder. The floor was a cold and greyish cement, making the room feel sterile.

We got in line for the scanners as the stern-looking guards greeted John: "Good morning, Mr. James. It's an early one," said one guard who finally cracked a smile. Mental note: this was a good sign that the guard was chummy with my lawyer.

Ironically enough, everyone in the lobby was instructed to "take out your IDs and present them before going through the machine." How could "the illegals" in the room be expected to present identification when the very nature of our presence was to obtain said documentation? All I had was my college ID. What would the guards have done if I told them that I did not have any legal form of identification to enter the building? The combination of my college ID and John James sufficed, and we were cleared to take the elevator across the hall onto the right. On the left-hand side were clear, glass doors that led to another room. It all felt so hypnotic that I could no longer rationalize anything or think clearly. The elevator only climbed to the third floor when we got out, but the ride seemed endless. We were greeted with an autographed picture of President George W. Bush Junior in the lobby of the third floor. At the sign-in booth, I was ordered to provide my alien registration and a signature. It was confirmed that I was an alien—an "alien"?!

Thankfully, John knew my alien number by heart.

The *Glamour* and *Marie Claire* magazines beckoned me as I walked into the waiting room, breathing a sigh of relief; things wouldn't be so bad. I always judged the nature or gravity of a situation based on the type of magazines available. For instance, when we sat in the Intensive Care Unit of the hospital the day Uncle Dan died, there were only two *National Geographic* magazines, one with a malnourished African child and another with a corpse on the front cover, which alluded to the heaviness of the environment.

Finally, our turn came and we walked into the courtroom and Heather and I turned left, where John instructed us to sit in the back row and wait for my case to be called. The confined courtroom had been sucked of all air, leaving us only with the thickness of contempt. The carpet was a dingy blue, releasing the odors of old coffee spills, mildew smut covered up by carpet cleaner. There was a lot of wood in the room, perhaps even the walls were made of the same dark oak. A matronly looking white woman with no makeup and clearly no sense of style, the court reporter Deborah, sat on the far-left-hand corner of the room typing away on a typewriter I'm sure had been around since Teddy Roosevelt. I later learned that the dirty-blond-haired white man who sat next to her was the prosecution, representing the DHS.

The judge sat high on his bench on the opposite end of the room on the left-hand side. Directly to his right behind him was a door that lead to the judge's chambers.

I felt a surge of euphoria when my case was called. I imagined that the judge would see me and think to himself, "Look at this poised, young woman," and it would dawn on him that I was very much an American in the cultural sense; he would obviously ascertain the clear waste of time and the honest mistake of my presence in his courtroom. When he immediately asked me if I understood how I offended the court, I felt like I entered a vacuum again where all sound had been sucked out. *Huh?* Did I understand the case that had been brought against me? Was this a trick question? John didn't prepare me for this. If I said no, would I be handcuffed immediately, put on a plane, and hauled to Deportation Land, wherever that was? Was I supposed to say yes? Wouldn't that technically be lying under oath? What do I say! It was like being asked your final statement before your execution. "Yes," I mumbled.

"Ms. Kalaw, it says here that your address is 198 College Hill Road, Clinton, New York 13323. Is that correct?" The IJ looked up to ask the question.

That's it? That's how he would open up this dialogue? Didn't he want to know why I believed that I was innocent? I planned to respond in a deep and assertive voice; this would be the impetus to a conversation between the judge and me, I was sure.

"Yes," I said with an assertive glance, which quickly turned into a nervous smile. I managed to project into the microphone that sat in a stand on the desk in front of me. I think he heard me.

"Your Honor," John, who was sitting to my right, stood up and spoke. "I was recently appointed to this case, and I would like to ask the court for more time to review this case with my client."

"How much more time?"

"July, Your Honor," John replied.

It was like watching a Ping-Pong game because there was so much back and forth but nothing substantial was being said.

"Mr. James," the judge resounded. "I'm running a court here. Deborah, what is the next available date?"

Pause. Deborah stopped her tapping on that stupid typewriter, licked her finger, and began to flip through the papers in front of her. *Yuck!* I couldn't stand when people licked their finger to sort through paper. She confirmed the date to Judge Colucci, which we all heard, so it seemed unnecessary for him to repeat it. Since he was the bigshot, I guess he felt the need to say it again.

"Mr. James, you and your client are due back in court on August 8, 2003, at 9:00 a.m. Is that okay with you, Mr. James?"

"Yes, Your Honor."

"Great. Mr. James," the judge said, "please explain to your client that if she should move at any point, she is to notify the court immediately. Any failure to do so could be deemed as your client disrespecting the court and attempting to flee."

"Flee?" I whispered to myself almost forgetting that I was sitting in a court room. Where would I go? I had no money and no identification, so how far could I get? I was trapped by the system and by my own psyche. The guilt, shame, and now paranoia was enough to keep me hostage for life.

"Yes, Your Honor." John started to get up, and I looked around the room in disbelief. Was that it? When did I get to speak? Why didn't the judge want to hear from me? Why didn't the judge ask me if I was okay with the next hearing date?

John and I walked out of the courtroom to meet Heather in the lobby. She was sitting in the back of the room on a bench the whole time. I guess she preferred to remain inconspicuous to the judge by waiting to speak after we left his court. My interrogations began: "What's the next hearing about? What date is it exactly?"

John replied in a patronizing tone: "Why don't we walk to my office to discuss this, okay?" Why did he do that? Add "okay" to the end of each question he asked as if he was commanding me rather than asking me.

We walked to his office in silence except for the banal questions that Heather asked about the weather in Buffalo or the history of Statler Towers. Statler Towers at one point was a lavish hotel during the 1920s, blah-blah. Why talk about this when my life was literally coming undone?

I was angry for making this long three-hour journey only to utter two words to the judge. It was insulting and a waste of time to have us travel out of our way only to spend about ten minutes in the courtroom.

"Our next hearing is scheduled for Friday, August 8, 2003, at 9:00 a.m.," John replied.

"That's such a long way away," I pleaded as I tried to untie the knot in my stomach. "Can we have it sooner?"

Graduation was in four months, and I had no plans; everything depended on this hearing to determine my next step. But even after this journey, I remained without answers or an identity.

By August, I would be homeless and jobless. I know I said that before, but I was certain this time.

"We are," he cringed, and his nostrils flared as he was speaking to contain his annoyance from my question. He shut his eyes and tightened his lips for a moment to suppress a growl or a yearning to scream at me. "We are trying to build a case, and we need time to build our case and to gather evidence."

Another pause, then he swallowed his saliva and began to enunciate making his words short and abrupt: "It. Is a good thing. That. We. Have. Seven months. To prepare. Okay?"

Heather didn't seem pleased with his tone either.

"What should I do in the meantime to prepare?" I complained, hoping that he would pardon me and magically make all my problems go away.

"Graduate. Focus on your studies. We need the court to know that you are a dedicated student and that you're an asset to the US economy. Now, August 8 will be our second Master Calendar Hearing, but it will also be my first appearance in court where I will get to present to Judge Colucci our case and our plea."

"So it's the same judge?" I asked.

"Yes, it will always be the same judge. Judge Colucci," John James commanded.

I only spent a total of thirty minutes in a courtroom with this judge, but I got a weird feeling about him. I cringed at the thought of having to see him again. It didn't help that a few months ago John hoped that we would get appointed to any other Buffalo immigration judge but Colucci. He had a bad reputation apparently.

"I need you to continue to do well in school and to graduate." What an asshole. I was like an annoying flee to him, and even though this was my life and my case, he would have been happier if he could swat me away. Could I even trust this guy? I was torn between hating him and desperately clinging onto him for dear life.

There was no further discussion after this point. While I knew what the intent was for August 8, I graduated in May, and there was no mention of how I could work legally in the US between the time of my graduation and August. Did it ever cross John's mind, or were such banalities too trivial to discuss? He had a case to prepare.

Why couldn't I be more normal like my friends? I wanted to take a hiatus from school like many of my friends who were getting jobs or taking the summer off. I wanted to be one of those kids who travelled across the world for a gap year or maybe had the luxury to join the Peace Corps and go to the third world and help fight malaria or whatever those volunteers did. It didn't matter; I wanted to rest like the old days.

I remembered the drives that Uncle Dan, Ya Marie, and I would take from Maryland to Columbus, Ohio, to visit Uncle Dan's family. Somehow the name Ohio always came out as "Ohowi" when I attempted to tell others where I was going. When I realized how much "Ohowi" sounded like Hawaii, I was positive that we were driving to Hawaii, which made the eight-year-old me all the more excited to share with friends. The drive was about seven hours each way, and I relished it. I had the entire back seat of our four-door blue Nissan that Uncle Dan bought from a used car manufacturer. Ya Marie packed sandwiches for the three of us. She always made the most delicious sandwiches, with toasted white bread, mayonnaise, ham, and cheese. She even sprinkled cayenne pepper on the inside part of my bread, which mixed with the mayonnaise and gave the entire sandwich an extra kick. I timed it perfectly so that I finished eating just in time for nightfall. I relished how the sky assumed a thick coat of a midnight blue, while the crescent moon followed us from the corner of my window. The best part was falling asleep to the sound of Ya Marie's light breathing as she dozed off in the passenger's seat while Uncle Dan hummed to one of his Marvin Gaye cassettes.

In practical terms, I needed a course of study that would buy time as I completed my immigration ordeal. I was officially an adult

ILLEGAL AMONG US

now, so I couldn't rely on anyone taking me in as they did when I was much younger. Until then, I wasn't sure how likely it was for me to work legally. No, I didn't fight so hard to graduate from these private schools just to end up working under the table. Besides, it seemed like a seedy subculture that I was scared to maneuver. How does one even look for jobs under the table? No, I couldn't do it. If only I could get into graduate school. But what would I even study? I had no more drive or motivation in working hard in school. What was the point?

At the suggestion of a college administrator with a master's degree in public administration, I glued my eyes to the computer screen later that night. Public administration. It sounded like the ideal degree for me, as its interdisciplinary nature would keep things exciting, offer the tools to study my own case. Eventually, the Heathers, Elizabeth Gileses, and John Jameses in my life would give up on me, so I had to be able to save myself. Most importantly, secure a home.

I could also pair public administration with law and take a sampling of what law school would be like, in case I decided to pursue a JD later. There were just a few minor hiccups. Each application averaged to about $85, and I only had enough money to apply to two programs. As if that wasn't stressful enough, hiccup number two was that I hadn't even tackled the subject of how I would pay for school.

The applications had been submitted to Columbia and to Cornell, but all the change in the world would not be sufficient for the Syracuse University's Maxwell School application. The program promised to pack a lot in one year, including an option to take immigration law courses and get a certificate of law. I always wanted to have an Ivy League school as part of my pedigree, but Maxwell's program seemed interesting. In reviewing my personal statement for the program, Hamilton's Career Development Counselor remarked: "This is fluff. You need to tell your story. Your story is powerful. It's compelling. That's what will set you apart from everyone else. Tell them that."

Was the counselor right? Was my story that authentic? I had grown so accustomed to living my crazy life. Sure, I knew that it didn't resemble the lives of my close friends, but was it worthy of being documented? I was doubtful but certainly willing to give it a shot. I didn't know what I would do if I didn't get into school, but one thing was for certain; I was leading up to my college graduation with no viable future.

It was April 2003, and I had not heard from Mr. James for some time. It was so frustrating to chase after him, just so he could read me my future. I wrote him in an email dated April 1, 2003:

Dear Mr. James,

It has been a while, but I have been working hard as you suggested. I recently got accepted to graduate school: Cornell University, Syracuse University, and to the University of Rochester. The Maxwell School at SU has offered me a full grant to attend their one-year master's program in public administration. In addition, I am pretty certain that I will also be graduating from Hamilton on May 25, 2003. So I completed the mission that you assigned me to, so to speak. I am inquiring as to how things are going regarding my case. Have you started filling out the paperwork for a congressional bill? Pardon me for being so anxious, but it's just that I am nervous because August 8 is right around the corner and I just want to have an honest opinion of how things are going. If there is anything more that I can do, please feel free to contact me anytime. Please get back to me with any updates.

Thank you so much.

Best,
Martine Kalaw

Weeks followed without a response. I needed John to respond to me before I lost my mind. Why wasn't he answering me! It would only be a matter of time before the seesaw of my life consumed me. One minute I was on cloud nine, and the next I was a wreck. Even if I tried, the magnitude of my nightmare broke down the walls that I built to shield myself from pain. I was an open wound. I couldn't even begin to imagine the type of journey that I would have to go on to heal.

CHAPTER 3

FANTA

His eyes were tiny slits like mine, but
they sparkled like stars in black night.

I. WE'RE IN AFRICA

Sixteen hours, four meals, and five movies later, Celeste and I arrived in Johannesburg, South Africa. Celeste was on a mission to find Wi-Fi to contact Ethan while I was itching to go shopping.

Celeste's pace was more of a sprint, as if she knew exactly where she was going, as if she had been here before. She managed to get in contact with Ethan, and then we did some quick shopping before our flight to Zambia.

We boarded the rickety, small plane. The leather seats were ripped at the seams. The screws that bolted the seats to the floor seemed to shift and creak when the fat man next to me sat in his seat. While there wasn't any food on this flight to keep her busy, Celeste was quick to make friends with the cocoa-brown elder man that sat next to her. I rolled my eyes, imagining how long this trip would seem if she decided to chat up everyone that we met during our eleven days. And did she have to speak for me and tell them my life story? There was no rhyme or reason with whom I chose to tell my life story to. It was random, but I wanted it to be my choice and not hers. My story was the only thing that made me interesting, whereas Celeste's very presence was magnetic. As the flight took off, I expected the scenic view to look like something from *Out of Africa*, but it wasn't; it was just a typical view from a plane because we were so high up. "My friend is Zambian, too, and we're going to Lusaka to visit her dad," I heard Celeste tell the man who responded with something.

Two hours later, I woke to the sound of the pilot indicating that we were descending into Lusaka in ten minutes. I tried to remember being on this land once before. *Martine, think! Try to remember being here when you were four years old.* But nothing looked familiar.

The Customs man, who had the complexion of a drop of water combined with a teaspoon of brown sugar and wore high cheek bones didn't seem to care that I was from Zambia or that I spoke Swahili. What was I expecting, a standing ovation? When I smiled, he just looked at me blankly from his enclosed Plexiglas booth. It was fine, I just wanted him to stamp my passport. *Ah!* My very first passport, and how cool would it be to have my country of birth appear as the first country I visited? Although I wondered if the non-smiling Custom's officer was on a mission to piss me off because he stamped a piece of paper instead and stapled it to a page in my passport. Why couldn't he have just stamped the blank page in my passport book? *Ugh!*

"Welcome home," he finally said. He still couldn't manage a smile. Maybe it was written in his job description: "Under no circumstances should you smile."

"Okay, let's get ready to deal with a bunch of taxi drivers and people trying to grope our luggage," Celeste remarked rather loudly. We both kept forgetting that Zambians spoke English.

I had gone over this a few times with Celeste like a game plan. We each had our carryon backpacks strapped to our backs, which gave me the flexibility to grab our suitcase from baggage claim while she feigned the aggravators.

Luckily, baggage claim was in clear site from where we landed. The Lusaka airport was of modest means. The one-story building felt more like a fortress that kept the blazing-hot Zambian sun from creeping in. You could see from one end of the airport to the other end, and from what I saw there were no food or clothing vendors. The Lusaka airport was purely functional.

"Hello, miss lady."

"Taxi, miss lady?"

"No, thank you," I'd dismiss cab drivers.

"Hello, miss lady," another man said to Celeste, ignoring me. "Would you like a taxi?"

It was like a procession of sun-kissed, dark-skinned men in T-shirts asking to drive us to wherever we wanted to go. It wasn't as overwhelming as we imagined, though, and the requests were polite. No one tried to grab our luggage, and everyone kept a respectable distance. I hobbled with the suitcase through the group of men. I was having a celebrity moment with all the attention, and while I feigned annoyance, I kind of enjoyed it. How did we manage to make this suitcase so heavy anyway? All we had in there were a stack of I Love NY T-shirts and dresses that no longer fit me. Oh, I forgot about the three pairs of heels that I packed to give to one of my sisters. We had notebooks, coloring books, and crayons to donate to an orphanage. We also had dried food. Yes, Celeste insisted that we bring her coconut protein bars and other foodstuff that we could snack on. I figured that I might as well bring a box of the fruit-flavored oatmeal packets. It was like we were packed to go live in the Serengeti.

Twenty minutes, and the airport shuttle had not arrived yet. The blazing heat seemed to make everything and everyone appear in slow motion. It penetrated my skin and even slowed down my cognition. A group of cream-complexioned women walked by in various shades of burgundy and black hijabs. Who knew that Zambia had a Muslim community! The arrival to Zambia was lackluster. Was I expecting a group of half-naked men and women to appear and perform a tribal dance for me like in *Coming to America*?

There was a normal parking lot like any other airport stateside. The only thing that distinguished it as being an African airport was the heat, the sign that read Lusaka International Airport, and the various African languages that flew around. I was thankful people also spoke English.

Our driver finally showed up, a slight man in a T-shirt and khaki pants who was probably in his midforties. When he saw Celeste's belly, he insisted that we sit in the car. Did anyone believe in air conditioning in this country? He had us sit for another ten minutes inside a scorching-hot van as he went searching in the airport for other hotel guests. I looked at Celeste's face and for the first time ever, she looked tired. Her cheeks were rouge from the heat, and her once neatly done ponytail was practically undone. Finally, Mr. Driver was back without any other passengers. Thank God, because I couldn't imagine being squeezed next to another body in this African heat. I got excited when he turned on the ignition, waiting for cold, air-conditioned air to blow out, but instead, he rolled down the windows. Great, more hot air but this time it was blowing in my face. African air—yes, I called it

African air—was different from the Manhattan air that I was accustomed to. While the air was warm, it had a lightness to it that made it breathable. It carried a fresh scent that could easily be bottled up and sold as a room deodorizer at a Bed Bath & Beyond or something like that.

"Just remember that the majority of the world lives in these conditions," she whispered like an apparition as we drove along the two-lane highway. "Your posh apartment in Harlem makes you a minority."

Celeste must have sensed my sudden silence as shock. It was a long, straight road engulfed by land on either side. The land was vast all around us with miles of red dirt and mostly leafless trees since it was dry season. The dirt was the color of cayenne pepper, and along with the fuel of the sun's rays, it's like we were driving through an inferno. The coloring of the ground magnified anything or anybody that contrasted it. It was exquisite like a blank, red canvas. I had never seen so much flat, barren land. Every quarter of a mile, if you looked far enough into the landscape, you could see a makeshift tent made of four tree branches dug into the dirt and tarp for a roof. Oh, there was a hut! It was my first time seeing one in real life. It was almost surreal standing no more than one hundred square feet or so with a straw roof and what appeared as dirt for the actual base. Did people live in those? What happened when it rained? Back there, there was another hut! So much land, but it seemed deserted.

A teenage boy who looked like a stilt walker with the longest and skinniest sticks for legs and a bright-red shirt with a Nike swoosh and shorts caught my attention. The blackness of his skin against the redness of the dirt underneath his legs made him seem isolated. Where were the rest of the Zambians? Wasn't he scared walking alone? How come no one was with him?

The teenage boy, the huts, the red dirt, and the lack of human contact all looked staged, it just couldn't be real. The thirty-minute drive went so fast that I resented arriving to our hotel. Now we were in the city, riddled with congestion, commercial buildings, and traffic lights. I couldn't wait to tell all the cynics back home that there weren't any lions wondering around Africa, people drove cars, and there were actual buildings here.

"Dude, we're in Africa!" Celeste's eyes sparkled once again as we unpacked, emailed friends and family back in the States. The hotel might have been rated five-star, but it felt bare and somehow incomplete. It wasn't just that hardly anyone was at that hotel but the twin beds in our room were smaller than I had imagined, and the cold, marble floors felt sterile. It was fine since we wouldn't be spending too much time in our hotel room. The plan was to have Sacha come pick us up and take us to dinner in two hours. We had to treat her to a meal to thank her for all her generosity. This dinner needed to be short and sweet so that we could sleep, we had been travelling for about twenty-one hours. Then we could meet my dad tomorrow morning. Oh my goodness, I couldn't believe that I was actually going to meet my dad the next morning. I was unable register what that meant. At least I had a night to think about it. I couldn't imagine how anxious I would have been if he picked us up from the airport like he insisted. It was difficult to talk him out of it.

"What you say? Can you say it again, my Doh'ta?" he had repeated on the phone four weeks ago. "I cannot understand you very well."

"Dad," I had shouted as if that would make it easier for him to understand my accent. "Celeste and I will be very tired. We will have the hotel pick us up. You can meet us at the hotel the next morning, okay?" Even if he was disappointed, he didn't let on, which only made me feel guiltier.

"Sho', my Doh'ta. As you wish."

Sacha was more pretty than cute in person. She had an oval face and shoulder-length hair. She was the type of Indian-girl pretty that could get away with looking unkempt while making it look fashionable. We sat at a table at the local hotspot waiting for her friends to arrive. It had a large outdoor patio seating with a full bar in the front and a scattering of occupied dinner tables. The cacophony of dinner-table conversations made the room boom with base even though it was devoid of music. At the dinner table, the combination of anxiety and exhaustion hit me just as fast as it had Celeste, but our reactions were opposite. I was so grateful to her for carrying the conversation with Sacha so that I could just sit and nod.

Two of Sacha's friends joined us for dinner. While they appeared to be Indian, they identified themselves as Motswana and Zambian.

I looked around the restaurant. This is not what I imagined Africa to be. There were a lot of expatriates from Australia, I later learned. Of course, there were a handful of other black people like me in the restaurant. How ironic that I was in Africa and happened to be the only black person at a table of four and only one of a handful of black people in the entire restaurant. The two men were curious about what brought us to Lusaka, Zambia.

"We're here to meet Martine's dad," Celeste said. "Martine has a crazy life story."

I listened to her trying to summarize my life as best she could while I mentally filled in the gaps of my immigration saga.

II. ANNIHILATION BY ICE

Buffalo, NY, was a hot zone for Immigration and Customs Enforcement (ICE) border patrols. ICE replaced the Immigration and Naturalization Services (INS) after 9/11, because it was near Canada—the concern centering on the potential havoc of illegal aliens crossing the Canadian border into the United States.

"They have been doing random searches on the Greyhound buses, so it's better for you to drive to court," Mrs. Washington cautioned over the phone. I heard her coffee mug shifting on the table. Even after having gone to my Master Calendar Hearing just months ago, I just couldn't prepare myself psychologically for the next one. It was dehumanizing and confusing. I wish there had been an available diagram to explain the procedure, aligned with my life schedule, which would've minimized my self-induced agony. Each subsequent appearance in Buffalo transpired like the first one in January 2003.

The August humidity greeted Elizabeth Giles and me when we arrived for my second hearing; surely, this had to be the final one. Mrs. Giles wore a crisp, white blouse and black slacks, as she liked to call them. Elizabeth Giles took on Heather's old responsibilities of driving me to and from each hearing, like Buckingham Palace's Changing of the Guard. I wished I had reconsidered my outfit, because it was much too hot for my Martin-Fit Banana Republic pants and matching jacket; it wasn't exactly a suit, but it came close.

"Hey, Mr. James," chimed the security guards at the checkpoint.

John looked somewhat disheveled, which wasn't unusual, carrying an overstuffed briefcase. He may very well have been wearing the same suit that he wore in January; outdated sneakers replaced winter boots and a baseball cap covered his balding head. The blue-tinted windows were a nice contrast to the florescent lighting, while the confused and overwhelmed looking people in the lobby mimicked my first visit there.

The chatty, Spanish-speaking attorney I saw last time was also there. With some eavesdropping, I determined her name: Camila. She seemed particularly agitated, quickly whispering to John before walking through the body scanner. The protocol was the same as the last time: sign in, wait for your alien number to be called, and then go into the courtroom with your attorney.

To our surprise, we were called into the courtroom immediately since we had arrived only five minutes prior to our scheduled hearing. We took up position in the pew-like seats. There were a few cases ahead of mine, and I could tell that Mrs. Giles was eager to understand this process.

"You have overstayed your visa," said Judge Colucci in a condescending tone. "Did you know that?" His glasses slid to the tip of his button nose as he looked down and stared at the defendant.

"Your Honor," Camila addressed, standing up, "my client has a six-month old baby that she has to care for while her husband is away with the US Army."

"Well then she and the baby will need to leave the country, or she can leave and turn her baby over to relatives or friends or the foster care system. Either way, she cannot stay here."

It was back-and-forth bartering as Camila pleaded her client's case with bravado. Judge Colucci didn't seem overly concerned about breaking up the family unit, or that the baby's father was a member of the US Armed Forces.

The client barely uttered a word, and when she did, her minimal command of the English language was smothered in a thick Spanish accent. *What could possibly be going through her mind?* I thought to myself. Did this judge expect her to just leave her baby?

Everyone in the audience awaiting their fate looked terrified; this was not justice at all, it was ICE. Judge Colucci was even colder than my previous visit to his courtroom. He seemed to have a personal vendetta against all violators. I wasn't going to back down, however. This was my opportunity to inform him that I was not at fault. Rather, I was a hardworking woman, and I deserved to be granted relief. I was confident he would grant me my power.

"It says here that you are now at 198 College Hill Road Clinton, New York 13323. Is that correct?" Colucci asked as he looked at the sheet from behind his little, round spectacles that seemed much too small for his big face.

"No, Your Honor. I moved."

"Mr. James, your client did not inform the court that she moved," the judge warned. "This is not something that I take lightly. When your client moves, she must inform the court."

My heart had stopped. I had informed John, providing him my new address when I moved months ago. Was I supposed to directly inform the court, or was it my attorney's job? John had never told me.

"I'm sorry, Your Honor," John replied. "It will not happen again,"

"I don't want to have to keep repeating myself." Colucci motioned to his clerk. "Please provide Mr. James and his client with a change of address form."

If this hearing was supposed to be about me, then why was I referred to as "the client," and why did I remain nameless, while everyone else under scrutiny was referred to by name?

"Now, Mr. James, it says here that your client is being charged with overstaying her visa. Is that correct?" Judge Colucci asked.

"Your Honor," John replied, "my client came to the US as a minor on her mother's travel passport and visa."

"Where is her mother?" the judge inquired.

"Her mother is deceased. My client has been diligently working and putting herself through school. Therefore, we want to file a motion to appear."

"Fine," Judge Colucci said with the eagerness of a person ready to be done with work and go home, "you are scheduled for your next Master Calendar Hearing on October 10, 2003, at 9:00 a.m. Anything else, Mr. James?"

Wasn't he going to ask *me* if there was anything else? Once again, the brevity of the proceedings baffled me. After my many months of agonizing, preparing, and worrying, it only amounted to a fifteen-minute beg and response. If only I had known there would be three more of these court appearances, I wouldn't have taken them so seriously. John's strategy was to stall the process with these Master Calendar Hearings so that he could develop my case; I wish he informed me of the delay tactics. Instead, I held my breath between hearings, frantically wondering whether my next visit would result in being deported.

My unanswered questions lingered, like why didn't the judge recognize me as an individual? Or what determined my next court date—something as trivial as his mood or as calculated as a calendar cadence? Regardless, every time Colucci banged his gavel to motion the conclusion of the hearing and stated the next date, my stomach flip-flopped. How much more of this could I withstand? It was infuriating and tortuous to be in limbo status; I felt like I was waiting to be sent to the guillotine.

Fleeting moments presented themselves during what I call my "Immigration Nightmare." I felt the cold thrill of living on the edge, never knowing what the next step would bring; it was often colored by the stark reality that this was not a sane way to live. I was within months of graduating with a master's degree, and I still had no "official" identity. Thus, no means to provide for myself. *"What will I do next year? Where will I live? How will I make money?"* I often asked myself.

At twenty-three years, I could not expect anyone to take care of me, but what options did I have? While my peers spent countless hours polishing their résumés and attending recruitment events, I sat in limbo, feeling like my access to education was a tease if my efforts resulted in deportation or working "under the table" at some restaurant.

I had ambitions, and I pursued dreams. With my interest in foreign policy, microcredit finance, and human rights law, I was determined to work for the United Nations. But how, though? It wasn't that long ago when the doors of the UN closed to my face because I didn't have proper identification.

"Ideally, I would like to assume a leadership position with the Secretariat branch of the United Nations in which I can . . ." I had appealed in an email to an old college professor, Professor Ndigo, as if I were writing to Aladdin the genie. Just like countless others, his advice was disappointing, taking me down a rabbit hole. The sheer absurdity of my situation triggered feelings of desperation from friends who tried to come up with a solution, anything. So many powerful individuals were at their wit's end over my immigration status—congressmen, college trustees, school administration, lawyers, alumni—they felt powerless because they could not help me.

When people offered their advice, I gritted my teeth: You should just get knocked up. I could marry you and that would make your problems go away. Here, call this number. Let me get back to you. Others prolonged their response because they were too embarrassed by their lack of immigration knowledge. Unfortunately, I bore the brunt of each absurd response and politely feigned gratitude—no matter how asinine the idea. "Okay, thank you so much. You are truly the best. I appreciate your efforts," should have been stamped across my forehead.

Meanwhile, each suggestion that really meant rejection was a direct blow to my ego and was shredding me on the inside. I wanted to scream, "If it were that easy, don't you think I would have done it by now?"

"Trans-border Feminism," led by Professor Aditi Singh, offered a small group of us a roundtable discussion where we critiqued feminism in both hemispheres. How sweet to have Professor Singh in my last few months of grad school. Singh was powerful and knew other powerful feminists, like Angela Davis. Of equal importance to my sanity, Professor Singh, who was aware of my immigration battle, would not let me retreat inward and become the victim.

"Talk to me for a few minutes," Aditi had politely commanded as class concluded one day. "I haven't gotten an update on your case. What's going on now?" It was just the two of us around a boardroom table. She slightly intimidated me because, as a feminist, I wondered if she judged me for wearing makeup and acting so girlie. She shook her head repeatedly left to right in complete disgust as I recounted the horrors of Judge Colucci's courtroom. Unlike anyone else I spoke to, she wasn't dismayed or befuddled; rather she was irritated and ready to march straight to the courthouse herself. "So how are you dealing with all of this, Martine?"

"Oh, I'm fine," I said with a weak smile.

"Fine?" Aditi asked while her eyes glared at me from beneath her raised eyebrow.

"I'm just really exhausted."

"I cannot believe you. Do you hear what you are saying? How can you sit there and be so contained? Your life is being controlled and they are telling you that you are powerless, and you aren't even a little bit angry? Don't you feel like screaming? Let it out!"

What did she expect me to do? After four years of back-and-forth theatrics, I was too tired to be angry. And what if I was angry, it wouldn't make a difference. No one seemed to care about me. I wanted to scream so loud that the vibration of my voice would shatter every window in the building. That's how enraged I was.

"But Aditi, I'm frustrated, and I feel helpless."

"But you are the exact opposite," this radical saint mentored. "There are two definitions of the self—the social definition and the state definition. The social definition tells us that we are who we are based on our relationships, our parents, our last names, our ethnicity, etcetera. The state defines us based on our nationality, our citizenship, our social security number, our driver's license, etcetera. The state tells us that if we do not have these definers, then we cannot exist in society, let alone succeed. You have lived and excelled despite your lack of access to these state definers. So in fact, you are bigger than the state," she said with conviction. She also carried an Indo-British accent, which made her sound more convincing. If I could have only seen past my own misery, I would have hugged her; my personal social empowerment was my guarantee of identity. But who cared about Aditi's academic, social theorist babble? This was real life and a pitiful one at that; I did not fit either the state or the social definition of the self: in my view, I lacked all the necessary definers to establish an identity— no mother, no father, no family—all I had was my name.

The simulation case study from Asylum Law class gave me an idea that I shared with John James. If Tousari, my hypothetical client, was eligible for an Employment Authorization Document (EAD), which would give her temporary permission to legally work in the US while her case was under court review, then surely something similar had to apply to me. An EAD, also known as an I-766, is a work authorization that comes in the form of a plastic card and permits noncitizens to temporarily work in the US.

"Interesting," John replied a few weeks later after my fourth Master Calendar Hearing. "Let me check." He grabbed a few leath-er-bound books from the shelf and sifted through them. "Hmm. You might be on to something. Let's get your application ready and then submit it in July."

He was the attorney, so how come I was discovering some-thing that should have been so obvious to him? This information was like Immigration Law 101, for God's sake. Was he stupid, or did he just not care about my case? Why wasn't I a priority to him? Was this my punishment for being pro bono? How would I be certain that he would file for my EAD in July? If I didn't get this

EAD, I wouldn't be able to work, and this time I wouldn't have a school to hide out in.

John made some indication to a biometrics screening where ICE would have to take my fingerprints and a photo.

III. IT'S SURREAL

The EAD was issued to me on July 1, 2004, and for the first time in my life, I tasted identity freedom, the nine-month expiration date notwithstanding—like going from slavery into indentured servitude. I could finally apply for and secure a job, earn money, and "be normal."

Three wonderful things emerged from that summer: I graduated from the Maxwell School at Syracuse University with a master's in public administration, I moved to New York City, and finally the Master Calendar Hearing drama was over.

I nursed a bottle of spring water while politely smiling at our company. I didn't want to be rude, but c'mon people, I was meeting my dad in less than twenty-four hours. Who could blame me for not engaging in small talk? I needed to prepare to meet Dad in the same way one would prepare for a job interview. While Celeste talked to Sacha and the two guys, I went over a checklist in my mind. First, I would write in my journal in the morning to chronicle my thoughts before meeting Dad. Would I wear my yellow shirt or my white T-shirt? How would I wear my hair? Neither Celeste nor I had an appetite that evening, so dinner didn't take too long.

We said good-bye to the two guys, and Sacha escorted Celeste and I back to our hotel, which was a seven-minute walk from the restaurant. The only caveat was the major highway that you had to cross. Apparently, Zambia is known for having one of the highest car-related fatalities in the world.

The cafeteria of the Radisson Blu hotel was about a thousand square feet of sunlit dining because of the floor-to-ceiling windows that decorated the wall facing the entrance. Faux-leather, cream chairs that sat at every table and booth added to the decorum, making the room appear even brighter than it was. The cooks' uniforms looked especially white against the deep-brown hues in their skin. There Celeste was, like a spec in the room, seated in one of the booths with two plates of mostly fruit, a bowl of yogurt, and a cup of coffee placed in front of her.

"Hey, the food in here's amazing," Celeste said as she waved over to me and poured cream into the mug. "Their coffee is so good. I got you some water." She spoke faster than I've known her for, which must have been a result of the coffee there and the eight hours of sleep that we got. While I was spending way too much time getting dressed in pretty much the same jeans outfit that I wore the day before, Celeste had already made her way to the breakfast buffet. The night before, she had warned me about not using tap water to brush my teeth. "This is a five-star restaurant, so you are safe eating pretty much anything in here. Just drink bottled water though.

The smorgasbord of food looked exactly like the pictures on the hotel's website, featuring the fluffy, bright-yellow scrambled eggs. The slices of cantaloupe felt refreshingly cool on the inside of my cheek. But my favorite remained the sautéed mushrooms and tomatoes. No wonder Celeste was excited. I was so engrossed in the food that I almost forgot I was meeting my father for the very first time.

"My dear, he is very excited to meet you," my newly formed relative, Constance, said as she stared at me from across the breakfast table with a toothy grin. Technically, she was a family friend. I couldn't remember from her initial text messages how she knew my dad. It was something to the effect of my dad taking her on as his child and walking her down the aisle on her wedding day. I guess when you already have thirteen kids, what's one more? She insisted on coming early to meet me since she would be late for the festivities. I was grateful to Constance's orienting me to my dad. "He is coming to the hotel in a little bit. I just spoke to him this morning. I have never heard Uncle sound so happy. You will be able to identify him as soon as you see him. He is a tall and slender man. Everyone loves him. He is such a happy and kind person."

What struck me about what she was saying was I could pick up on most of that just by talking to my dad on the phone. Perhaps, like me, he wore his emotions. It was like a game of Double-Dutch at this point, because one minute I accepted him as a kind and loving man, and the next minute I questioned my own judgment.

How was I so sure he was not pretending to be nice only to lure me in and steel my money? Constance also claimed he was tall, whereas another relative had told me he was short. There was only one way to find out.

"Okay, so the GoPro will be set right here so that it captures your dad walking to the hotel," Celeste said. Her mouth was moving so fast in contrast to everything around me, which moved with a snail's pace. "Just don't forget that the camera is right here, and be sure to get closer to it so it can capture everything that you guys are saying," she said while looking through the eye of the camera to make sure it captured the scene. She propped the GoPro on a stool that sat across from the table to test the angles. Celeste staged the entire reunion, from ordering enough spring water for the table, to making sure that we sat outside where the video would capture us under natural light. To ensure that no one got too hot, Celeste moved us to the canopied table on the far left that offered a good combination of sun and shade. *Whew!* We were all set for my dad's arrival according to her.

The sun was a scorching ninety-five degrees. Even the canopy on the veranda outside could not contain the heat that accompanied it. I wore my yellow and red 2014 World Cup jersey that highlighted all the African teams. How had I managed to put on ten pounds in the last year so the only jeans I could fit into were my GAP Boyfriend jeans? My outfit was the opposite of my usual chic that I insisted on, throwing on a bright-pink, floral-print, cotton scarf around my neck to accessorize. If only *Women's Wear Daily* could've suggested the perfect outfit to wear when reuniting with your father after twenty-nine years. How could Celeste be envious of this getup?

"You're so lucky. Whereas, I cannot even fit into anything."

Oh, my sweet Celeste. Didn't she know how lovely she looked with her little belly; the best accessory ever. She also wore loose jeans and a salmon-colored T-shirt.

"So I would like to interview you before you meet your dad. That way you can chronicle this for your movie." She pulled a chair and sat across from me with her GoPro in hand. Celeste was fully equipped to capture every moment for me. For as long as I could remember, she was always taking photographs or in a dark room processing them. Come to think of it, Celeste did my very first photo shoot at STAB for my senior yearbook photos. I trusted her direction with the GoPro camera. Where would we have been if her friend hadn't loaned her the GoPro when he found out about my journey story?

"Words cannot begin to express how I feel," I said. "I never knew that I needed a dad until I got a dad. I'm both excited and nervous to meet him." The truth? I was no longer sure that I wanted to go through with meeting him. I had just travelled across the world to meet a man who abandoned me from the time I was four. Based on what one of my siblings told me, he terrorized my mother to the point that she had to kill him off in her own mind to find peace. What kind of a real man beat his wife? At his core, he must have been ruthless. What if I reminded him of everything he hated about my mother? He sounded sweet over the phone but maybe that was just his ploy. Why had I agreed to travel halfway around the world with my friend for this? All this time, I was worried about my stepmom poisoning me or a relative stealing my passport, but it was my father who could be the biggest perpetrator.

I wasn't even sure if I was speaking English at this point. My mind was in a million places, none of which I had ever been before. The most trivial of things began to occupy my mind, a sheer sign of my anxiety taking over.

Celeste drank a ton of water to keep cool, and I just did it to pass the time, which felt like eternity. What if one of us had to go to the bathroom when my dad arrived? That would ruin our reunion and the movie. It was settled then, I would hold my urge to pee until after I met my father; it wasn't worth the risk. The one time Celeste excused herself to use the bathroom, my heart flip-flopped, but she must have had the same concerns I had: "If for whatever reason you see your dad walking over while I'm away, just press this button and don't run to him. Make sure that you are standing here to hug him. I'll be back as fast as I can," her voice trailed as she skipped to the restroom. Trying to remember where Celeste directed me to stand when my dad arrived and while also remembering to turn on the camera when dad arrived caused me to suffer temporary memory loss. Where was Celeste going? All I could see were her salmon-colored Toms shoes.

Where is he?

"Dude, Africans are just like Filipinos," Celeste said with a surpassed impatience on behalf of both of us after she returned from the bathroom only to find me sitting in the same position she left me five minutes prior. "I'll be there in an hour . . . but it's actually like three hours."

After forty-five minutes of holding my breath every time a new car entered the parking lot or a black man walked towards the hotel, in hopes that it was my dad, I grew lethargic. The anxiety finally wore off since he was nowhere in sight. Maybe this was a joke. I wasn't going to meet my father.

Is this a dream?

It was surely surreal.

IV. HE'S SO HYPER

A skinny, tall man wearing a gray suit and a hat laughed increasingly louder as his pace picked up and his arms started to open towards me. He had a commanding presence but not intimidating, like he was some sort of president or something. I knew right then the man walking over was my dad. I had an incredible urge to run over and throw myself in his arms.

Oh my goodness, Celeste. That's him.

Instead of my heart racing, as I had expected it to, it skipped beats, and I felt pulsation all the way down to my stomach. My entire body stiffened, and my feet were glued to the concrete floor, causing me to become immobile. If I had attempted to lift my leg, it would have felt like I was lifting the entire world underneath my shoe. First, I felt it in just my toes but then it moved up my entire foot, just below my ankles. My God, this is what it meant to have cold feet! It's possible that even the air held its breath in anticipation for what would happen next. He was getting closer, and I wondered if I should have run to him, but I remembered Celeste's camera rules.

"Dad!" my muffled voice managed to let out through his armpit, which is where my face ended up as my dad proceeded to hug me. All those pictures he sent me of himself were deceiving of his size; he was so thin.

"Mwanji. My doh'ta. Oh, my doh'ta, Mwanji!"

He may have repeated those words for almost five minutes while planting kisses on my forehead and cheeks and hugging me incredibly tight. The sun reflected against his freshly oiled, mahogany skin. I looked at his nose, and it was a slightly bigger version of my button nose. His eyes were tiny slits like mine, but they sparkled like stars in black night. His grin was wide with thin, shapely lips like mine. His teeth were a tarnished off-white with one baby-bottom front tooth that sat shorter than the others. I cannot believe that he wore a suit and hat for me. Was my arrival that much of a celebration to him? My mind was on delayed reaction mode. I was like one of those old Bruce Lee *kung fu* movies where the mouth movement and the actual words were out of sync. While he was hugging me and showering me with adoration, I was still processing the fact that I was meeting my dad.

I turned to see the light-skinned black woman who was walking with dad, also crying on my left. Celeste was holding her tears back by pretending to focus the camera on my right.

"Mwanji," he said, "this is your elder sister Beatrice."

I had no idea who this person was, and I wasn't sure if I was supposed to know but she cried for me in that moment as if she were at my funeral, so I couldn't help but throw myself into her arms. Calling what I was going through overwhelming would be a gross euphemism. It was more like a state of shock where your body is present but you're not sure where your mind is, so you keep going, you keep asking: "Mind, are you there?"

"Mwanji," Beatrice was barely able to let out through her sobs. "I miss you, my Sister. I have not seen you since you were a baby." She was about 5'6" with a round face and innocent eyes. She struck me as a good Samaritan, someone who gives everyone the benefit of the doubt.

"I miss you, too," I lied.

Meanwhile, Celeste introduced herself to my dad to which he exclaimed: "Mama Celeste!" and had given her a big hug. I made a mental note to explain to Celeste our Central African custom of calling someone Mama. It was similar to the Mrs. and Ms. pronouns in English and regarded as a form of respect for women, just as calling an adult male Papa was respectful.

"Why don't we all sit down, and I will ask the waiter to bring two more large bottles of water," Celeste suggested seconds later when she sensed my awkwardness creep up. Now that we had officially met, what came next? I had been replaying my reunion with my dad for months, and it came down to a fleeting moment that had just passed. Thankfully, he had all the plans for the day. "We will go to Chawama today so you can meet the rest of your family," he said while maintaining his coffee-cup-wide smile. He looked at me with such compassion and adoration.

We were soon walking to the parking lot to get into Beatrice's Toyota sedan. "Yes, this is definitely okay," Celeste whispered into my ears, indicating that she was comfortable getting in the car. I partially wanted to make sure that Celeste was okay, but I also needed her to take care of me because I was with family but without faculty. I looked at my dad who sat in the passenger seat and answered phone calls like a police dispatcher: "Yes, we are on our way. Yes, we are all in the car with Mama Celeste." I became mute not knowing what to say.

"So we're going to Chawama?" Celeste broke the silence. She could have been in Chicago for all she cared; she was perfectly content and taking everything in. I on the other hand was holding my breath, anticipating another shock to my system like the huts we saw on our way from the airport. So far so good, though. The two and three lane highways, the billboards and the traffic lights all seemed normal to me.

When we got off the highway diving into the neighborhoods, gravel appeared, the car tires kicking up red dirt. On this part of the ride, all I noticed were rows of one-story shanty houses made of tin roofs and a type of cement. People were outside, walking, standing by the little makeshift bars to get a cool beverage. There was a 200 square foot hair-braiding salon. I saw a house with no door, seemingly with no electricity. This was poverty. It was the spitting image of Africa that Americans saw on those pathetic famine infomercials. The realization that my family was red-dirt poor made me embarrassed in front of my white friend.

"Remember, what you are seeing is very normal for a majority of the world," Celeste whispered to me, sending a wave of calm into my tense body. We drove to what appeared to be one of the bigger houses in the neighborhood elevated with bricks; probably to prevent flooding. A battalion of women and children stood in front of the house waiting to greet me when we got out of the car.

"Welcome home, Sister Mwanji. I'm Imani."

"Hi, Sis. It's so great to finally meet you. I'm Fifi."

These two younger and lighter versions of me came over with a bouquet of flowers. They had a bouquet for Celeste as well. It felt very much like a homecoming. I was a cross between a show pony and the Pope, here to bless everyone with my presence. It was all quite daunting and unrehearsed, so I just slapped a grin on my face and hugged the next person in line to meet me. "This is your stepmom," my dad offered. "And this is your cousin," he introduced everyone as if I was somehow familiar with these people previously. Everyone looked at me as if they knew me, but I was

ILLEGAL AMONG US

very lost and couldn't tell the difference between one person and another.

"And this is your other stepmother."

What?!

It was in this moment that I could not contain my emotions anymore. They came out in the form of an ugly cry, where my face contorted and I couldn't maintain a pretty composure. I was being swallowed up by a herd of Africans who were supposedly my family. While I wanted to surrender and have my family take care of me, I didn't know them. Who were they? Worse yet, I think I threw myself into the wrong stepmother's arms. I couldn't tell which one tried to kill my mom and which one was best friends with my mom. I would later learn that my stepmoms didn't get along.

In his excitement, my dad beckoned us to get into the car so we could go to the next neighborhood where more people were waiting for us. How could there be more people? I just hugged what seemed to be about fifty people. He was so excited that he couldn't contain himself. "We need to get something to drink at the store for everyone," he motioned to Beatrice to drive to the nearest grocery store. The ten other people coming with us, including both stepmoms, couldn't fit in Beatrice's car, so they had no choice but to walk.

A sudden guilt came over me; maybe I should be walking, too. How come I was being treated like a princess while my older stepmoms had to walk? The neighboring village was a fifteen-minute walk; in this sweltering heat, it could easily take thirty minutes when holding a little baby. That didn't stop my dad from wanting to give Celeste and I the ultimate treatment. The grocery shack resembled the grocery store I used to visit on Mott Street in Chinatown, New York City. It was a dimly lit, one-store dungeon with no air conditioning but shelves of imported goodies from Trix cereal to traditional staple food.

"Would you like some Fanta? Let us get you some Fanta."

This was my first introduction to Fanta, a drink that I had only seen in commercials with women wearing bikinis and sarongs chanting "Fanta, Fanta, Fanta." I wasn't much of a fan of soft drinks, but there was no harm in trying a little Fanta.

"Martine and I will drink water," Celeste jumped. "We are so thirsty for water." She gave me a look as to say, "You want to trust me on this one."

The waters were 1 kwacha, equivalent to a hundredth of a US cent. How could 1 kwacha buy you a bottle of water in some places but buy you a meal in other places?

We drove up to a 500-square-foot house with a driveway. Later, I'd find dad had borrowed his friend's house for my welcome. Nearly thirty more people were waiting to meet me inside. I was like the Bearded Lady in a circus where everyone eagerly waited to touch my hand to confirm that I was in fact very real. The living room was cramped with people sitting on sofas, on arm rests, and on the floor. How would I meet everyone? But dad had a plan to walk me around every corner of the room to hug each sweaty person. I wondered if they had rehearsed the day prior, because everyone took their cues and no one stepped out of line.

"Shesheme wangu," which translated to "my Shesheme" were the words that my sister Zalika uttered when she came into the room. It was the very first time seeing my mother's daughter since I was an infant. She looked so much like Ya Marie that I almost thought I had seen a ghost. Her skin was coffee complexion with a beautiful, red undertone. Hers was just as flawless as my mom's, with her pouty lips and deep-set, almond eyes. She was stunning in her simplicity of a red blouse and a skirt. I almost forgot that Zalika was in Zambia. My dad must have adhered to my request when I was thirteen and brought his ex-wife's daughter, my sister, to live with him and his children in Zambia. She was leggy and supple, what Ya Marie would have looked like if she wasn't ill during most my life. She called me by my nickname, Shesheme, a name that I had not heard since I buried Ya Marie back in 1996. It was as if the room stood still as everyone held their breath and watched two soul-mates unite. While Zalika was technically my half-sister just like my father's kids, coming from the same womb made our bond feel that much deeper. In that moment, when she held me tight, I imagined Ya Marie's spirit being in the room, rejoicing that her children had reunited.

As if conducting a wedding procession, Dad hurried me along so I could meet all the people that were eager to see Joseph Kayembe's long-lost daughter, or the person who was closest to the deceased Ya Marie.

"You know, I knew your mother very well." A saucy, fair-skinned woman caught my attention. She possessed a handsome beauty and looked to be in her midsixties.

What could she tell me about my mom? I was dying to gather information about this stranger whom I referred to as Ya Marie.

"We worked together at the Congolese Embassy in Zambia. She would complain about feeling sick and pregnant and not feeling like working. I told her 'shut up, cunt, and work.'"

Oh my goodness! Did I hear her correctly? I was pretty sure she said *cunt*, but I dare not ask again. Maybe cunt had a different connotation in Africa; maybe it was equivalent to idiot or imbecilic. It didn't seem to faze her after she whispered it to me in a francophone accent and winked.

"You knew my mom when she was pregnant with me?" I hung onto anyone and anything that brought me closer to my mom's memory. This cunt-calling woman began to feel familiar all of a sudden. Dad scooted me along to the next person in line before I was ready, but I had to make sure to come back and talk to this woman.

"Please, no, don't pour powder on my face," I complained as my dad's wife—I still couldn't distinguish between stepmoms—sprinkled what seemed like baby powder on me and other attendees. It may have been tradition, but no one seemed amused by it but her. It was almost as if she made up this ritual by asking herself, "What would be the most annoying thing I can do to a group of adults?" She would splash baby powder in our hair and faces. It was more aggravating that she poured a mound of the powder in her hands and then threw it on people like a potion. I feared that it would affect the quality of the pictures and video that Celeste was capturing. If she tried to pour anymore stuff on me, I was going to slap her right in her face.

Since graduating from the Maxwell School, I was at the mercy of my next hearing to determine my fate. It was scheduled for August 9, 2004, and July was nearly coming to an end. In mid-July, I had safely arrived in the Big Apple but still lacked job prospects and a home.

With only $1,000 to my name, I sought shelter. The hardest part about being homeless was the pressure of the "what's next" from immigration court, I had to decide whether to spend my precious time looking for a home and a job or preparing for my hearing. This next hearing needed to be the denouement, because I couldn't handle any more juggling of my life. John assured me that everything would go smoothly, as this August 9th appointment was an actual hearing, rather than a Master Calendar appointment. I would be able to testify and present witnesses on my behalf, namely, Señora Castillo, Mrs. Smith, and Judge Wells. Mrs. Giles offered to drive me to my hearing once again. Finally, I would participate in a court hearing on my terms. My overconfidence about the following day's outcome was contagious at the dinner table.

I was like Dorothy going to see the Wizard of Oz with my Scarecrow, Tin Man, and Lion protectors. Judge Wells was a powerful man, and surely when Judge Colucci recognized that his peer was testifying on my behalf, it would ensure my credibility, dismissing the case.

I didn't meet Judge Wells until the day I graduated from STAB in 1999. In fact, I didn't even know that I had a benefactor. Judge Wells didn't want me to know. He didn't want me to feel like I owed him and his wife, Tiffany, anything. Judge Wells and Tiffany were close friends with Harriet Johnson, STAB's Head of Admissions, whom I interviewed with. Over a meal, Harriet shared with the Wells, "We have this incredible young woman who is an invaluable addition to St. Anne's, but we have absolutely no funding left to supplement her education and to live in the dorms." It only took a night for Judge Wells and Tiffany to determine that the previous night's conversation was a sign for them to sponsor the young woman. Judge Wells got in his car and drove to Harriet's home to share the news as Harriet was in her car getting ready to drive off. Judge Wells flagged Harriet's car down to a stop and said, "You know that young lady you mentioned at dinner yesterday? Tiffany and I would like to help." That's how another stranger saved my life. After I met him at my graduation, he was no longer a stranger but more of like a father who watched over me from afar.

I was unable to focus on and appreciate the lovely five-star, candlelit dinner that Judge Wells hosted for my "angels" and me in advance of my victory. These angels, my lawyer, benefactor, fairy godmother, and advisor, were the arteries that pumped lifeblood into my heart, and I was immensely grateful for them. I was revved up for the hearing. We were going to present a case against my abusive aunt, specifically Aunty Amelie. I could not wait to testify to Judge Colucci about the abuse that Aunty Amelie inflicted upon me, forcing me to work as a minor in her consignment store in violation of child labor laws.

The hearing proceeded as follows: first, I would testify, but not in the presence of my witnesses, then Judge Wells, Mrs. Smith, and Señora Castillo. They would each testify individually. I tasted freedom in the air and couldn't wait to take a gulp. If only I had known that this was the turning point in my life where I would be forced to testify against my own dead mother.

After every utterance to the judge and his court, a voice in my head pleaded, *Ya Marie, forgive me. I have to do it; I have no other choice.* My other concern was whether I answered John's interrogation correctly, because we had prepared for testimony regarding my aunts, not my mother. After every question, I wanted to ask: "John, was that the response you were looking for?" I learned from watching legal dramas on television that when you are on trial, always respond to the question in a complete sentence. For example, if the prosecution asks if you were aware that your neighbor was lying in a pool of blood in his living room, you should respond: "I was not aware that my neighbor was lying in a pool of blood in his living room." Simply giving a one-word, close-ended response of "No" was not sufficient. It made for a longer trial, but it sounded more sophisticated. Unfortunately, I was hypersensitive about using this approach; judging by the transcript of my testimony, which I was later privy to, my inconsistency was obvious. At the completion of individual testimony, we were all called back into the courtroom. I sat on John's right, and my posse sat behind me in the first row of benches.

Dad changed the greeting process because he was on a mission. This time I was supposed to remain in my seat, and he would bring people to me to meet. He was the usher who pulled people away when time ran out. When a family friend was speaking to me about all the great things she heard about me, my dad tapped her on the shoulder and said, "Okay, Mama Mwanji must say hi to everyone please, please," while politely placing his hand on their shoulder to move them along. How could you get annoyed with this man when he spoke so politely and was clearly full of wonderment of a kid in a candy store. Dad was having so much fun and clearly had planned this event as if it were my own wedding party. He was like a kernel of popcorn, one minute he popped over to the door and greeted more people, the next minute he was back by my side introducing people to me, and the next minute he was adjusting the music. No wonder he remained so thin, the man never stayed in one place!

It was Judge Colucci's turn to speak. "Mr. James, the information that you provided displeases the court. There is no evidence in any of the paperwork that you submitted that indicates or suggests that your client's mother battered her. In fact," he stared me dead in the eyes, squinting as if he were trying to hex me, "I have reason to believe that this claim is false and has been presented to the court in the 11th hour. It seems to me that your client felt the need to make up stories in the 11th hour to change the outcome of her trial and the court's decision. But the evidence points in the other direction. Even your client's three witnesses have no awareness of the abuse and battery that your client charges against her deceased mother."

My entire brain circuit shut down in complete shock about what the IJ was saying. I hated John from that point forward with every fiber of my being. John promised me that by telling the truth, the whole truth, and nothing but the truth, I would be saved. Instead, the judge accused me of making fraudulent statements and creating lies. He emphasized the 11th hour so much that I wondered if that infuriated him the most. Furthermore, I was mortified by the thought of my posse, who sat directly behind me and witnessed the entire debauchery, listening and making their own judgments. Would they believe me, or did they also think I was lying? Why was it that John allowed the judge to talk down to me in that way and not come to my defense? Of all the people in the courtroom, I couldn't look Judge Wells in the eyes for the shame and embarrassment I must have caused him.

Judge Wells was headed back to Virginia when he stopped into John's office to say good-bye to me. "Just know that your past does not determine your future," he said to me. If only he understood the circumstances that preempted the shift in how evidence was presented. It wasn't my fault. I didn't plan on wasting his valuable time and money, only to make him and my other witnesses look like fools. If only he knew of my lawyer's incompetence. In that moment, if it were possible to silence the torment of Colucci's words by putting a gun to my head, then I would have. As he stumbled on his thoughts to prepare for March 10, 2005, I watched him with sincere loathing. I trusted him with my life, and he disappointed me. How could he force me to reveal this traumatic experience only to *not* have my back? I hated him. I felt so defeated, so broken and ashamed. Caught in a web of my own creation, under the "guidance" of my lawyer, I saw no way out.

Now that the court knew about my physically and mentally abusive mother, I either had to prove it to Judge Colucci, or risk deportation. The bareness of John's office made my cries more obvious; they were tears of humiliation and frustration. How could this backwards immigration process push me to such desperation that I would expose my darkest secret to a room full of strangers? These people didn't even see me as a human being; I was an alien, a number. I was sorry for dragging my poor, restless mother into this saga.

Without the pressure of it being our very first encounter, I finally had a chance to fully take in the image of my dad in the grey, polyester suit and grey hat. I was like a newborn seeing her father for the very first time. He looked like a caricature of himself. His suit was baggy on him, making him look like he was shrinking by the hour. His laugh was light and breathy, but it came from deep within and weighed the room down. He smiled with his teeth the entire time, which revealed the folds that ran between his nose and cheekbones. He was like a young man pretending to be an old man who was pretending to be young. At the core of him, he was full of vitality and seemed to see everything through the eyes of a twelve-year-old boy. Despite the blows that life must have dealt him, he still insisted on remaining lighthearted. My return home was a mark of hope for him.

"The judge was angry and accused me of presenting evidence in the 11th hour. Between now and my next trial, we just need to gather more evidence to support my claim," I explained in a mass email to friends as I sat on the floor with my laptop and a bowl of ramen noodles. There was a collective exasperation from all walks of my life—so hopeful that this was the final court drama for me. It was agonizing for my friends; they were at odds about what to do or how to respond. Life certainly had to go on for all of us. While seeking fresh witnesses, gathering evidence, and dealing with the trauma of my next hearing, I also had to find shelter, food, and secure a job. In the following two months, I was housed in ten different locations throughout New York City's five boroughs. Frustratingly, within a week or two of each move, I inadvertently overstayed my welcome.

"Oh, Martini, my mom and dad love you, and we have a spare bedroom so you should just move in with us," a Hamilton classmate promised. It was easy to believe her—this woman had fully recovered from a terminal illness, and she had the strength of will like no person I had ever met. I tolerated all her seemingly stupid or uninformed questions simply because this was a woman who earned her war wounds. I departed this arrangement because Alexa, my friend from STAB, was going away on a three-week vacation: "Martini Weeny, you can stay in my room for the next two weeks, free of charge."

Six months later, the New York City Office of Management and Budget (OMB) offered me a job, with a $45,000 annual salary. It was certainly more than I ever had, and I was just relieved to have authorization to work legally, even if it was temporary. My workday provided distraction and escape as I waited for the next trial date. I forecasted inmate population at Riker's Island, New York's most famous jail, which influenced the mayor's policies with the police force and courts. Otherwise, I consistently harassed my peace of mind with dark projections: would immigration services just show up at my doorstep one day and handcuff me?

He was only twelve when he became an orphan. "My mother and father died of an illness and then my sisters and brothers," he once told me. What illness? What kind of illness could wipe out an entire family so fast? They all died within weeks of each other. "Like you, I tried to take my life. I felt that God had forsaken me," my dad recounted in one of his letters to me. At twelve years of age, he was left in the world to fend for himself. He wasn't able to continue in school, but he taught himself to draw and paint. He was already gifted with a paintbrush, but he started to teach himself some basic techniques. And he continued to read whatever he could get his hands on, particularly as it had to do with world events. He vowed never to experience the loneliness he felt after losing his family. To me, that didn't justify his polygamy. But in his eyes, he wanted to have a lot of children so he would never be alone, and in turn, they would have each other.

Nine months flew by very quickly. It was now April 2004.

"Martine, let's go, let's go. We only have a few days left!" This cheerful email from OMB's human resources office was their pleasant reminder that my EAD clock was ticking. While sitting in my cubicle one day, numerous spreadsheets surrounding me, I cupped my hands over my eyes and sobbed, hoping that my supervisor wouldn't walk by. John James, who oversaw the renewal process, was nowhere to be found. Even more frustrating was that I had reminded John a few months ago, and he was inexplicably stalling. He knew very well that the card is issued for nine months, but it takes a few weeks for a renewal application to go through the immigration system. As the deadline approached, my anxiety increased, as did the risk of not having my EAD, and therefore unable to hold my job.

"We will apply for your EAD renewal in April, okay? You need to speak to a counselor. Learn to relax." No doubt that I was a headcase, but my lawyer's ineptitude had a lot to do with my wracking stress.

"I think what you are trying to say is that your lawyer is in the process of going with you to the Federal Building to get your EAD?" OMB's attorney interrupted as I attempted to confess to the vice president and director of HR that I was an illegal alien and in deportation proceedings. I thought that if I begged my superiors, they would have mercy on me. In his austere British accent, he continued to speak to the two women, the vice president and director: "Valerie and Denise, if I may, I will reach out to Martine's attorney after this meeting and we will figure this out. It doesn't seem as bad as we imagined." The two women breathed a sigh of relief and entrusted the reputation of the agency with their colleague.

"Please close the door," OMB's attorney instructed as I entered his office later that afternoon. "Look, I stopped you a few times in there because you do not owe any of us an explanation of your status. All we need is proof of your ability to work, and that is in the form of an EAD. What is going on with your lawyer? Has he submitted the paperwork for your EAD?" OMB's lawyer recommended that I go to the Federal Building and apply for an EAD on site, rather than wait for one to be mailed to me.

At 4:00 a.m. the next day, an unsightly image of Judge Colucci came to mind and a sudden bolt of fear hit me as I prepared to face those immigration monsters on my own. What if they arrested me? What if these representatives scolded or humiliated me the way that Colucci had? What if they turned my application down and refused to give me a new EAD?

It was surprising to ride a crowded East-Side subway train at 4:30 in the morning; judging by their attire, many appeared to be blue-collar workers on their way to the job site. We all sat, various hues of blurry eyes, from the brownest of browns to the blackest of blacks—a lot of accents and non-English was spoken over the din. While the construction workers wore their Timberland boots, others wore dilapidated sneakers, jeans with visible stains, limp T-shirts, and Salvation Army used jackets. I caught my reflection in the subway door window and looked at my cropped hair, pearls, and trench coat; I hoped that I stood apart. Were these daily, hardscrabble commuters curious about me? Did they recognize that I was out of place?

The line in front of the Federal Building was filled with a myriad of spoken tongues, ranging from Spanish, French, Creole, and what sounded like a Slovak language. As daylight arrived, pedestrians walking by glared at us with contempt, as we resembled a welfare line. The diversity of represented nations inside the waiting room, which seemed remarkably like the DMV, was much broader than I expected. People of all skin tones wore suits and ties, carrying briefcases—this certainly wasn't the immigrant image portrayed by today's American media. In the far-right corner of the room stood a stunning black woman who appeared to be a model from the streets of Milan or Paris. Of course, there were some unassimilated immigrants, otherwise referred to as "fresh off the boat," that looked just as nervous and confused as me. Regardless of our immigration status, the mere fact that we understood the frustration and anxiety associated with something as miniscule as the EAD process bound us together.

For the first time, I felt like there were others who could genuinely relate to me. "Why are you here?" the attendant behind the glass booth asked with an edge of annoyance in her voice.

Although I thought it was obvious, I mumbled, "I'm here to get an EAD because mine expired. My attorney told me to give these to you." I slid the sheets of paper that John faxed to me under the glass partition. She looked at the documents the same way I felt about them—confused and unclear. I would have benefited from reviewing the documents beforehand, but that's what lawyers are for; I was depleted of the needed focus. Beads of sweat began to pour down from my forehead as this woman called her manager over to decipher the message.

"It says here that you are currently in removal proceedings, so we need to verify your eligibility for an EAD."

"Yes, she's right over there. I know, she just arrived today." Dad carried over the phone to another relative. He was able to speak for me in the way that one speaks on behalf of someone that they have great familiarity with. This was new to him, but he took pride in being able to speak on my behalf as he did his other children. It meant he knew me. It was nice being spoken for, especially by your dad. I was not alone in the world having to fend for myself. I had someone who was there to protect me. So even with what seemed like a thousand sets of eyes on me, I felt like my dad would take care of everything. How could I have even questioned this man's authenticity just a few hours earlier? He was far from scary. But this was the very same man that berated and abused my mother. How could that be? I couldn't even imagine him yelling let alone beating someone. I was trying to paint him as Ya Marie's villain, but it was impossible to do. Was he just good at acting or had he changed his ways?

If this immigration attendant could just keep her voice down! Even though the room was filled with immigrants, I couldn't handle anyone knowing that I was in removal proceedings; it was humiliating. In the world of immigration, I was the lowest ebb.

"I know, but I have been in proceedings for a while now and was eligible for a work permit before. I'm sure that I am now," I spoke in a stern whisper.

"Okay, we will need to verify your status. Please have a seat, as it may take time to get through to their phone lines."

Thank you! They would make their stupid calls and straighten this out and give me my renewed EAD. Then I could go back to being semi-normal for a few more months until this process started all over again.

As luck would have it, they couldn't verify my status and denied me the EAD. My employer's lawyer, whose job was at stake over my situation, insisted that I go back to the Federal Building again. Of course, John finally remembered the correct document that I should have provided on my first visit. I made my second trip the following day, riddled with anxiety, because if this attempt failed, I was out of a job, unable to afford my home, and, once again, professionally unemployable. I submitted all the documents as required.

"Have a seat, we will call you up once we review your forms."

It was a different woman from yesterday's visit, but she had the same irked tone in her voice. I went back to the same seat, shuddering from sheer anxiety. I also felt a nervous giggle; I think I was delirious. A young Asian couple sat directly across from me; they seemed agitated as they shuffled through the documentation, bickering back and forth. "Do you need help?" I opened my palm and extended my hand as if that was the universal sign for assistance. It turned out that neither of them understood English and needed assistance filling out the forms. Wasn't there an interpreter in the building? You would think that a government agency, charged with engaging international people, would either have an in-house translator or the forms printed in multiple languages.

"Your name here," I said slowly and loudly, forgetting that they were not hard of hearing. "This is where you arrived when you came to America. Did you come to La Guardia? Or John F. Kennedy? JFK?" I asked as I pointed to the blank spots on the page.

"Yes, JFK," the man nodded in excitement.

"Okay, let's write that in here," I said as I took the pen and began to fill out the section. We got through the front page of the sheet just in time for their number to be called. "Okay, great. Good luck!" I was happy for them, and I hoped that they would be okay. But once again, my own burdensome reality hit me, which only left an unsettling feeling. Here was a foreign couple, barely able to speak English, and they were seemingly progressing further along in the system than me. I watched as their EAD applications were approved and they got in the line to snap their ID photos. I was left alone with my thoughts, waiting, contorting myself in that neurotic way, which Aunt Frances always warned me about.

I began gnawing the inside of my cheek, crossed my legs once, and crossed them again so that they looked like a pretzel—this feeling brought me great comfort. My number was called. Finally, the process worked in my favor, and I was issued my second EAD, valid for another nine months. Instead of relief, I could only consider how I would have to endure this process every eight months without any certainty that it would result in approval of my temporary employment. I didn't just have to worry about being a good employee to keep my job; I also had to make sure I was eligible to get documents to work. One false move and everything would come tumbling down. It felt like the system was set up for me to fail.

"Sis," she said, "you can borrow Papa for the next few days, because I know that you haven't had any time with him. I don't mind you being his favorite for the week, just as long as you give him back afterwards," she said, laughing.

She was perched on the arm of the sofa like a little bird. My youngest sister, Imani, was only twenty-one. Although she must have been my height, she was thin as a rail, which made her appear taller. I discreetly envied how her clavicle protruded under her T-shirt, a sign of a waif. Even her red pencil skirt was baggy on her. She was the only one of the siblings that I had met so far that would be able to fit into my clothes, which would be loose fitting on her. I saw so much of myself in her. She was polite, sweet, and her doe eyes carried so much hope about what the world had to offer.

The family, specifically our dad, poured his last hopes in escaping poverty in her. Imani lived on campus at the nearby university and was on her way to campus in a few hours after my arrival. She was sincere in her compliments of how happy she was to finally meet me. Clearly, she was dad's favorite, but now that I was back in the picture, perhaps we were tied.

Before I could breathe much relief for my legitimate life, temporarily forgetting that I was illegal, I got a call from Aunt Frances, whom I had not spoken to in nearly three years. Her tone was curt:

"I'm calling to let you know that your Aunty Amelie passed away." Aunty Amelie? I hadn't heard that name in years. Somehow, she seemed larger than life, immortal.

After a long pause, my aunt continued. "She died in her sleep, of carbon monoxide poisoning. Emanuel was gone from the house, probably at a friend's house, and I guess they didn't have a carbon monoxide detector. So the fumes leaked into her bedroom while your Aunty Amelie was asleep. She never woke up. Emanuel came home to find his mother dead." This was shocking. But why did she keep referring to her as "my" Aunty Amelie, as if I was somehow responsible?

Ironically, at the time, Mayor Bloomberg had launched an initiative to mandate that all NYC buildings install carbon monoxide detectors. I always wanted to escape Aunty Amelie's wrath, but I didn't wish for her to die, no one deserves to be punished in that way. I was just so afraid of her and only wanted to get away, never to see her again.

After eight years of absence from the Kalaw clan, the idea of being confined in a space with them terrified me.

"Martine," Señora Castillo advised. "I am not telling you what to do but go for your mom. It is the right thing to do."

"Go and pay your respects," Mrs. Smith said. Later that weekend, standing nervously in the Silver Spring, MD, Greyhound bus station, I saw the tall and sturdy black figure walking towards me. *What do I say?* My awkwardness kicked in.

"There she is," he said with a wide grin, revealing an array of ivory teeth. "How is my girl?" he asked and gave me a big hug. I didn't realize how much I had missed Claude until that moment. But I wasn't sure if it was that I missed him or if I missed looking into the eyes of someone who looked exactly like me. As my mother's younger brother, he knew me from birth and that was comforting and rare.

"Hi, Claude," I said bashfully. As he gripped the steering wheel, I noticed the palms of his hands were blackened from working in his car shop. He owned his own business as an auto mechanic. "So, young lady, how are you? I feel like I have not seen you in years. But you still have that same smile." Who can forget my smile? For many years, I plastered a fake grin on my face to hide the pain. It was reengaged for this very special occasion.

"You leave, and you forget us all. You don't even call. Look at how much you have grown. My God," Aunty Dominique began her rant the minute I walked through the door. I wanted to defend myself after each accusation, but I was more absorbed by the drastic physical changes of my aunts and uncles—they were all overweight and bloated, with round faces and bellies. This was in stark contrast to my mind's image of them from eight years prior.

A myriad of theatricals occurred at Aunty Amelie's wake; the "best performance award" went to Aunty Dominique. I'm merely suggesting that she may have been acting, when she literally threw herself inside the coffin while screaming: "Amelie, Amelieeeeee! You left me! You left us. What are we going to do without you? Let me die with you!" It was startling and would have brought tears to anyone's eyes. But a flashback to the day of an enraged Aunty Dominique kicking me out of her house came to mind: "Your Aunty Amelie is a witch!" Aunty Dominique ranted. "She uses people, and she has taken advantage of all of us. She has probably done voodoo and cursed all of us! She is evil. You can get close to her if you want, but you will see how quickly things will fall apart. She is bad luck! She is evil!"

Already, I began to count the hours until I could go back to New York City and be with my friends. Right now, my only security was my cell phone where Roxana and I exchanged text messages: "Are you there yet? Are you okay?" she wrote. My body was present, but my spirit was on its way back to New York City.

"Hey, listen," Claude said as he placed his large hands on my shoulders and looked me squarely in the eyes, "Martine, I could see it in your face since you walked in. You wear your heart on your sleeve and you give your heart so openly. Your mom was the same way. We abandoned you. Do you hear me? We were the ones who were at fault, because we left you. And trust me, I remember—I was there when your Aunty Dominique kicked you out of her house. It hurts me to see her lie and act like she didn't. And now they see how successful you are and the fact that you did it on your own. And they feel shame and embarrassment. And they are full of pride, so they won't say it. But on behalf of the entire family, I want to say that I'm very sorry. We are sorry that we abandoned you. I ask for your forgiveness on behalf of all the Kalaws. If there is ever anything that I can do to make up for what we did to you, please do not hesitate to ask me."

Claude's offer came at the perfect moment, because I needed a witness to corroborate my accusations of physical abuse at the hands of my mother. My medical transcripts emphasized my issue with anorexia and bulimia, which were influenced by past trauma, but we never breached the topic of Ya Marie; we ran out of time.

"I was not able to get in touch with any of your step-family. We need more evidence that your mother battered you. Is there any-one in your family who would have witnessed the abuse and who would be willing to testify?" John James pressed for a possible source of damning information against my mother.

"Well, my Uncle Claude feels a tremendous sense of guilt for how my family treated me. He said that he would do anything within his power to make it up to me. He knew of my mom's tem-per, and I think that he witnessed a lot of the abuse."

"Could you give him a call? Let him know that he would be testifying in court. Then have him call me." I was ecstatic, because it seemed that this would be my breakthrough. I was sure that Claude was present when my mom beat my sister, Zalika, with the iron rod back in the Congo, and he must of have seen a few of the beatings she gave me. I remember him trying to stop her from beating me once. I felt confident that his testimony would provide the necessary evidence to win my case.

"Claude," I said in a tender voice over the telephone. He just had to say yes. "Remember how I was telling you about my im-migration case? Well, I have a trial on March 10 in Buffalo, New York, and I would like to ask you if you would be willing to testify on my behalf. The subject is touchy, but it is about my mom and how she treated me. I know that this is a hard thing for me to ask you, especially because she was your sister. But I need your help." I held my breath, prepared to not take no for an answer.

"Of course, sweetheart," he replied in the most calm and reas-suring tone.

"Really? Oh my goodness. Thank you so much, Claude. I'm going to give you my attorney's name and number. He asks that you call him right away. Thank you so very much." We didn't speak again until the day of the trial.

"Just be consistent with what you said in the past and an-swer in complete sentences," was the only advice John gave me in preparation of my testimony in court. Claude was asked to wait outside of the courtroom as I took the witness stand. John began a line of questioning, which appeared to be curveballs, thank goodness. The white attorney, whom I deduced was on the opposing council and represented the state, listened and shifted through a stack of papers that John handed him before the trial began. I didn't like this man being here, and as far as I was concerned, I did not feel comfortable with him learning details of my personal life. The curveballs became more direct, and my answers grew rawer and unnerving.

"Be specific," John had coached me a few hours before the trial. "Don't say 'my mom beat me.' You need to detail what she used to beat you with and how. Where did she beat you? What part of your body? How did you respond? How did she stop? This is how you need to specify your answers."

"Mama Celeste, this way," my dad directed. He motioned to her to capture him in the GoPro as if he were directing my movie and was the supporting lead. He shushed everyone because he was about to say a few words. This man had a captivating presence. While slight, he morphed into a giant in any room. My dad had charisma. When he laughed, you wanted to be in on the joke. When he told a story, you wanted it to be about you. He was one of the eldest men in the village, which surprised me, because he didn't seem old. At seventy-one, he was considered ancient. People must have died young in Zambia. Maybe in their sixties? I wondered what they died of. How had my dad managed to bypass death, especially under harsh economic circumstances? There were so many unanswered questions about who this man was, with only ten full days to find out. He took a seat on the black, leather sofa directly across from me. He bowed his head almost as if he was about to say a prayer but didn't.

"Please, everyone be quiet," my dad commanded. "Mama Celeste, please sit next to Mwanji over there. I would like to make an announcement." The room grew silent. I never got a chance to explain to Celeste that my family would refer to me as either Mwanji or Shesheme, both names I went by. At this point, I figured that she caught on. What shocked her the most was that I spoke another language—Swahili. It was like a whole other side of me that she never knew existed.

My scabs were being picked open, exposing my deepest wounds all over again. As I answered each question, I would have flashbacks—I moved seamlessly through two traumatic worlds that day: the first was having to openly present my entire life on the witness stand to a room full of strangers; the second was reliving the tragedies of my childhood. When it was all said and done, I stepped down from the bench, raw and paralyzed. Claude was asked to take the witness stand. He was a hero, unselfish. I held my breath, not knowing what would come next.

As he clearly described Ya Marie's abuse, it was uncanny how his phrasing mimicked my own. "My sister, Marie-Louise, had a bad temper," he told the court. The Kalaw family euphemistically termed my mother's rage as "a bad temper," and it was certainly well known within our ranks, but rarely discussed openly.

"It's over, we won," was the feeling coursing through my mind and body—the weight of the world dissipating. I waited for Judge Colucci to deliberate in his chambers and arrive at a final decision in my favor. There was no jury as is the case in all immigration courts, only John, Claude, and I on one side of the courtroom and Judge Colucci, opposing council, his assistant, and the law clerk on the other. Surely, Claude's testimony added another dimension, which would be all the proof needed. But this never-ending nightmare was not over.

Colucci walked back into the courtroom and began to spit fire: "Mr. James, it seems that your client communicated with her uncle prior to the trial, so I have reason to believe that they conspired and conjured this story. They used the same wording, which seems unusual if they were not falsifying the story." My mind went blank, like a computer being zapped of all its data. What did he mean by us conspiring?

John didn't tell me that I couldn't speak to Claude before the trial. In fact, he asked me to call Claude and connect the two of them; I never spoke to, or prepared, my uncle prior to his testimony. I only informed him about the reasons for the trial. This was John's fault. How could this be happening?

"Your Honor, if I may. My client had very limited interaction with her uncle except for giving him my phone number."

"With all due respect, Mr. James, I cannot believe that your client did not discuss and prepare her uncle for this testimony."

Then his rage was geared toward me. He looked at me with intense loathing as if I were some sort of insect that he was prepared to annihilate: "Ms. Kalaw, you should be ashamed of yourself. Defaming your dead mother's name in the court of law just to further yourself is despicable. You are a liar, and you should feel horrible for making a mockery out of my courtroom. You deserve to be deported." His words struck me like bullets, and I practically blacked out as he continued. My mind wandered off into the blank space between my thoughts to block out the verbal abuse.

"There is a story in the Bible about a man with one hundred sheep, and he loses one sheep and only has ninety-nine," Dad began while making sure he remained in the camera's purview. No doubt my dad loved being in the spotlight! It was the most heartfelt speech I had ever heard, and it was all about me. It was as if I was his freshly discovered new world. Only the words of someone who created you could be this profound. He even took the time to type out the speech so that Celeste and I would have a copy to take with us. He loved me and had always loved me. He had been looking for me since he had lost me. He didn't fail to acknowledge Celeste. "I am thankful for Mama Celeste. If it was not for her, I know that I would not have this opportunity to see my daughter Mwanji again."

My heart was mush because every syllable that my dad uttered penetrated my heart. He had read the first draft of my memoir, this book, so he was fully aware of the pain I endured as an illegal immigrant. He acknowledged my pain and validated my struggles. I reflected on the years when my immigration nightmare culminated to what I felt was unbearable.

I became Shesheme again, begging Ya Marie to stop screaming such horrible things. Colucci's words became muffled in my ears but no matter what, I could still make out everything he said. "Please stop, you're killing me!" the little girl within me pleaded.

"You are a liar," the judge said ruthlessly. I left the courtroom, feeling violated and ashamed. Claude took all the blame, and he felt that he had failed me. But it was all John's doing. I hated him with all my might.

"So now what?" I asked John with disdain; it pained me to even look at his face. I would have fired him on the spot, but my $45,000 annual salary and temporary work permit—guaranteed for only eight more months—severely limited my options. Was he resentful and acting out because I wasn't paying him? Hamilton College paid him an initial $300 retainer, and he offered to take the case pro bono after that. Every time I offered to pay for any filing of paperwork, like the EAD application, he objected.

"Now we will appeal your case with the Board of Immigration Appeals in Falls Church, Virginia."

What does that mean? How long will that take?

V. WORTH AUTHORIZATION

Dad's speech left me raw.

"Thank you everyone for coming," I managed to say. "Please don't think that my life in America has been easy. It's been very hard. I'm so grateful for this opportunity to be here."

I wanted to say so much more. To recount every detail of my agony and pain, but I couldn't even find the words.

"Mama Celeste, would you like to say anything?" my dad asked rhetorically.

"I just want to say," Celeste jumped in, "that I have grown up with Martine. I have seen her struggle so much in her lifetime, especially in growing up alone. It's so amazing to be here to see all the family that surrounds her and loves her. I feel lucky to be able to be part of this journey with her."

I lived a lot of secrets and never fully disclosed my entire life to Celeste, but she could have not said it better. It was uncanny how she could still sympathize with me despite not knowing full details. She was right; there was a time where I felt alone, especially after I felt betrayed by John James.

If I didn't find a new lawyer, I would surely go insane; this risk was greater than being deported.

"So right now you're in removal proceedings, and your case is being appealed by the Board of Immigration?" an attorney who was referred to me had asked on the other end of the line, as I held my breath, not knowing what to expect. I was sneaking in a call in my cubicle, hoping no one could overhear my conversation. "Do you understand how rare it is and highly unlikely that the Board of Immigration Appeals (BIA) will overturn the judge's decision?"

"Well," I had muttered, filling up the silent space in the conversation while the question of taking on my case gnawed at my gut.

"Seriously, you're better off getting married," he commented with a light chuckle. "I'm not trying to sound trite, but you should probably go for extra security and get pregnant and get married. That is a sure way to increase your length of stay in the US. That way your case can be based on extreme hardship for your baby and your spouse."

Four years of immigration madness had come down to this: a legal expert recommending that I put aside my values, all principle, and try to deceive ICE (and now BIA) through a false marriage. Many friends who felt desperate about my situation would suggest this well-utilized tactic; in the end, where would it leave me? To save myself, who would I drag into this drama, only to risk creating severe challenges in his life? Didn't anyone else see the wrong in marrying someone for papers? It was not as glamorous as many Hollywood movies depicted, and there was no guarantee that marriage (or becoming pregnant and having a baby) would ensure my stay in the United States. The procedure was drawn out and complicated: papers had to be filed, numerous fees paid, and multiple, ongoing evaluations conducted. A social worker or investigator could drop by, unannounced, from time to time to ask questions and observe "our" living situation. These evaluations determined the legitimacy of the marriage, which lead to the issuance of a green card. The entire process could take up to two years. Above and beyond all that, Judge Colucci had a vendetta against me and would probably accuse a false marriage, which, ironically, would prove to be his first *accurate* accusation. He would order me deported, regardless of having a child, just like he did to the Latina woman almost four years ago. I heard of and witnessed too many stories that ended badly, where women married men out of desperation for a green card and ended up in physically and mentally abusive relationships. After all I had already been through, I wasn't willing to take such risks.

As I contemplated firing John James, I spoke over the telephone with a Nigerian friend. "Well, all I can say is be careful with the attorney that you choose," she warned. "I knew people who lost thousands of dollars, money they barely had, with empty promises from their immigration lawyers. These people are still without papers and finally had to get married to start the process. If I were you, I would steer clear of shady immigration lawyers, especially the African ones who may try to take advantage of you because you are also African. Honestly, you are better off just getting married to a nice man. Are you dating anyone? I can hook you up with some nice Nigerian men—they're all doctors and lawyers," she chuckled to lighten the mood.

Why did it always have to come down to marriage as the final solution? I refused to succumb to marriage just to secure my status. Despite my desperate circumstances, I believed within my heart that if I remained honest, justice would prevail. My intentions of "someday" falling in love and getting married were at a standstill until my case was finalized. I didn't want my future husband to ever question my motives for marrying him.

Celeste's 35-millimeter lens made her famous among my family. Did they think her photos of them would end up on the front cover of *Vogue* magazine or something? I was surprised by how comfortable my stepmothers and sisters got in requesting photo ops.

"Let's go outside so Mama Celeste can take some photos of the family," Dad announced. Celeste maintained a consistent amused face with her eyebrows arched higher than usual, suggesting she was excited in a good way. She didn't seem to mind at all that she was the designated photographer. In fact, it gave her a specific purpose. It was I who awkwardly followed the crowd down the dirt driveway. My two sisters insisted on being in the first two photos with me, one standing on either end. I knew Imani a little bit better by this point, but I hadn't spoken to Fifi. Who was she and which one was her mom? She looked like a cupid doll with big, bright eyes, a round face, and a cute mouth. I was the big sister in this trio, and I felt special. With our powdered heads and faces, we took reels of photos.

Virtuous or not, my debilitating agony continued, and work became my sole refuge as it provided a forced and focused distraction. I was running out of options; even my law professor, Sharon Pratz, became exhausted of my cause. She was the expert, who elevated my knowledge of immigration law and claimed that nothing was impossible with the right research and analysis. Frustratingly, I realized that even Professor Pratz had, had enough when she began to redirect me to "other people." I'd been on the receiving end of this form of dismissal before: Whom in Clinton's office should I contact? Was there a specific staff person in Charlie Rangel's office that I knew? These questions were simply a reminder that this was *my* problem. I was like a hot potato getting passed on from one person to another. It did not matter whether I appealed to a judge, law professor, or staffer in a congressman's office—no one knew how to help me.

"Take down this name and number," Judge Wells began during a phone conversation. "Charlotte England." Despite my skepticism, I wrote down the number, because I trusted him. I held my breath and dialed her number. Would I receive the typical disdainful response?

"Well, it's a pretty convoluted story," Charlotte England responded after I gave her a five-minute synopsis of my situation. Although she was technically a stranger, I spoke to her with significant ease. I felt she was listening to me and cared about my feelings rather than only to the facts of the case. After so many recounts of my story, I had perfected the pauses, and I could always anticipate the questions. Charlotte did not have the usual questions, but she did ask the one that would ultimately change my life.

"Would you mind coming into my office for a consultation? I think we should meet in person." After a brief pause, she added. "I do charge a fee for the consultation and a retainer if we decide to work together." I knew it; there was always a catch—money was the *only thing* these weasel lawyers cared about. Charlotte's law office was located on Madison Avenue, near the *Le Tigre* store. There was no way I could afford a prime-time attorney like her. Bamboozled once again, naively, I had been hypnotized by her sympathetic and nurturing tone.

"With all due respect, I have several clients who don't even have a job but find the means to pay. I will work with you but do need some form of compensation. My retainer is $2,000. I would be happy to set up a meeting so that I can meet with you in person."

In my mind, a $2,000 retainer was an obscene price when there was no guarantee of a successful outcome. We were in the post-9/11 economy of New York City, and that kind of cash was not growing on trees, especially by withered money vines.

"Mrs. England comes highly recommended. I don't think you have to worry about her taking advantage of your situation. She sounds like a dynamite attorney," Judge Wells advised when I told him about my consultation. This was my chance to ask for a loan, but what if he said no? This gentle giant of a man supported me time and again: he funded my private school education, corresponded with local Virginia congressmen, flew to Buffalo to testify on my behalf, and cosigned my apartment lease in Manhattan. What more could I ask of him?

"Martine, Judge Wells is like a father to you. He cares about you very much. You should not be afraid to ask for his help," Señora Castillo's words came to mind.

"It's not necessary for you to repay Tiffany and me," was Judge Wells's response to my request. "We just hope that someday you can help someone else when you have the means."

That's how I found myself in the waiting room of Charlotte England's office later that week. The office looked like a stage set from a television law series, like *The Practice.*

"Martine?"

I smiled, expecting to see someone more rigid and surly looking.

"What a pleasure it is to finally meet you," Charlotte said with a firm handshake. She stood at about 5'7" with short, cropped, blonde hair and her cool, red-framed glasses, making her look more like a fashion editor or a PR agent than an attorney. Her glasses sat squarely on her narrow face, and she did not wear makeup, except for a hint of pinkish-orange-colored lipstick. She wore a beautiful, brown jacket, complimented by a silk scarf perfectly draped over her shoulders. I was obsessed with shawls and scarves; the draping effect was the most playful part of any ensemble, which always completed the desired look. Despite all the reservations that I had about Charlotte, there was no doubt she complimented my fashion sense.

"Let's go into the conference room so I can look at your paperwork while you recount some of the details." She walked softly in her heels across the hardwood floor.

"Now, I just want to say that it is such a pleasure to finally meet you," she said again with reassurance. This must have been a truce for any past miscommunication. "I read through the bio that you sent me, and it was quite remarkable, all the things that you have been through."

Charlotte won another point, along with her fashion savvy, for validating me. She was the exact opposite of John. "I want to look through the documents that John submitted to the court during your trial. I want to see if I can gather substantial evidence in preparing your brief, if John has not already submitted it to the Board of Immigration Appeals (BIA). But first let me just begin by reading through some of these documents."

I sat in silence next to her at the oval table and felt assured, for once, that here was a person who was equally, if not more, dedicated to my case as I was. I trusted her and was confident that she was smarter than me when it came to the legal and political aspects of my case.

I caught Fifi from the corner of my eye ogling over Celeste. How could she be so mesmerized by Celeste's long hair and white skin?

"I can braid your hair," she said something to that effect while attempting a quick French braid on Celeste. She should have been more fascinated with me, her sister whom she had never met. Fifi was about two years younger than me, which meant that if we had grown up in the same household, we would have either been the best of friends or the worst of enemies. She would have been my competition with boys and my dad's attention. Her daughter reminded me of my favorite baby doll from my childhood. She was a pretty chocolate complexion with the largest eyes and the darkest curly hair that looked like midnight painted on her head. "She could be your daughter, she is the spitting image of you," Fifi said, and she motioned her daughter to come to me. While the little girl was gorgeous and possessed my complexion, she didn't look like me. What was Fifi really up to?

"Oh my. It states here in one of your mother's applications that she had an alcohol problem. If John had read this carefully, he would have discovered this, and he could have used this as further evidence of abuse."

Charlotte looked up from her new casework and viewed the person sitting before her. "Oh, my dear, I'm so sorry. I cannot imagine what was going through John's mind when he was preparing your case." She gave me a comforting look, which said, "We will get through this together." That was all it took for my tears to surface, which I had been fighting back. "Let's read through everything and see how we can fix this." She sifted through more paperwork and drew out the inconsistencies, explaining it all to me in detail, as if she were teaching her apprentice. I soaked in the knowledge because it was *my life*, and I finally had a teacher, an advocate, and friend showing genuine concern.

"And do you see here? This is your mom's statement of travel that is still in French. John had it translated, but he should have had the translation notarized to make it legitimate. And your eating disorder therapist's (Dr. Burk) transcripts and testimony should have been notarized as well."

It's true, I had suffered from an eating disorder since the time Ya Marie became gravely ill. It worsened after each visit into that immigration courtroom with Judge Colucci. It started with forced vomiting and taking laxatives while I was in middle school and became an obsession with over-exercising in college. By the time I was in graduate school, I just stopped eating altogether. I would go days without food, and compliments about my being thin fell on deaf ears and only encouraged me to further starve myself. I was sick, but I just couldn't stop. After a routine medical checkup at the clinic associated with my university, the nurse said, "Since you are a student at Syracuse University, I am obligated to send you to an eating disorder clinic based on your exam results. If you don't go, it could affect your ability to continue going to class." It was basically a threat, and I couldn't afford to get kicked out of school. It was in Dr. Burk's office where we discussed how my intake of food was my false sense of control of the life swirling around me. Dr. Burk prescribed me Zoloft to reduce my anxiety, but it only made me numb to all emotions. Perhaps that was better than being in a constant state of pain and living in a mental torture chamber.

Charlotte removed her glasses and ran her thin fingers through her hair in an exasperated fashion. I suddenly worried that she would quit my case—after only one day—because of the huge mess to clean up.

"So, my dear, the next order of business would be for me to reach out to the opposing council or to John to get your entire file transferred to me. I want to look over everything to see if there is anything that is missing. Then, if there is still a chance, I want to prepare your brief to the Board of Immigration Appeals. And if John has already submitted it, then we will need to figure out how to remedy the situation. But automatically, I'm leaning on going public with your case. You have a compelling story and your circumstances are quite unusual. I think that the public should be made aware of what is going on with the undocumented immigrant population. We need the country to hear your story."

"Really? I guess I'm a little scared about going public. What if I anger people or they see me as a threat? What if they attack me in my own home because of it?"

"Dear, I think you will experience quite the opposite. There will be an outpouring of compassion, and people will want to know how they can help you. It might be the only thing to shake Judge Colucci up. So before I do anymore, I need to know that you are willing to be my client. I will draw up a contract with a pay scale and, as needed, I will send you a receipt of expenses."

With little hesitation or thought, I agreed. I finally took my first peaceful breath. I wasn't alone. I knew that this was the turning point in my case, but there was no telling if it would ever conclude.

There was lightness in my step as I exited the building; maybe everything would work out after all. I deserved to have a good attorney who understood the law and my case. My right hand quivered as I attempted to sign my name on the dotted line of the contractual agreement. By doing so, I was agreeing to a fee of $200 per hour for the first ten hours and then $175 for each additional hour. The $2,000 retainer would be used toward my fee. I also had to commit to a minimum of $400 a month, plus any miscellaneous costs, such as copying and filing.

"We want to reach out to local congresspeople to see if we can get a private bill for you. If a new bill is introduced to Congress that will benefit you, we want to have clout with congressional representatives so that they can support the bill. If and when necessary, we will go public with your case because the media is very influential. It may be a way to further intimidate the Buffalo courts."

Representative Jerry Nadler was a bulbous man wearing a tie and a crisp, white shirt with standard buttons that begged to be relieved of their duty.

"Representative Nadler, my name is Charlotte England, and I'm representing my client, Miss Martine Kalaw, in what I believe to be one of the most compelling legal cases I have ever encountered," she began.

She must have been in sales in her prior life, because she was able to squeeze in so much into one sentence before stopping for a breath.

"Unbelievable," Nadler remarked, glancing at me and trying to paint Charlotte's recount to the black woman who sat directly across from him. Nadler maintained the same quizzical look that most people had after my story was told. He was trying to formulate questions but was so overwhelmed with the details that he just didn't know where to begin. My case went beyond his frame of reference about justice. It made no sense whatsoever and there was very little context for him to relate. "You have my complete support," Nadler said after some time.

When the American Immigrant Lawyers Association (AILA), of which Charlotte was a longstanding member, organized speakers for Senator John McCain's *Town Hall Rally on Immigration* in New York City, Charlotte convinced them that I needed to be one of the featured speakers. Exactly one week before the event, we were revising my speech.

"You have five minutes to tell your story; we want to give everyone the big picture and we want to make it clear that you fear for your life if deported either to the Congo or Zambia." Charlotte informed me that we needed the support of as many Republicans as possible, and McCain's rally could help leverage that. Since the Senator from Arizona was in support for some version of comprehensive immigration reform, this was my opportunity to appeal to him. All I needed was a nice suit to match my polished speech.

"What a steal! You would look dynamite in this crème suit, but I also just love this heather grey on you. If I were you, I would get both. You cannot beat these prices, Martine!" Charlotte was unable to control her enthusiasm, as we shopped the racks of Lord and Taylor. Hopefully she didn't notice my eyes rolling back with utter annoyance. I could barely afford her legal fees and my rent, let alone the funds for two new suits; was she hallucinating?

Alas, placing myself in the scope of the public eye required a certain look. Thankfully, each suit cost just under $150.

My ego took flight, as I believed that my story was the most compelling compared to the other speakers. I also considered myself to be the most polished—I forgot that this was not a pageant but a rally for immigration reform. I had a hard time accepting the fact that I was not the only undocumented immigrant in the world with a powerful story to tell. During the dress rehearsal, though, my ears perked up, my eyes grew misty, and my ego finally took a back seat. The sweet-faced, blonde-haired woman with a thick Polish accent spoke about her never-ending battle with immigration; the balding man with tired, blue eyes mentioned that he woke up at 3:00 a.m. every day to go to his minimum wage construction job. It was difficult to bond with these individuals, as we were being wired and had microphones shoved into our faces. But I wanted to know them and follow them on their journey. Somehow, the success with my case depended on theirs.

When I did have a moment with these peers of mine, I didn't even know where to begin. Our battles were so long and drawn out, and the unspoken understanding between us spoke volumes. We empathized with one another just by the very nature of sharing a common plight. We were in the same battle, just assuming different roles. With each person I met under these circumstances, I vowed to keep in touch, knowing that at some point we would lose touch. Somewhere along the way, one of us would eventually want to forget. It was too painful to live in hardship and then be constantly reminded of it by seeing someone else who acted as your mirror. Would I be able to see Senator McCain? How would it go with him?

During the reception, I finally saw Senator John McCain in person. He was smaller in stature than I imagined seeing him on TV. He walked over to me, and I introduced myself as one of the speakers. "And where are you from?" he asked.

"I was born in Zambia, but my family is from the Congo."

"Those are very difficult places to come from . . . thank you for your courage," he replied with sincerity. He shook my hand finally, and he wished me luck. Although I did not agree with many of his political views, Senator McCain earned my respect because he validated my fears of deportation to the Congo or Zambia. On this day, I was introduced as the first speaker at the town hall. There were hundreds of colorful people in the audience; judging from the faces and the signs they held up, most the audience was of Hispanic origin. I wondered where the black, white, and other brown faces were—surely, the Hispanic community was not the only one affected by immigration reform. As I stood at the podium and projected, I looked to see my own reflection in the faces of the onlookers. I knew then this was not my struggle alone and it was not in vain—there was a reason why I went through this. I felt a sudden surge through my body. I was ready to tell my story.

I was thrilled when, the following week, *The Immigrants Journal*, a Brooklyn-based organization that provided legal aid to immigrants, asked me to speak at their immigration rally. I called my friend, Gisselle, who helped me to perfect my speech.

"Gisselle is dynamite," Charlotte said. "I would love to hire her as my intern assistant in your case." Gisselle was indeed a gem. She always made time for me, to listen to my complaints, revise speeches, edit narratives, and laugh with me as I waxed poetically about a futile love interest. Although not officially in Charlotte's employ, Gisselle advocated on my behalf.

"And Malcolm X once said, my Brothahs and Sistahs," the second and most long-winded speaker began that evening. Gisselle and I snickered about the nonsense that characterized this rally at the Brooklyn Museum. It seemed unorganized, and the speakers became flakier as the night progressed. I was the tenth speaker listed on the program; there was no telling if any sensible person would stay long enough to hear my saga, as it was nearing 9:00 p.m. Finally, my turn arrived, with Charlotte and Gisselle cheering me on. I walked onstage in my pinstripe grey suit, note cards in hand.

I stood at the podium, took a deep breath, and drew the crowd in. I learned to relax my facial muscles, and then I began to speak. The room stood still, even the air froze in place; everyone was engaged in my words and voice. I spoke slowly, enunciated, and where I felt necessary, paused. I allowed the tears to roll down my face, because Charlotte advised me to show the audience my pain, but I was so overcome with waves of emotion and adrenalin that my tears were too real. My throat grew tight as I uttered my final statements.

"Martine," Gisselle said with tears in her eyes, "you're such a captivating speaker. I'm so lucky to have you as a friend."

At the end of the night, various individuals approached me, ranging from local magazine editors and publicists to other suffering immigrants. That evening, I became a D-list celebrity, and I realized that it was just the beginning. The essence of the night was beautifully captured when a young, dark-skinned black woman with wavy, black hair approached me and stated, "I just want to thank you for telling your story up there. I'm going through the exact same thing, and it inspired me to see you standing so bravely up there. How did you gain so much education when you had everything against you?" This was a question that I was not fully prepared to answer. "I guess I never gave up on myself no matter what the circumstances looked like," I answered. "When I was told that it was impossible, that motivated me to try harder. My primary goal was to just get *one person* to hear me, in the hope that he or she would want to help me."

For an instant, I had become someone's hero; this lovely woman's face softened and her eyes watered. In that moment, I wasn't a frightened, little girl awaiting a beating from Ya Marie, nor was I a shaken young woman taking in Judge Colucci's verbal abuse. I had expanded. I felt bigger than the system that imprisoned me. It was then that I finally understood what Aditi Singh was trying to tell me all those years ago.

The momentum picked up around my case and all my friends were motivated to help—it was like my own movement. Charlotte drafted letters to the offices of Senators Charles Schumer and Hillary Clinton, and we sent a thank you note to John McCain's office. We wanted to positively influence the DREAM Act (Development, Relief, and Education for Alien Minors) legislation in Congress, which would benefit me; otherwise, we hoped to win support with one of these senators so that they could potentially sponsor a private bill for me when the time was right. We did all this while awaiting the BIA's decision.

"Hey, Martine, please send me your timeline and a narrative. My aunt is an excellent writer, and she edits for the Theatre of the Deaf. She has offered to review your narrative before we send it to our local Connecticut senator," my friend corresponded.

"Tini," another referred to me by my nickname, "I have a friend and coworker who is affiliated with Hillary Clinton's office and he has offered to help get your story to her. I have copied him on this email, but I have attached his name and number. Please feel free to call him."

By April, Senator Arlen Specter of Pennsylvania introduced to the 109th Congress the Senate's Comprehensive Immigration Reform Act of 2006. It was most certainly a hot topic; if passed, then I would be entitled to permanent resident status. The bill needed sixty Senate votes, but sixteen senators had yet to give their consent, like Olympia Snowe and Charlotte Collins from Maine or John Warner from Virginia.

"I'll try to reach out to Warner's office," Judge Wells assured us.

We all went back inside where the music was playing louder this time. It was time for a real party. This festivity was tame compared to the African parties that I was raised on. It was primarily due to the boring, non-secular music that my dad insisted on playing. The music complimented the giant poster of a white, blue-eyed Jesus that confronted me from across the room. The music eventually picked up in pace and became more tribal, with no words but the *buh-bump* of drums. This was the kind of music you were supposed to gyrate your hips to. While it probably seemed vulgar to outsiders, it was just part of the culture and didn't seem odd to even the Seventh Day Adventists in the room. It was just me who took discomfort in moving my hips like that. Besides, I couldn't move my hips like that even if I tried. I stuck myself in the corner chair and kept busy talking to my mom's best friend from the Zairian Embassy, the c-word lady.

It was truly a whirlwind year. In March 2006, following my invitation to Gracie Mansion to meet New York Mayor Michael Bloomberg, Charlotte called me with more news.

"Lauren Ackerman, a reporter from *Metro New York*, an urban newspaper, is doing a piece on 'Undocumented Immigrants' and both your name and mine somehow came up. I'm happy to provide them with your narrative but they need to do a photo shoot. Isn't that exciting?"

ILLEGAL AMONG US

A photo shoot meant my face would be in a free newspaper distributed in every subway station in New York City. I couldn't imagine the thought of my mug all over New York City. Fear quickly took hold of me, and I started to wonder about strangers on the street recognizing me. What if people were offended by me, the illegal immigrant, and attacked me?

Was I truly ready to be the face of illegal immigration? What were the consequences? I was instantly mortified, and I wiped back the tears because I had forgotten that Charlotte was on the other end of the line waiting for my response. I couldn't disappoint her; we were such a strong force, and I did not want to ruin our momentum.

"Okay, that's great," I said with little conviction.

"Are you doing okay, kiddo?" After undergoing minor foot surgery the prior morning, I was home and heavily medicated with both feet stuck in orthopedic shoes.

"Sure. I'm just in a lot of pain, and I'm feeling groggy but I'm so excited, thank you," I had lied.

There was very little time to contemplate. I donned my "fashionista hat" and went straight to work in search of the appropriate attire for the photo shoot. I paired my favorite *Red Engine* jeans with a white and navy-blue stitched blazer and a colorful blouse. Of course, the photographer had to keep my booted feet out of the pictures.

"Don't worry," the gentleman reassured me; three cameras strapped across his shoulders and a light pod. We stepped into the hallway of my apartment building to capture the natural light that blazed through the windows. After a few minutes of contorting my face to look "relaxed," I finally remembered Tyra Banks's advice from *America's Next Top Model*: "Relax your face and smile with your eyes." I tried to feign a look of deep reverie, and somehow my face and hands relaxed just enough to capture my true essence. Afterwards, I had a telephone interview with Laura Ackerman.

VI. FAME

"Martine, you're on the front cover!" Giselle shrilled.

"What?" I froze with my phone in my right hand. I was in tight quarters with my bed and just two drawers fitting into what constituted as a standard-sized Manhattan bedroom. I often had to crawl over my bed to get to the window because there was no walkway at the foot of the bed. What did Giselle mean I was on the front cover?

Then my coworker called me from the office, and it was obvious that she was whispering from her cubicle: "Oh my goodness! I went to get today's paper and there you are; I'm so proud of you, Martine." I couldn't hang up fast enough before another call came in. Each call seemed so hazy as I was waking up.

When I finally got hold of a copy of *Metro NY*, the infamous photo stared back at me on the front page—an eight-by-eight with my hope-filled eyes and my hands cupped together. I flipped to the article and began to read: "Ms. Kalaw is an orphan . . ." I was mortified to be exposed to the world, but especially when I considered the professional relationship I had maintained with all my coworkers. I wasn't prepared for this type of coming-out party.

This article triggered an avalanche of emails into my inbox, some from colleagues I barely knew. "Hello, Martine. My name is Evan, and I work for the Tax Policy Unit. I know what you are going through, and I have a few questions for you and your lawyer. Have you considered filing asylum? Can you claim persecution on any grounds?" While I appreciated the gesture, I rolled my eyes at the rhetorical questions.

I phoned Giselle back hoping that she could somehow use her humor and wit to calm me down. "Giselle, I feel so exposed. I'm embarrassed to ever face my coworkers. Now everyone knows that I'm illegal," I cried with an immense level of shame. I felt somewhat robbed of my dignity, even though I consented to the article.

"Martine," Giselle began, "but don't you see. You might be illegal but you are illegal among us. There is overwhelming support of you. People love you and see you as a part of us. You belong in America just like the rest of us."

We were set for my work authorization appointment at the Federal Building on May 25th at 9:30 a.m. and Laura Ackerman, the reporter who wrote my *Metro NY* article, asked to accompany Charlotte and me. To expedite the process, Charlotte suggested that I get a letter of recommendation from my employer, which she hoped would be persuasive since it was an agency presided over by the mayor.

"Martine, look at what you wrote," she replied in an email. "Worth Authorization" was the subject line of the email that I sent to my boss, my director, and to all human resources. What a Freudian slip! Deep down, I did feel like I was at a live auction: "Black African girl, 5'4" and 120 pounds, she's illegal . . . going once, going twice!" If even one person didn't approve of me, then it could wreak havoc on my status. Nevertheless, I did receive a letter of recommendation from my employer.

Laura reminded me of a former Girl Scout with her brown hair and pink cheeks. She was more like a cross between Mary Poppins and no-nonsense GI Jane. She found my story to be so riveting, she was prepared to write a follow-up piece. "I promise to come alone with no cameras, just a notepad and a pen."

She was phenomenal, a real firecracker. When she started to jot down notes from the conversation between Charlotte and the ICE officer who declined my application and asked why Laura was there, she replied, "I'm taking note of the conversation."

"You cannot do that in here," the security guard commanded.

"She is with us," Charlotte interrupted.

"And who are you?" the guard asked with insolence. He must've been of Southeast Asian descent, with an Indian accent. It was inevitable that all three of us were going to get kicked out of the Federal Building.

"This is my client, and we are here to obtain her employment card," Charlotte spoke with calm and clarity. "And this is our friend, who happens to be a reporter who wants to document Martine's story." There was no wonder that she was good at what she did.

"But what is she doing with that?" He pointed to Laura's note-pad and pen. He was obviously infuriated that these three women were mocking him.

"I cannot write?" Laura asked condescendingly. That's why I liked Laura—she challenged and intimidated those who impeded her efforts. Of course, it helped that she was a wholesome-looking white woman. When you had a topnotch lawyer and an aggressive, fearless reporter, you were bound to win any argument. We were like a watered-down version of Charlie's Angels. You know, because there were three of us and we were all kind of badass in our own way. My files were not in their system and they denied our application for my work permit.

Memories from my previous experience in this place surfaced, but Charlotte quickly morphed into a lion protecting her cub; with Amy by her side scribbling away, she finally got someone's full attention. "Miss, my client's case is filed in Buffalo. Please check your records again thoroughly. I also have copies of her pending case." I watched the two of them standing up there, fighting for me. I refused to budge from the warm spot that I discovered in my chair. I figured that the delay in getting my EAD was because my case was filed under the Violence Against Women's Act (VAWA), a law that protects violent crimes against women. Since my immigration case was based on my mom's abuse, it was filed under VAWA to protect me. Therefore, my file was much more difficult to access.

Let them deal with it, I'm tired.

Getting another EAD was a small victory that I thoroughly relished. Amy insisted on sharing the news with concerned *Metro NY* readers. They had sent a barrage of emails to *Metro NY* asking about the outcome of the young woman without a country. I felt empowered by the media this time, and I had a chance to raise my voice.

I respected Charlotte's hustle. Her goal was to get me in the public eye to evoke sympathy, therefore cornering Judge Colucci. Just when Charlotte and I were looking for our next big break, a particularly arresting article about a young boy named Djibril Seck in *The New York Times* railroaded us. He was a teenage African boy, an illegal immigrant. His story seemed more arresting than mine. Of course, he was going to steal my thunder.

"Plus, he's younger so he warrants more sympathy," Charlotte said.

If only one illegal immigrant could win the award for "most traumatic story," then Djibril would take the Oscar. I believed that the media and mainstream America had a limited threshold for news about immigration before apathy set in. It was like the holocaust syndrome—after a certain number of topical movies and books, it was arguable that people grew reticent to the message. We had to get my story out there before the public grew tired of hearing about undocumented immigrant strife. Now this kid won the hearts of New Yorkers. To make matters worse, he was a genius, and only thirteen years old. Although bright, I was anything but genius. I couldn't compete with his saga.

"I have a brilliant idea!" Charlotte said. "We need to connect with Djibril's attorney. I have started putting in calls. They have an in with key legislators who can pass the DREAM Act. And if we work as a team, your story and Djibril's combined would blow people out of the water! It will be a huge success. It will be fabulous." Charlotte could barely breathe with all her excitement. She realized that using the adjective "fabulous" was the key to persuade me to do anything. I imagined that Djibril, myself, and perhaps one other individual would tag team with our posse of brilliant lawyers to devise a strategy that would change the course of immigration history—similar to *Brown vs. Board of Education,* the landmark decision of the Supreme Court. I wouldn't allow the details to cloud my fantasies. Sure, the premise behind *Brown vs. Board* took years to develop, but ours would be hugely successful as a concept brought to the national spotlight overnight.

Charlotte did most of the work, namely, finding the stories, the affected individuals and their lawyers. First, it was Djibril, but then came Arnan Bosque and Abdel Shuayb. Arnan, a college student at Princeton, was invited to speak on TV with Anderson Cooper, and Abdel was a graduate from Cornell Law.

The day came for all of us to finally meet at Charlotte's condo on Riverside Drive. We were the "DREAM Act Team," aptly coined by Charlotte and me. Our childlike spirits emerged as we began to envision what this new group would be like.

"We will host a fabulous brunch at my place with you, Arnan, Abdel, and Djibril. You will each share your stories for us to bond, and then we will start to devise a strategy on how to lobby on the Hill for the DREAM Act," Charlotte said, following with all the seriousness of her former statements. "So I'm thinking of having bagels, lox, fruit, and cheese. What do you think?" What did I think? Would this ridiculous catering bill show up on my tab or not? Thankfully, it didn't. It came out of Charlotte's pocket.

Djibril was not at all whom I expected. It was reassuring to see that he was just a quiet kid, easily bored by adult conversations, who happened to be in this precarious immigration situation. Shamefully and ironically, I shared many of the same stereotypes towards these undocumented youth as the average American shared towards me. I expected African immigrants to look and sound a certain way, but Djibril had no trace of the stereotypical African accent. He was just a socially awkward, tall, and lanky teenager. Djibril said very little—his lawyer wasn't even present to speak on his behalf—and was extremely shy. How astounding that such a normal-looking kid could have suffered so greatly at such a young age. This must have been how people perceived me.

Arnan was unafraid as well as unapologetic, which resonated deep within me, because I suffered such shame for being undocumented. On the other hand, he did not feel the need to justify himself; he was simply his own advocate and felt entitled to status as a US citizen just like everyone else. He must have been smart to carry on a conversation with Anderson Cooper not just about his own journey, but on the topic of immigration itself.

The room was filled with many type-A personalities, making it impossible to engage in deep, personal conversation. It was an ego trip, where one council would suggest some legal clause, and another would rebut with their idea. If it was this hard in our current setting, I wondered how the heck anything got accomplished in a law firm. It was a warm spring day but we all sat around her unlit fireplace. The smorgasbord of cheese and bagels went untouched. My eyes bounced from one boy to another like a Ping-Pong ball. How did I fit in? I was older than them, and I was a woman. But here we all four were united by this common demon. There was a moment, however, when the attorneys were wrapped up in their own conversations, leaving us, their clients, alone to ourselves. I witnessed something powerful as each of us was free to drop our guard and relax for the first time that morning—perhaps for the first times since our respective nightmares began.

It was as if all the air simultaneously released from our lungs. Arnan shifted from the articulate, poised young man who was always being interviewed, to a recent college grad unsure about his future: "If I pursue this amazing opportunity in London, I may not be allowed reentrance into the US. Then I'm stuck in London with potential immigration complications there, too." Djibril just wanted to be a kid, hoping to be a part of the school science competition and itching to play basketball later that afternoon. It was Abdel who most intrigued me; maybe it was his modesty or his nature to be a curmudgeon. Perhaps it was the fact that, at twenty-five, he was the closest in age to me.

Abdel's story struck me as a testament to the cruelty of life. How could it be that his brother won the immigration lottery to obtain a visa and remain in the US while he was going to be deported? He resolutely denied each of my attempts to create a silver lining; once again, I was reminded of myself. Was Abdel my reflection? Had I sunk so low in my own self-pity that it would take a shovel to dig me out? At what point had I lost my faith? Whereas Djibril was preoccupied with being a kid and Arnan worried about going to London, Abdel lost his conviction, and for that reason alone, I pitied him the most. And if he indeed was my own reflection, then I, too, was feeling sorry for myself.

"Well, I think we did it, kiddo! I think we will have this DREAM Team ready to go public soon enough," Charlotte remarked as the last of the DREAMers left. We sat across the table from each other and picked at all the leftovers.

Apparently, our meeting couldn't have been that much of a success. It turned out that Arnan and a few others were invited to Washington DC to speak on behalf of the DREAM Act. Of course, Djibril and Abdel did not go for their own reasons, but no one thought to invite Charlotte and me.

"I have to admit that I'm hurt that they did not invite us to DC," Charlotte confessed. I was, too. "Well, we will just keep trying, kiddo."

Instead of trying to ride on the coattails of others, Charlotte and I quickly calculated our next steps over a few glasses of wine. Gisselle joined us on rare occasions. Gisselle quickly became my sidekick, except she was the one with more poise and ideas. She stood about 5'11", and while she dressed sporty, she had the face of a 1940s Hollywood actress. She could have easily been Hollywood starlette, Ava Gardner's, child. Charlotte's husband would periodically chime in, but it was Charlotte who livened the conversations.

"You don't mind if I smoke, do you?" I watched in complete shock as she lit a cigarette and crouched, Indian-style, while carefully blowing smoke so that it wafted towards and out through the chimney. "I don't smoke that much anymore," she said, beginning to share her life story. Gisselle and I listened, fascinated by this womanist. Charlotte was so real, so natural, that you couldn't help but be mesmerized. She had rebel written in the lines of her face.

"Oh my goodness, Charlotte is just so cool," Gisselle said. Like me, she was hooked by the allure of Charlotte's charm, supreme intelligence, and her luxurious apartment on Riverside Drive.

Even in my happiest of times, I had the looming presence of this deportation, and that alone prevented me from fully enjoying life. No more than three weeks after I started my new job at the New York Public Library, John James's office submitted a $2,000 bill to me. Knowing him as I did, John was too disorganized to have come up with this itemized bill for all the work conducted; his assistant, Leslie Vidal, must have been behind its creation and delivery.

"What do you think this is? This is not free!" Leslie screamed at me over the phone when I questioned the bill. "This is his job, and this is my job. We need to earn a living, too. I think that you can afford to pay this bill, especially considering that you are living and working in New York City and you have a hotshot New York City attorney that you can afford. I'm sick of all of you expecting things for free. Don't you think that you owe him something?"

At that moment, I was beginning to see that this was not about John but about Leslie and what she felt she was owed. As far as I was concerned, John didn't deserve anything for ruining my case.

"I'm not paying this, Leslie," I said sternly. The audacity of her to demand something from me and make sweeping judgments about me. How dare she. She didn't know me.

"You need to pay! You better pay! I will have the collectors come after you! How dare you!" Leslie screamed over the telephone. Did John even know that his assistant was calling up his clients and threatening them? Did he put Leslie up to this? I reacted out of karmic fear and negotiated a payment plan. Call it bad luck, or whatever else, but it was after me. Technically, John James was still my attorney presiding over my case, so it was not going to be that simple to get rid of him. Until Judge Colucci gave Charlotte permission to manage my case, John still represented me. Essentially, I had no right to select my own attorney at my discretion at any point in the process.

She read the appeal that John James submitted to the BIA, and then handed me a copy of the document to keep while looking deeply into my eyes. "Martine, I'm so sorry. This is one of the worst briefs that I've ever seen. The evidence is inconclusive; there are spelling mistakes and grammatical and syntax errors throughout the entire document. It's all just wrong. There is no chance the BIA will approve this. It would be almost insulting for them to read."

My heart ached at hearing the truth. The BIA seldom overturned cases; if my chances were one in a million with a well-written brief, then they fell to one in twenty million with this lousy brief. I certainly was not that lucky. My fate was now sealed, and I just knew it was a matter of time before I would be deported to God knows where. Why did John hate me so much? What had I done to warrant such a cruel twist of fate: a bad mother and cruel family, an incompetent lawyer, and now deportation? There was no good in life, so it seemed. To Charlotte, this fight would go on until it was won; if necessary, she would take this to the Supreme Court!

The opposing council in my case, Brad Doherty, informed Charlotte that the BIA remanded the decision back to Judge Colucci's courtroom; it was now up to my judicial nemesis to make the ultimate determination. Generally, when the BIA remanded the decision back to the court, it meant that they did not care to deal with it, most likely due to the thousands of backlogged cases. The intent of this action was to alleviate their workload via the judge's assistance—relatively standard protocol. By not granting relief, however, the possibility remained that my case would never end; rather, it would just bounce back and forth between the BIA and the court for years.

Judge Colucci submitted documentation to hold another hearing on November 15, 2006, and properly notified my attending lawyer; John failed to inform me. It was November 5th, less than two weeks before the scheduled hearing when Charlotte called me with this astonishing news that she had recently come upon. I had left John a dozen messages in the previous two weeks, asking to discuss my payment. Leslie remained in contact with me via telephone, email, and fax because she wanted to ascertain that I would pay my bill in a timely manner. She even had my new work number, yet not once did she mention this critical information. How could both have neglected to inform me that the court had scheduled another hearing, knowing full well that my failure to appear would automatically result in deportation? I was no conspiracy theorist, but it certainly sounded like sabotage.

A disconcerting web of issues surrounded this upcoming hearing: Charlotte was not officially my council in Judge Colucci's courtroom, since he had yet to approve her request for a change of council and a change of venue. This meant that John James had to represent me in the Buffalo courtroom on November 15th. To add to my difficulties, Charlotte was scheduled to be out of the country on that day—she could not even accompany me upstate. Did I forget to mention that just days earlier I fainted while running and was now dealing with a concussion? Physically, I was in no condition to face Colucci on my own.

"Obtain a letter from your neurologist stating that you are undergoing serious neurological tests, such as the MRI that you've already done and the CAT scan that will soon be administered," Charlotte said. "I want to request a motion to change council and to change venue because you need to be at work and because you are undergoing medical evaluations. I also want to request a motion to change the date of your hearing." Charlotte's ambition was admirable, but she had not yet encountered Judge Colucci's wrath. I knew already that every request would be denied, which he ultimately did.

Four days until the hearing, Charlotte and I started to scramble. Dionne, a mutual friend, insisted on traveling to Buffalo with me. She was originally Charlotte's friend who took an interest in my case, and since she also happened to be African, I saw her as a mentor. I was uncomfortable with the imposition placed on her—of both time and money—simply to act as my emotional support. Furthermore, I wasn't sure if I trusted anyone to see me at my most vulnerable. My acquaintances knew me as a strong and motivated woman; few had witnessed my fear-filled, cowering persona that revealed itself once within the confines of the Buffalo court system. This side of me had no voice—she cried and doubted herself—I detested this display of frailty. But I just couldn't face Colucci alone. It was worth the risk of my friend seeing this part of me. This judge had deeply traumatized me. I would rather get hit by a bus than have to go back into that courtroom with Colucci. I would do anything to keep from being violated by Colucci again.

VII. FINALITY

I stopped caring about the possibility of living in purgatory, which was what one of my friends used to say to scare me out of taking my own life. In my view, I'd rather be dead than have to continue with the insanity of these hearings; or worse, suffer in a detention facility or survive, destitute and alone in DRC. If I could just rid myself of the burden of this immigration stronghold, then perhaps I could be at peace. But I had lost my will to fight; I was exhausted by the numerous battles that had led me to this point. Besides, Colucci would only continue as my unrelenting foe. He had more ammunition—the law, the government, and the courts. I would end my life because that seemed like the only viable option.

I needed for life to be over with, once and for all. All those past suicide attempts were for amateurs. I couldn't trust taking pills, because they hadn't worked in the past, and I couldn't get my hands on anything lethal enough. Should I hang myself? I needed to figure out a way to do this so that no one would find me for days. Yes, there would be pain involved, but that pain couldn't be greater than being abused, losing your parents, being tossed from home to home only to be told that America was not your home either. The unknown is tormenting because it's an abyss you go into alone. It's like death but worse because you are still alive. I was just tired of fighting against the hand that was dealt to me in life. No matter how hard I tried, how optimistic I was, nothing was going to change.

I grew recluse and spent my evenings crying on the barren living room floor of my apartment, researching websites that promote suicide to find the quickest and most effective method to kill myself. I mourned my own death as my funeral flashed before my eyes: I saw Señora Castillo and Mrs. Smith broken, feeling as if they had failed me. I wondered about where my corpse would be sent, since I had no homeland. Deep down, I didn't want to die, but I could not envision any other solution. I was exhausted of living this life; dying offered solace.

"Martine," Jimena consoled over the phone, "maybe this isn't your battle to fight." An interesting thought; perhaps I had to go through this for a greater good. But I didn't want to be a martyr. Why me? If no one could give me an answer to that question, then I wasn't willing to live through any more pain and anguish.

"Martine, if you take your life," she paused as she began to sob over the telephone. "I'm going to be very sad. It will break my heart. I will never be the same," Señora pleaded. I did not want to make her cry, but I also knew that, in the long run, my not being around would relieve the burden she carried about my immigration.

"But, Señora," I also began to fight the tears back, "I'm very tired."

"Please, please hang on," Roxana typed on Google chat from medical school in Poland. "Your story will change the world."

But perhaps it was my friend who was a model turned aspiring actor who said it best. "M, I know that you think suicide is the answer, but it's not. I've been there; I know that darkness. It will consume you before you have the chance to kill yourself. Stop trying to run and acting the part of the victim. You just got to fight. It's not easy but you have to do it, you don't have a choice."

The same colleague, Evan, who contacted me when my *Metro NY* article came out in May 2006, gave me his therapist's number during my lunch hour at work. "I know that her name sounds funny, but she is good. She specializes in cases with immigration. She is a forensic psychologist. Just call her now and tell her how you feel, and she will make time. If you want, you can take my next appointment, which is for tomorrow evening. It'll be okay, Tini," he said in the most compassionate tone that brought me to tears in my office. "She's amazing with immigration cases. Unfortunately, she doesn't take insurance, and she is very expensive."

In the past, this fact would've brought immediate objection; but today, I was desperate. I was scared to call. I already knew how these therapy sessions went because I had been going to them since I was fifteen. Therapists were always fascinated and perplexed by my immigration saga, and I ended up spending more time educating them on immigration law than getting treated. They were also a trap. You wanted to tell them enough so that they could help you but telling them too much could put you on medication or send you to a mental facility, both of which I wanted to avoid.

Under no circumstances could I admit what I was really thinking, which was that I wanted to end my life. I went online and researched ways to do it so that I would succeed this time. Kind of an odd statement, I know. But I didn't want any false alarms like in the past. The throbbing pain of being illegal had to go away. How could anyone else understand my hurt of not existing in this world? I was like a shadow. People could see my silhouette, but no one actually *saw* me. I wasn't as strong as people claimed but instead I was fragile. People admired me for being poised in spite of my circumstances but that was just a show, deep down I was broken. I had an immigration judge whom I was deathly afraid of. He scared me just as much, if not more, than Aunty Amelie.

I phoned and left Dr. Saltz a message, and she returned my call an hour later. The first thing that I noticed was the extremely soft and soothing cadence in her voice.

I waited in the lobby of Dr. Saltz's office on 72nd Street and Columbus Avenue until I was greeted by a middle-aged, white woman who stood about 5'5" with short, grey hair, wearing a plain, grey sweater with *Martin* fit khaki pants. She wore glasses and looked like she played golf on the weekends. Her office resembled that of a typical therapist—leather couch, bookshelves, and a big clock. She had a white noise maker, something I had never seen before and left me fascinated. It was a small detail, but it seemed like a gesture. Almost as if Dr. Saltz was offering that I could share whatever secret I had and no one else would overhear.

I sunk into the leather chaise lounge as she asked me, "Now, what is going on?" She had an inviting smile; not overly exaggerated, but it offered reassurance. It was a concerned smile, which would have seemed appropriate even in the most tragic of circumstances.

"Dr. Saltz, I'm afraid that I might kill myself." And so began our relationship. She knew Judge Colucci, as she had to testify for an immigration client in his courtroom once.

"Oh, he is awful. He is really cruel," she completed my thought. She validated my experience. She understood how I felt. The anxiety that I felt in explaining my immigration with past therapists was nonexistent with Dr. Saltz, because she quickly picked up on everything I explained and even asked questions to show that she knew exactly what I was talking about. After our first session, I no longer sat at the edge of my seat, feeling like I was on a witness stand. I was able to recline on her leather sofa and let my head rest on the pillow. While I felt like a cliché, I was at ease. Dr. Saltz's office was the single place where my breathing was tranquil, and I didn't fear judgment.

"Sure you hate being in his courtroom. He traumatized you when you were already suffering from post-traumatic stress disorder from your mom's abuse and your aunts' abuse."

When I began to tell her about my doubts and fears she responded: "You need to turn off the cassette. These awful things that you think about yourself are not your thoughts. They are thoughts and words of Aunty Amelie, your mom, and Judge Colucci. You have played this cassette so many times that you are confusing their voices for your own. That's not how you truly feel about yourself—you haven't had the opportunity to see yourself and to formulate your own beliefs about yourself. If you hated yourself and you thought you were worthless, you would have given up years ago, and you would be dead. Every time you find yourself repeating something negative, I want you to recognize that it's a recording. Then I want you to press the stop button." Dr. Saltz was eccentric because she used terms like cassette when I was sure cassette players had been extinct for at least two decades. No matter, I got what she was saying.

As simple as that advice may have seemed, it was profound to me and it altered my entire universe. I saw Dr. Saltz twice a week for an hour and sometimes it seemed like, aside from Charlotte, she was the only person who understood me. Dr. Saltz diagnosed me with trauma not too long after our initial consultation.

Three days before my departure for Buffalo, Charlotte called to give me the name and number for Owen Frost, whom she asked to accompany me to my hearing in her stead, even though John was technically my council. Owen Frost's role was to protect me, to intervene when necessary, and to report back to Charlotte about all the legal details of the hearing.

As Dionne and I waited for Mr. Frost at the baggage check in Buffalo, I noticed a small caricature of a man with thick-rimmed glasses come over to greet us. He had the advantage in recognizing us because it was not often that two stylish, black women hung around the Buffalo airport. He was very polished in a crisp suit and fit the profile of a typical attorney. He opened his mouth to reveal a small, mousy voice. The voice sat somewhere between a whisper and a whine. His name was Owen Frost, he said. I struggled between calling him Mr. Frost and Owen. Dionne thought it was more courteous to refer to him as Mr. Frost.

We collected our luggage and got in his car to drive to his office. Oddly, tonight was the one night I was unable to make small talk, which came as a complete shock. When I opened my mouth to speak, nothing came out except air and silence. Thank goodness for Dionne who jumped right in and began to chitchat with him. This gave me time to absorb everything that was happening, and to reflect on it all. Unlike downtown Buffalo where John's office was situated, Owen's office was in a more suburban setting. I didn't even know that this part of Buffalo existed. He and his wife owned their own law firm, and she acted as company accountant. The office was covered in eggshell-white carpeting—these people must have been quite meticulous to have white carpeting throughout.

"Please have a seat in here," he said, sounding a bit frazzled. "I need to continue with a call from Brad Doherty."

Brad Doherty, the opposing council who represented ICE informed Mr. Frost that John would not be able to represent me in tomorrow's hearing because of a medical condition. Had Owen not reached out to Doherty, he would not have known about the change in events until arriving in court the next day. An even more daunting projection: had Charlotte not asked Owen to accompany me to my hearing, and had I travelled to Buffalo alone with the expectation that John would represent me, I would've walked into Colucci's lair alone. God only knows who would have appeared as my council. My next thought was very legitimate: who was legally representing me in tomorrow's hearing?

"That is exactly what I'm trying to find out. Please excuse me as I take a private phone call in the other room," Owen said as he laid down a piece of paper he had recently collected from the fax machine. As soon as Owen exited the room, Dionne retrieved the printed fax off the desk. I couldn't believe she had just done that, something I would be too much of a coward to do. She sensed that something was going on and that no one would tell us; we needed to take matters into our own hands. As she read the note aloud, I sat frozen.

"Can you believe that? What do you think it means?" she asked as she memorized verbatim what the piece of paper read.

"Well, I don't know," I lied. I knew what it sounded like, but that notion seemed much too crazy.

"It sounds like John had a nervous breakdown of some sort. This is unbelievable," she whispered as I looked past her, imagining Mr. Frost walking in and catching us in the act. But we had nothing to worry about, because Mr. Frost was absent for at least thirty minutes. If John had in fact gone crazy, then that explained everything—his condescending nature, disappearances, forgetfulness, impatience, his verbal bite and overall incompetence. Maybe he was crazy all these years. Maybe that is what spawned his assistant's venom that fateful day over the telephone.

Owen walked in to find us still in our seats, free of any incriminating evidence, as the paper lay where he had left it.

"So right now, it is unclear if John's request to be absent from the case has been granted or not. We will know tomorrow." He wore a forlorn look about him that went perfectly with my I-cannot-believe-my-lawyer-beat-me-to-a-nervous-breakdown look. It was painstakingly ironic that John was undergoing an MRI after I just had one. While I was denied a reschedule of this hearing, he was rewarded absence from it, and we had suffered the same symptoms.

"So what's next?" Dionne boldly asked. The outcome of my trial was probably inconsequential to her, so it was easier for her to ask the daunting questions. "I guess what I mean is, what should we expect from tomorrow's hearing?"

"Well gosh, with these things anything could happen. And Judge Colucci is so scary. It says that the case was remanded back to him, and, ideally, he should grant you relief but there is no telling what he might say or do. I'm not a big fan of these immigration cases." How comforting that this individual—a stranger charged with being my shield from my immigration Goliath—was timid, small, and a weakling, just as I felt when in court. How infuriating to have to pay a whopping $300/hour for such mediocrity.

On the drive to the hotel, Frost alluded to the fact that Colucci also traumatized him: "It's a long story, but in my past, I was very much involved in immigration cases under the Buffalo Court system. I was very attached to my cases, and for the most part, I thought that I was making a difference. I had one extremely depressing case with a young woman who had a child, and she was from a very impoverished part of the world. Anyone with remorse would have seen that she could not survive in such devastation, except Judge Colucci. He denied her application several times to the point where both she and I became disillusioned about the immigration courts. She was eventually deported, and her child was left behind in the States. After seeing that, I vowed never to get involved in these types of cases."

Here he was, being forced to relive that trauma again; I'm sure he didn't realize what he was getting into when he agreed to do Charlotte this favor. As for myself, I learned that the pain of ICE litigation did not just remain with the clients; to a certain extent, the lawyers carried the same burden. Some grew small and meek, while others literally went mad, as in John's case. What kind of system could reduce immigrants to being subhuman and break down the spirits of their attorneys? Where was the justice in that?

It was comforting to see the cute and feisty attorney who spoke rapid-fire Spanish, whom I had seen on previous courthouse visits. She walked over to Owen Frost and with bulging eyes demanded to speak to him: "Immediately please." How odd that she considered the conversation private, if all she was going to do was speak loud enough for the entire room to hear. "I just heard from John this morning, and he isn't doing well. He has been excused from the case for good. But I have been assigned to all his cases for the time being. I know that she was your client, so I do not mind if you would prefer to represent her today, because I'm hardly prepared."

Was this some sort of a joke? In the last week, my case had been transferred to not one or two but four lawyers. But the only person who was truly prepared to represent me, and who actually wanted to, was also the one person lacking permission to do so.

What kind of cruel joke was this? Dionne was equally as dumb-founded. Would anyone ever believe this story? This was stranger than fiction.

I was more worried about Owen; he had clearly suffered major distress as an immigration attorney, and my hearing triggered that old darkness. Owen Frost walked into the courtroom terrified of Judge Colucci. My instinct was to protect him but what could I do? I prayed for a miracle to renew Owen Frost's faith.

"Your Honor, I wish to turn the case over to Mr. Frost, who is actually representing the defendant," the fiery, Spanish-speaking attorney said.

"Mr. Frost, it's nice to see you," Colucci said, tilting his head down so that his spectacles slid down his nose. "Do you object to this, Mr. Frost?"

"I agree with that, Your Honor," Frost responded, nearly losing the little that was left of his voice.

"The Board of Immigration appeals remanded the case back to me to render a decision. Mr. Doherty, what is your take?" he turned to look at Brad Doherty who sat in his usual seat looking around the room with his steel-blue eyes.

"I have no objections to grant the defendant permanent resident status by approving her request for adjustment of status." After the conversations that the opposing council representing ICE and Charlotte had, perhaps he recognized our honesty. Or maybe he just knew when to give up. I mean, we were going into year six of these trials, and, frankly, he must have been just as worn out as me.

"While I respect your decision, Council, I have to object. I'm denying the request once again. In fact, I'm prepared to take this case to the attorney general." He spoke with such malice and intent. Had Charlotte been in the courtroom, I believe she would have objected and presented a counter argument. Owen Frost was a complete nonfactor; he seemed on the verge of breaking down if he had to be in the courtroom much longer.

"Court dismissed," Colucci said as he beat down on the gavel.

We all proceeded to hurriedly leave the courtroom. Colucci apparently had the same notion as he headed to the judge's chambers. He stepped down from behind his throne, and I could not believe what I saw. Right there, in front of my very own eyes, stood a little man, no more than 5'6" in an oversized robe. In heels, I was taller than him. This minuscule man had fooled me all these years. Colucci was real, but his superiority was a figment of my imagination; he was a small and insignificant impediment, and he could not stop me. I was bigger than him just like I was bigger than the structures that attempted to confine me. This realization was my subconscious slaying of Goliath.

I felt confused that day. Who was my lawyer? Frost was no better than John; they were both cowards who didn't speak up for me. Were they all part of a conspiracy to sabotage my case? Also, how was the attorney general to be involved, and who knew that this office held jurisdiction over my case? It was clear that Colucci was on a crusade against me when he disagreed with the government's council, who was ready to close the case and grant me a green card.

Dionne and I glared at one another with the same obvious thought running through our minds during our return flight to New York City. "Nah," we both said in the same breath. Was it possible that the young, professional-looking man sitting in front of us was Judge Colucci's son?

"Yes, I'm from Buffalo. I grew up there. My name is Thomas Colucci," he remarked to someone on the other end of the line. Maybe it was just a coincidence but most certainly an odd one.

VIII. MR. K.K.

I watched as everyone did a celebratory dance for me and my friend. Celeste seemed to feel right at home despite the all-black cast. Fifi had gotten Celeste a traditional sarong and tied it around the top portion of her belly. The music was booming, and everyone was dancing in celebration of my homecoming. How could Celeste be so comfortable with my family, whereas I just sat on the couch and watched the happenings? In a matter of hours, a significant piece of my history had been uncovered. Here I was with my father, my father! No vile of blood could be a better indicator that we were related than just our phenotypes. Meeting all my mom's friends from DR Congo and Zambia seemed to bring her memory to life instantaneously. When the samosas were being passed around, my stomach made a hungry noise to remind me that I had not eaten in hours. I did tell my dad that we couldn't eat food from home, but it was the fear of being poisoned by my stepmom. But I was so caught up in the celebration that the idea of being poisoned seemed superfluous. Celeste must have felt the same because I turned to her as she was taking a bite out of a samosa.

"I think this is fine for us to eat," she said. Was this just her hunger talking? I wanted to pull her aside and ask her to reassess the situation, but she was already intoxicated by the fever of the party. The samosa tasted just how a samosa was supposed to taste with a crispness on the outside and a meaty center made of potatoes and other vegetables. The house didn't offer an oven, so these samosas must have been warmed by the sun or a fireplace in the back of the house.

We opened Pandora's box by eating samosas, because after that both Celeste and I were presented with a mound of Congolese food. How could they possibly think I could eat almost three cups of rice? The rice was topped with what resembled my mom's signature dish of cassava leaves sautéed in tomatoes and palm oil, when I was growing up. The palm oil added so much flavor and carried the same richness as butter—yum! The chicken was questionable though. It was some odd version of a smoked turkey, but it looked dry. The rice and cassava reminded me of home and now that the plate was placed in my lap, I would insult everyone if I didn't eat it. It was hard to eat while kneeling on the concrete floor on the porch while sitting an inch away from three different people. I had my first taste of Fanta. No wonder Celeste objected to it. It tasted like orange syrup, which overpowered all the other flavors that sat in my mouth. I felt guilty for putting Celeste in this situation of having to eat African food. I figured if I ate the food, she could afford to say no. Celeste surprised me, again.

"I will have a very little. A very little because I'm vegetarian," she said and assumed the logic I had, which was if I spoke louder perhaps they would understand me better.

"So, Celeste, tell us about your husband," my younger sister Fifi asked, in awe of this white goddess. Celeste's belly, which seemed to have grown overnight, made her relatable to the other African women in the room. I was one of the few among the women in the room who had never experienced the pangs of morning sickness and childbirth. It was Celeste who had more in common with my sisters than me.

"He's so handsome." I could see Fifi looking at a photo of Ethan and feeding into the colonial notion of white being pure and better than black. It bothered me, because while that was not what Celeste represented to me, to Fifi, she was a white goddess.

"And your husband just let you come to Africa without him?"

"Well, he didn't just let me. We discussed it, and I wanted to be there for Martine, and he supported that." I watched as Fifi looked in awe of what must have seemed like Celeste's defiance.

"And how many months along are you?" another female relative asked her. I was grateful once again for the distraction as I contemplated how I would finish the food on my plate when my stepmom motioned for more food to be put on my plate.

"No really. I will throw up." Rude or not, I had to draw the line somewhere.

"See, you need to marry a white guy. Don't waste your time with these lazy black men," my stepmother said to me as she asked me about boys. There were a lot of great black men out there, and I happened to have dated one, Barrington. He was great until he dumped me over the phone. After her ignorant comment about lazy black men, the realization sunk in. My dad's younger wife hated my mother but it was only after the greetings that I was able to make out which one of his wives was the younger one. The same stepmom who poured powder on me and whose arms I threw myself around was in fact the one who tried to poison my mom. But she seemed so nice. She was handsome, but my mom was prettier.

In meeting all my dad's wives, I decided that my mom was the most sultry and striking. Powder pouring stepmom did have a seductive quality about her, and I could see how she could have my dad in a trance. Her skin was taught, her hair fell thick and long down her back, and she unapologetically offered one-liners. She was like my dad's hot, young thing. My sister Beatrice's mother-in-law was lying in the corner with my sister's baby, amused by the conversation. Her eye sockets seemed to have a mind of their own. She had a way about staring at you so that it looked like she was putting you in a trance; it scared me. Celeste and I would later name her Crazy Eyes, and the powder pouring stepmom who tried to poison my mom as Scary Stepmom.

I wondered if I appeared to be a walking ATM to some of the family members in the room. My suspicions served me correct when Zalika's son, a gangly teenager with the face of a Gucci model, approached me and publicly asked me for money. "Aunty, I need money to go to school. I'm a very hard worker, but my mom is struggling." His mom was struggling? What about me? I, too, was struggling. It's like the room stopped, and there was laser beam focus on me in that moment.

"You have to keep in mind that I'm just reuniting with a dad, two step mothers, thirteen siblings, and I have another six in the Congo," I responded. "Everyone is going to ask me for something. If you were me, who would you chose first?" Perhaps posing the question that was plaguing me would get him off my back for a bit. Zalika's son was dumbfounded by my audacity and wasn't prepared to answer. Suddenly, the guilt I had about the colorful tale that Celeste and I shared about our friends contributing to our trip to Africa became a nonissue.

"We must go, Mwanji and Mama Celeste," my dad beckoned. Everything was done in haste. Under normal circumstances, I would have grown irritated by the sudden movement, but I saw pride in my dad's eyes, and he just wanted everyone to see his long-lost daughter; he wanted me to see my home. We got in the car and headed to my dad's oldest child's house, Joseph. It was impossible to confuse him with my dad because although he was my dad's namesake, my dad was often referred to as Mr. K.K., rather than Joseph.

By the time that we arrived at Joseph's home in what seemed to be a thirty-minute drive through more shanty towns, it was pitch-black out. The African night was blacker than any other night, which made seeing in Joseph's house particularly difficult, because he had one lamp. The village was so quiet that you would have thought that we were the only humans in sight. The darkness and the silence felt eerie but familiar at the same time. I sat on an old and dingy couch and imagined the germs crawling up my leg. When were we going to leave? Like Cinderella, I felt like the clock had struck midnight and everything that appeared magical was reverting to its original, ugly self. I felt absolutely no connection to this brother of mine, whom I had never heard about until today. He was very tall and lean and lived inside a competing duality of hardness and softness. I could tell that his life was difficult. His mother, my dad's very first wife, ran away from my dad but left my brother with my dad. He wore the hardness of life in his jaws, which remained clenched, but contrasted the softness of his eyes.

"We need to get our guests some Fanta," I heard dad whisper to my brother. God help us! Why did everyone insist on force-feeding us with Fanta? I found it to be the most repulsive taste, and a mere swallow left me feeling like I was a candidate for severe tooth decay. Even worse than drinking Fanta, I had to go the bathroom. It didn't seem like we were leaving anytime soon, and I had not used the bathroom in over eight hours. My brother's wife passed me a flashlight and motioned for me to walk outside with her. A sudden panic came over me. There was no bathroom. I was being motioned to use an outhouse. I looked to Celeste to save me. "Help!" my eyes screamed out to her.

"Just squat very low," she whispered back.

"I can do this," I told myself on the way there.

It was a long and tortuous walk. I finally knew how convicts felt on their final walk to their execution. I was so terrified that I could have peed all over myself, but I reminded myself that if pregnant, white Celeste was able to use an outhouse earlier, then Martine Kalaw from third-world Zambia should have been able to. She pointed to the outhouse and stopped three feet away to give me privacy. In that moment, it didn't even matter that there was no toilet paper. I just wanted to get it over with. It was like a life-size shoebox with a latch on the door. I couldn't image who would want to be locked inside. I opened the door and peered down for the hole and saw it. I inspected the ceiling before stepping. At the site of two giant roaches, I shuddered and held in my scream.

Get yourself together, Martine! They are just bugs. Do you want to pee on yourself?

My internal dialogue began. What would happen if I didn't pee now? I wasn't sure how long this night would go. I proceeded to step into the dungeon. No! I couldn't do it. I imagined dying in the shoebox from shock after the bugs fell on me and ate me. I ran from the outhouse as if it was about to explode. "I'm done," I lied.

"Did you do it?" Celeste's eyes asked when I walked back into the house. How do you say, "hell no" with your eyes?

I sat next to her and muttered under my breath, "I couldn't do it." She started to feign exhaustion, something that she could get away with.

"Let us go so that Mwanji and Mama Celeste can sleep," Dad said. In that moment, the heavens opened and took pity on my bladder.

CHAPTER 4

MATERNITY AWARD

I felt it in my bones that I had been in this place before.

I. 1981

Yesterday was emotionally exhausting. Celeste and I fell asleep the minute our heads hit our pillows when we got back to our hotel room. I almost forgot that she was pregnant because her endurance had exceeded mine. This time my dad was punctual in meeting us at the hotel. He had the entire day planned. His crisp, white, pinstriped suit was so big on him it gave him the appearance of a little boy wearing his father's clothes. The cream-colored newsboy hat that sat on top of his head was a stark contrast to his skin, which had gone from mahogany to a sun-kissed black in what seemed like overnight.

"Let us go!" he motioned to Celeste and me as we crammed ourselves into Beatrice's car. Celeste looked rested and rosy-cheeked in the long, burgundy, striped sundress that I gave her, whereas I felt grungy in the same jeans I wore for the past two days. At least I was wearing a new shirt.

"We are going to the late president's memorial," he finally revealed with unnecessary enthusiasm for a trip to the cemetery. "First, let's go to the University of Lusaka."

Now I was excited. I wanted to see the campus and get a feel for the educational community in Zambia.

"You know, Zambia is known for high cases of car accidents," my dad shared as we drove down the highway. First off, I already knew that. His comment was highly inappropriate, considering we were in a car, but the man had no filter, which was endearing in a way. He was like a living Wikipedia for the African continent. I appreciated the traffic, because it gave me a chance to gaze out of the window and take in my birth country. The sides of the highway were decorated with more red dirt and the most exquisite trees. They were shaped like bonsai but had bright-orange flowers as leaves. "We call them flamboyant in French." My dad emphasized his francophone accent. I assumed my dad was embellishing and that they had another name; they certainly couldn't be called "flamboyants."

"And, Dad, that's a beautiful looking church. What religion is that?" I asked as I remarked what looked like a white temple on the far right of the highway.

"Hmm? Oh yes. That is a very bad place. That is where they sacrifice bodies to worship the devil," he said with conviction and caution. A guffaw came over me.

"Dad, I'm sure that no one is being sacrificed. That seems crazy and would be against the law."

"It is true, my Doh'ta, it is a very bad place. If you go in there, they can sacrifice your body," he warned.

"Dad . . ." I was compelled to argue, but Celeste gave me a look to encourage me to let it go. I was disappointed about my dad's ignorance. How could he believe something so draconian? Africa was developing but we weren't living in the dark ages. No one was being sacrificed on an alter for goodness's sake.

As we drove up to the university and drove by passengers, they seemed intrigued by us. I almost forgot that Celeste was white and that would draw a lot of attention. As we got out of the car to begin our walk around the campus, it sounded as if thousands of foot soldiers were stampeding towards us.

"Get back in the car!" my dad shouted. I panicked, and all I could hear was Ethan's voice asking me to take care of his wife.

"Celeste, quickly get in the car." I was worried the invaders would immediately attack her because she was white. *God, please let us get out of here safely*, I thought to myself. I had never witnessed a riot before. This one was more like a protest by students regarding the interim president, which was slowly growing into a riot. I was slightly irritated with my dad, who swore that we would not encounter any of this. I refused to look at Celeste for fears that my terror would frighten her.

"This was just a protest," Dad said. "But it is too dangerous, so we will go to the president's memorial."

Duh, it is dangerous. Celeste seemed more exhilarated than anything else and started cracking jokes: "We definitely have to leave this part out of our recap."

"I'm not sure if I should smile or not," I told Celeste, as my dad shooed passersby out of the picture. We were at the memorial of the Zambian president who had died less than a month ago. Was it appropriate to pose in front of his gravestone and smile, or should I have looked like I was in mourning? I couldn't be sure. That didn't seem to concern my dad. He was acting like we were at Disney World taking pictures with Mickey Mouse.

"Mama Celeste, move this way. Beatrice, come up front," he went on, forgetting it was Celeste's camera that he was getting carried away with. Before we could overthink it too much, my dad scurried us back into the car so we could go onto the next stop.

"Yes, she is here. Yes, you can speak to her," my dad said into his flip phone, then handed it to me. Who were these people he was making me talk to? "This is your aunty. She wants to say hi," he exclaimed.

"Hi," I uttered, trying to control the annoyance in my voice. "Yes, it's so wonderful to speak with you, too."

I was growing impatient having to speak to random strangers whenever my dad felt like I should. He seemed to take so much pleasure in showing me off, so I just didn't have the heart to tell him. "We will not have time to go to the embassy where your mom worked, but we will go to UTH."

It took me a minute to decipher the acronym. "You mean University Teaching Hospital? Where I was born?" I asked, my heart having skipped many beats.

"Exactly. Where you were born. Yes."

I felt the tears welling up again. It never occurred to me we would get the chance to go to UTH. There was a point in my life where the only thing I knew about my birth was the name of the hospital I was born. But now I was going to see, touch, and smell the very first surroundings I was exposed to as soon as I came out of my mother's womb. I held my breath, not knowing what to expect. UTH was a campus to itself with large and small dormitories and concrete buildings large and small, which sat on a lot of land covered in red dirt and flamboyant trees.

As we drove up to the maternity ward, we saw a sprinkle of medical staff in crisp, white lab coats and stethoscopes. They had an air about them that only medical doctors would have, as if to say, "I'm special because I save lives." A sea of nurses walked by wearing candy-striped uniforms with matching white caps. They were so stylish in their getup that it almost resembled the nurse uniforms I have seen worn in Halloween parades. Then another group of nurses walked by carrying notebooks, but their outfits were light blue with matching little hats.

We walked into the main corridor where Dad began to explain the story of my birth. "Your mom went into labor so we called a taxi, and we came to the hospital, and we walked through this door, and the nurses took your mom." He couldn't contain himself. I realized that reliving these memories was as essential for him as it was for me.

The blue-painted, concrete walls, the long, linoleum hallway, and the tarnished, metal staircase put me into a dreamlike state. There was an acrid, stale linoleum scent that smelled so familiar I was taken back to January 1, 1981. I felt it in my bones that I had been in this place before. That realization and realizing the power of sensory memory gave me goosebumps.

"Mr. K.K.," Celeste said as she discreetly held the GoPro at her side, "where does that corridor take you? Where are all those people headed?"

"Yes," he said, turning to me. "That is the emergency room for mothers. The day before you were born, your mother went into labor, and we took a taxi here and came through these exact doors. Meanwhile, your twin sister Rose was being born at home."

I wasn't sure whether I should be amused or annoyed that my dad was referring to my sister, who was born a day before me by his other wife, as my twin. It only suggested that my dad had sex with both wives around the same time and got them each pregnant—disgusting! It was like he was in a reenactment of what happened on New Year's Eve 1980.

He spoke to me with a plastered smile on his face, which contradicted the painful events that he was recounting. "Your late mother visited that area many times. She suffered many, many miscarriages. Before you were born, she was pregnant and lost too much blood. The doctors told me she would die that day," he said as his eyes glazed over, and he began to relive that fateful day. As he shared those words his expression changed from amusement to regret as his voice dropped an octave. Dad was lost in a deep meditation with images from his past. As he spoke, I felt the blood being drained from my body.

I had no idea that Ya Marie had experienced so many miscarriages. The hospital, while somewhat functioning, was visibly a public hospital with old and possibly unsanitized equipment. I couldn't imagine my poor mother having to return to this place time and time again as she lost another baby, and nearly her life.

"They gave her a blood transfusion and, thankfully, she lived."

I got the chills thinking about my mom getting a blood transfusion from this kind of facility. Everything about her illness and death started to make sense. As I stared through the window that lead to the wing, I started to contemplate who this stranger was whom I referred to as Mom and, most often, Ya Marie.

At thirteen, it was hard for me to understand, but my mom was just looking for someone at whom she could unleash her frustrations. These were more like crazy spells that could be sparked by a mere look or misperceived tone of insolence. The switch happened so fast, it even surprised her; one minute Ya Marie would be relaxed, and then her Shesheme—the lone child she brought to the United States—would say something, seemingly innocent, that sparked immediate rage. Suddenly, she would chase her terrified daughter down the hall into the bedroom, literally wanting to kill her. I would drop to the floor and curl up into a fetal ball begging lenience: "Ya Marie, I'm sorry! Please forgive me! I'm sorry! I'm sorry!" But my pleading only aggravated her to greater violence. Her foot often became the weapon of choice, as she tossed aside the high-heeled shoe and stomped on her young daughter's back and kicked her in the ribs and shoulders. Ya Marie also made good use of her fists as they landed blows to my head. The attack was brutal, and every punch was further intensified by the harsh, unrelenting words: "Who do you think you are, you, you bitch! You imbecile! You animal. Whore!"

When her arms tired from punching, it only incensed the kicking, as her rage intensified. Finally, blood oozing from my nose signaled her to stop, as she realized that she had inflicted adequate physical pain. But the assault did not end there. Next came the voices of the men who hurt her, the shame for the diseases that plagued her body, and the feeling of guilt for losing these same men, whom she lured in with her sexuality to care for her and the children. All this swirled through her mind like a typhoon.

"You better be careful, Shesheme, or I will kill you. I will cut out those little eyes of yours and cut off that nose. Just who do you think you are? You are a nobody; do you hear me?"

It was a torrent of hatred exhumed from Ya Marie's past and thrashed onto my persona.

"How can she hate me so much? Why does she hate me so much? Why?"

These questions raced through my mind as I plugged my ears to blunt the force of her words. Suddenly, the crazy spells were countered by euphoria—almost minutes later. Ya Marie wanted the pain and hurt to disappear as quickly as it arrived, so I had to plaster a smile on my face and act like nothing happened. Alcohol was the best lubricant to soothe my mother, which relaxed my fears and helped us both to forget. She drank, and I got drunk off her intoxication—in a sense, we were both addicts. In fact, Ya Marie's wine provided solace for the two of us. Any embarrassment that came from our walk along the highway carrying groceries, because we were too poor to afford a car, was flowered with the knowledge that we purchased a $5.99 set of boxed wine that would last three whole days. I was like a battered wife.

I was interrupted from my catatonic state by my dad nudging Celeste and me to take the stairs to go to the birthing ward. "See this birth ward? This is where your mom gave birth to you." My dad pointed to the 8.5 X 11 paper printout that had an arrow signaling the birth ward. A nurse rolled her eyes as she passed by us to signify our ignorance. Did we look like voyeurs? Because we weren't. I was born here. My dad also felt the need to explain and get permission to go into the birthing ward. He wouldn't allow for Celeste and me to object, because this was his gift to me, to truly know where I came from.

He found a little office where a hospital administrator was having her lunch of rice and meat sauce, and interrupted. "Excuse me, can we go into the maternity ward? My daughter was born in this hospital in 1981, and she is here visiting with her friend. I want to show her where she was born." The woman, who was clearly not going to enjoy her lunch today, looked at my dad, then looked at Celeste and me who stood next to my dad as if to say, "So? Do I look like I give a damn?" My poor dad was trying so hard to impress me, but little did he know I was already blown away to a point where I wasn't able to process anything else.

We still snuck into the birthing ward where new mothers were lying on cots in single files. Some were bare breasted and looked exhausted from having given birth. They looked at us with complete disbelief but too exhausted to put up a fight. Were men even allowed in this section of the hospital? Immediately, I felt embarrassed. What were we doing here? We were encroaching on these women's privacy, and Dad, especially, should not have been there.

"Do you see where that woman is lying down? That is the cot where you and your mom lay after you were born. Before you came home from the hospital."

"Woah," I said, as if I had seen some sort of war relic. "That's the actual cot?"

"Well, I'm sure that's not the *actual* cot. It's been like thirty years," Celeste said, trying to make sense of it all.

I know that I'm gullible, but what if it was? After all, this was a dilapidated government hospital. Only I could say that. Celeste was not allowed to say that. It was the same thing as a black person being able to say the "N" word but not a white person. I think she sensed that.

"Celeste, I think that's the actual cot," I said, wanting to believe it to make my moment that much more dramatic. As we were debating on the authenticity of the cot, dad was taking photos of the cot and the woman for me to chronicle.

"Okay, Dad. Enough. I think we should go."

"Yeah, let's get the fuuuu . . . outta here," Celeste muttered under her breath.

In all her travels to the developing world in South America and Asia, Celeste hadn't been exposed to the hospitals, so what we were seeing left even her speechless. She couldn't help but want to capture each nook and cranny to share with the people back home.

A tall Middle Eastern man who was wearing a white *topi*, the traditional cap that is used for prayer, stared at me menacingly as he walked past Celeste and me. He looked to be in his midthirties, but his full beard masked his true age. He wore a knee-length lab coat and a stethoscope around his neck. Why did he look at me like that? He looked at me as if I was selling out my own kind to Celeste's camera lens. I felt a tinge of guilt.

"Celeste, maybe we should just put the camera away. That guy was looking at us."

I didn't want to seem any more neurotic than I already was by telling her what I thought the strange, good-looking Middle Eastern man might have been thinking about us; it just seemed a little odd.

"I wouldn't want to give birth in this place," Celeste said as she snapped her final picture. Just what did she mean by that? Of course, I wouldn't want to give birth here either, but I could say that. Her saying it just made her seem like an entitled white woman who was looking down on poor black Africans. I was born here, so it couldn't be that bad. I wanted to rebuttal her statement, but was I being hypersensitive? Celeste travelled all this way with me and had been exposed to so much in the last twenty-four hours, so I had to give her a break. After all, she was human and could stick her foot in her mouth on occasion. I wanted to forget that she ever made that statement. Dad had enough planned for us that it was easy to forget.

"Now, we must go to the house you lived before you left for America," he said.

"You mean the house that I grew up in?" I asked with complete dismay. I couldn't believe that my childhood home was still standing and that my dad would go through the trouble of making sure I saw it. He planned this trip so thoroughly and thoughtfully. How could he have known that I needed to see so much of my past?

I looked at him from the corner of my eye and saw an incredibly poetic man of seventy plus who perhaps had played and replayed this moment in his head for years, not knowing if it was just a fantasy. I suddenly became a child headed to Disneyland; this was the moment I had been waiting for, and I didn't even know it. Where my dad was taking me was where my story began. Beatrice was still acting as our chauffeur as Celeste, Beatrice's baby and babysitter, and I sat in the backseat.

"The new president must put gravel on these side roads to make them into real roads," Dad said to defend what we were seeing around us.

"Mr. K.K., where are we going?" Celeste asked.

"We are going to John Howard compound. That is where Mwanji grew up until she left for United States."

I had grown accustomed to how my dad answered a question by restating it; it made him seem so austere. I had never heard the term "compound" used in reference to where people lived. Celeste didn't question it, so I pretended to know and assumed that I would soon find out.

As the car slowed down, and we started to drive into another gated neighborhood, I noticed that this neighborhood was perhaps a little bit more expensive than the one my brother lived in, because I saw less shanty and more stucco houses.

We got out of the car, and I looked at Beatrice, who was surrounded by nostalgia. My dad was on a mission to give me back my childhood, but the only things that stood in the way were the tenants that currently resided in his old home. It occurred to me that my dad had a childlike innocence where he didn't understand the concept of boundaries. In this instance, he eagerly wanted to barge into his old home so that he could show me around, even though this was no longer his property.

"Mr. K.K., maybe we should ask the current residents if we can look around the outside of the house."

At least my dad was open to feedback. Each time my dad proceeded to tell people of the exciting story of his daughter coming back home, people seemed more inconvenienced by his explanations. We were permitted to walk around the house. The husband and wife couple just wanted us to hurry up and get out of their space.

"This is where we lived when you came home from the hospital. This window is to your late mother's bedroom. You stayed with her in there. And this house had four bedrooms, and I put a bathroom in there." Even my dad must have known that the conditions he lived in were not comparable to his old and much bigger house. "And do you see this mango tree?" he chuckled. "I planted this mango tree when we built this house and it grew so big." He took so much pride in reminiscing. The tree was tall as it was wide, and its branches flowed in various directions around the house.

"I planted this mango tree!" He caressed the tree as if he was about to make love to it.

Enough with the damned tree! would have been the words that sat on top of my cloud bubble. The tree represented the house and the family that my dad created.

Back in 1981, his four-room home with indoor plumbing, a toilet, and a tree full of lush mangos made him the richest man in the neighborhood. It was a symbol of his success and not only that, but his manhood. And now here he was in a one-room shanty with an outhouse that encompassed at least six people, with no job. He had every right to want to hold onto that mango tree for dear life.

I was quickly interrupted by a dozen pair of white pupils that bulged like a swarm of moths near Celeste. They didn't approach her like the stereotypical African kids in the movies that are so taken by a white person. Instead, they just stared at her; some seemed startled while others were amused, as if they had just encountered an inanimate object. A child's curiosity is so innocent. This was the first time some of these children had ever seen a white person before. Maybe some of them had never even seen a picture of a white person. What she looked like to them, I wondered.

Celeste seemed so humbled by the experience. Nevertheless, I was still angry with her for saying what she said about never wanting to give birth at UTH. Did she think that she was better than me?

"Habari kani," my dad greeted the neighbors in Swahili. It was as if he knew them. He pointed to me and then went over to hug them and motioned for me to come over and say hi. The elderly man and woman stared at me as if they had seen an apparition. "My dear, it has been many years. We have not seen you since you were a baby like those little ones over there."

The neighbors had been living in the same house since the 1970s.

"We knew your mother," the wife said.

It was as if she knew what to say to pull at my heartstrings. I was in search for anything or anyone that could reveal more to me about my mom, who remained elusive to me. In the 97-degree heat this husband and wife looked at me as if they knew me, and that further validated my existence.

When dad asked Celeste and me if we were hungry and we said yes, we didn't realize we were going to eat at Scary Stepmom's house. The credit goes to Celeste for coining that name after she confirmed, "Yeah, that woman is being overly nice to you to compensate for something she must have done to your mom." Celeste didn't have to say it, because I felt it. I worried about being left alone in a room with her because she might try to poison me, too. That's why I grew nervous when Dad suggested that Scary Stepmom make us dinner.

"You and Celeste can have a little shima." Even Celeste, who was usually tough about this matter, was casted into my step-mom's spell, and we found ourselves coalescing just a little bit.

"I will eat a very little, Mr. K.K., because I don't eat meat," Celeste mentioned.

What seemed like a minute later, Scary Stepmom brought over a plate of that same chicken from the other day that looked like it had recently been tarred and feathered.

II. STEPMOMS

"Dad," I grew annoyed by all the force-feeding, "Celeste just said she doesn't eat meat."

"Yes, but it is just chicken," my dad protested.

"Dad, she doesn't eat meat!" I exclaimed.

What didn't he understand? I was angry that we were being forced into these eating situations when I specifically told my dad that we could not eat at his house. I was even more frustrated that I was such a pushover, and I was making Celeste be the enforcer.

We were able to dodge the food after I ate two bites, but my dad insisted that he serve us something. "Let us serve you mangos."

Mangos seemed safe enough until I noticed that Scary, who was sitting to the left of me, had a giant butcher knife that she was using to peel the mango. I imagined that knife slashing my face by "accident." Celeste sensed my fear, "I can cut the mango," she practically screamed.

The two of us must have appeared hysterical to them. Scary lived in an exclusive neighborhood. The roads were still made of dirt, but the houses were not shanties. They were little, white-brick, concrete homes that sat in endless rows. The houses were pristine and were the equivalent of what I would consider sub-urban living by US standards. I didn't see any outhouses, but I figured that the goal was to make outhouses discrete, and they were not meant to be seen in this neighborhood. I didn't quite understand the purpose of an outhouse. Did people use it to bathe as well, or was it solely used as a toilet? I felt guilty for my igno-rance and even more guilty for not wanting to know.

When the kids from across the street came outside to take a sneak peek at the white woman, it was I who became the stereotypical Westerner who wanted to take a picture with the little barefoot African children. The littlest one was so pretty with her big, beautiful eyes and braids that I imagined I would one day have a daughter that resembled her. I asked Celeste to take a picture of us.

"Uh. That doesn't look good," Celeste said. "You mean to tell me that you want to take a picture with someone's kids, just so you can post pictures with you and African kids?"

I was so caught up with capturing every moment to share with my friends back home that I hadn't considered how patronizing I had sounded.

It was only two hours later that we found ourselves at Sad Stepmom's house. Why Sad? Because she seemed melancholy. She wasn't dad's hot, young wife, so she was his afterthought. My presence seemed to bring back memories of her kinship with my mom, which must have made her even more nostalgic. It was evident that Sad Stepmom and my mom were friends and neither of them got along with Scary Stepmom.

Sad Stepmom lived in what seemed like the opposite side of town from Scary. Her house wasn't in a quiet suburban neighborhood. Her face was in a battle with the aging process, and the only indication of her being over sixty were the deep creases in the corners of her mouth. They were the kind of creases that develop from years of smiling to cover up pain or anguish. Otherwise, Sad Stepmom's eyes sparkled, and I imagined that her plump body was the cushion for so many tears from others. Unlike Scary, she spoke in a loud whisper, which was very strong and sturdy up close. There was no doubt that she was the true matriarch of the family. I relished looking at her face not just because she was pretty, but because her softness towards me made me think of the fleeting moments of love that my mom showed me. I imagined her and my mom being best friends and sharing secrets about being married to my dad, who probably treated both like shit. They probably exchanged stories about morning sickness and childbirth. Sad Stepmom bore my dad eight children and most of them congregated at her house during the evenings. This evening, there were about ten people packed in a house the size of a toolshed.

I couldn't believe that dad was having Sad Stepmom cook for us when no more than two hours earlier I told him I could not eat at his house because of the water situation. Sharing food was a way of communing, and he wanted to do something nice for me, but it was difficult to eat hot *foofoo*, also called shima, in a sweltering-hot room where personal space was not the norm. I was practically sitting on my sister's lap as she watched me eat my food. While the tastes of the soups and the fresh fish was reminiscent of my childhood, I felt obligated to add some extra "yums" and "ooohs" to make everyone happy. *Foofoo* is a dough-like substance made of cornmeal that you eat with your hands alongside meat, soup, and vegetables. This food was tasty, though, and I felt more comfortable and safe at Sad Stepmom's house.

I was relieved to get back to our hotel room, where I could process the whirlwind of details I just experienced within the past two days. I felt a surge of resentment against Celeste when I quickly remembered how she had insulted me and my people at the maternity ward. Should I bring this up or just ignore it and hope that I would get over it? We still had nine more days together, and it was bound to manifest in something we said or did.

"So I was a little hurt by what you said earlier at the hospital," I began. The truth was that I wasn't hurt at all but, rather, I was offended and irritated. I seemed to suffer from being overly passive aggressive or extremely confrontational, so this was my attempt to improve my communication.

"Oh no, it's not what I meant at all, and I should not have said it that way. I thought about what I said after I said it. It wasn't that I was saying that there was anything wrong with the hospital. I just couldn't imagine not having access to proper healthcare when I needed it. Also, I'm against giving birth in US hospitals, too."

Oh! That made sense. She was reading all these books about midwives and doulas and I knew she planned on having a home birth. Thank goodness I brought up my concerns and Celeste was able to explain.

"Like I was thinking about your mom and everything that she must have gone through. And like your neighbors at John Howard and your mom's friend from the embassy. Maybe they were involved in helping you and your mom escape." All that my dad had told me was one day he came home, and my mom and I were gone. We were on our journey to the US by way of DR Congo. "Think about it, these people were looking at you because they knew you, they must have known the pain that your mom was enduring, and they may have plotted with your mom to get you out of Zambia."

"And you know what's also weird? I think my mom had me when she was thirty-three. It's the same age that I'm right now, and I literally walked in her footsteps during her birth of me."

"And you saw your mom's daughter for the first time since you were a baby. And it must have been so emotional for you, because she has a strong resemblance to your mom." Zalika was the carbon copy of my mother physically, but I wondered how much she resembled my mom in actions.

Within weeks of departing the Congo, she fell into a crazy spell, and almost murdered her daughter, Zalika. I witnessed the brutality; something I will *always* remember. It's like her hands and mouth developed a mind of their own. "I'm going to kill you, you whore!" she screamed, as she beat her with a metal rod. Ya Marie didn't seek out this weapon, but it was the closest thing she could find, and with all her might, she landed blow after blow across her daughter's body. She could hear little Zalika's screams, but if anyone dared to try to stop her, she would kill them, too. With each drop of blood splattered, she grew angrier. It was only after she felt her father pull her away that she dropped the bar: "Marie-Louise, stop it! You have to stop it! You are going to kill her!" The image was paralyzing. At four years of age I had rejected her from my heart, which is probably the real reason I began calling her "Ya Marie," instead of mom.

On particularly great days, Ya Marie would begin sipping wine prior to my arrival home from school. "I just want to feel good today," she'd say, and this was the only way she knew how. It felt warm as the mind-numbing nectar slid down her throat, settled in her belly, and tingled her solar plexus. *Ahhh*, sweet comfort; soon, all the concerns about her health would dissipate. The distant truth of not seeing or speaking to her children for nearly ten years was forgotten, and finally she could hear the melodic voice of Congolese chanteuse Mbilia Bel singing to her. In these moments, she was grateful to have me, her Shesheme, and she wanted to make me feel special.

Sometimes the blissful feeling energized Ya Marie to go on a shopping spree, snapping up all things Mickey Mouse, as I was obsessed with the Disney Channel. She also loved to buy chocolates and cookies for me, even though I didn't appreciate junk food. Instead, she knew exactly what I enjoyed most: that spicy aroma wafting from a pan of yellow rice, shrimp, and sautéed green peppers, alongside a dancing pot of stewed chicken. On many Friday nights, the food was ready to be devoured when I arrived home, and Ya Marie would do a Congolese rhumba as she served the two of us. The music, the wine, the dancing made even the most tragic memories fade into bearable, and this was the only time she could speak about it.

One Friday evening I approached Ya Marie, albeit delicately, to help me with a school assignment. I was required to interview my parents on their background and write a report. It was critical that I massage the questions to prompt her thinking memory, rather than spark her anger and despair.

"When you were in Africa, did you ever encounter war?" I sat at our dining room table looking out large windows, which provided a panoramic view of our one-acre backyard; the weeping willows swayed under the daylight sun. As she began to speak, I was carried back in time; I was lifted away from our little home in Columbus, Ohio, and transported to Ya Marie's Zaire [DRC]. I was absorbed.

"Never forget the name Patrice Lumumba. He was a great leader of Zaire [DR Congo] and helped us gain our independence. He was the prime minister of Zaire. He was your grandmother's second cousin. Anyway, people gunned him down and mutilated his body, and they even shot him in the eyes. Patrice Lumumba was a great, great man, and if he were not killed, Zaire would have been a better place than it is today. When Mobutu became president, everything changed. Suddenly, women were not allowed to wear pants, and he didn't want anyone to speak French, the imperialist language. We were only allowed to speak Lingala. The war started shortly after Mobutu became president. He was so evil, and he would send his soldiers to kill anyone who opposed him—that's how corrupt he was. You know that even that cane that he walks with is actually a sword? When I was married to Alexandre, Mimi's father, who was a big-time political figure,

Mobutu wanted him dead. One day when I was about nineteen and I was at home cooking, Mimi was at my side and I was pregnant, a soldier came to my door. It was one of Mobutu's soldiers. He came to warn me that Mobutu was looking for Alexandre to have him killed, and his family was in danger as well. This soldier, out of the goodness of his heart, wanted to warn me so that I could flee. I remember leaving the pot cooking on the stove. I grabbed my babies and the clothes on my back and fled to my father's home in Likasi."

By the time Ya Marie finished the story, she was enjoying her final glass of wine, and we were curled up on the couch. We laughed and drank up each other's company; on this night, Ya Marie was the least threatening.

Another ever-present stress for Ya Marie was money, or lack thereof. Beyond the monthly social security death benefit (due to her American husband's passing), she needed to find extra income. While living in Maryland, she had run a child daycare business from her apartment, which helped pay the bills and kept tummies sated. To establish a similar initiative in Ohio, it required financial backing as well as a business partner. But it was only Ya Marie and me, her fourteen-year-old daughter, so that dream was lost. The saving grace was discovered with the sewing needle. Demand for African-inspired women's clothing was high, and Ya Marie put her talents as a designer and seamstress to good use. Every morning she would wake up with boundless energy, ready to create and get paid for it. Her sewing jobs provided a decent and consistent source of income.

One summer I was away from home visiting my cousins and Aunt Frances in Massachusetts. When I returned, my bedroom was redecorated; Ya Marie created the most beautiful floral canopy above my bed, with a matching comforter and shams. The craftsmanship was amazing, and she remembered my favorite color—pink. What had I done to deserve such a wonderful gift?

"You are so smart. You are so hard on yourself when you get just one *B* on your report card. Never got those kinds of grades when I was your age. And look, you are doing all this on your own."

Ya Marie looked at me with admiration. She had dropped out of high school to get married and have children, so she was proud of her daughter, who seemingly was not headed in that direction. In this regard, Ya Marie only had appreciation for her late husband, Dan Cooper. He instilled the value of education and provided Shesheme with a structure on how to excel in school. He was the only man that genuinely cared for Ya Marie, as evidenced by his devotion to her daughter. Yet, tragically, even he did her wrong. As her foot pressed down on the sewing machine pedal, she strategically planned her children's future, because hers was a lost cause.

Ya Marie was consumed with grief and worry about her children in the Congo. Were all six of them even alive?

"Since I have a green card I can sponsor my children to come to America. I will also start applying for my citizenship; as an American, it will be so easy to bring them all here. Shesheme will be fine; she's attending an American school already." My mother was least concerned about me. That evening, Ya Marie pondered all this in her newly refinished basement, which her brother, Samuel, had just completed. "I need to try to save Gaston first; he is homeless, and someone could kill him or recruit him into a gang or God knows what."

A few weeks later, I asked Ya Marie with wide eyes and a fluttering heart: "Is Gaston coming to America?" At that moment, my life was coming back into perspective; even the plague of my teenage acne wasn't going to break my stride. We last saw Gaston in 1985, and he had become a legend to us since that time. My eyes fixated on the only photo that I had of him—it was an image of a dark, lanky eighteen-year-old man, with big, blank eyes, a slightly used tan suit, Goodwill sneakers, and a scar under his eye—standing in front of a corn field. God knows how he got that scar, which only heightened the curiosity about my brother. There was a deep sadness in his eyes, which became increasingly familiar to me as I recognized it in Ya Marie's gaze.

My mother bought a used car for Gaston, a white, four-door Honda that sat in our gravel driveway. "So he can have his own car when he arrives," she envisioned. Ya Marie applied for and received his visitor's visa, and along with thousands of dollars, sent it to Gaston, through trusted family friends, the Bembas. The next step was to bring his American visa to the Congolese Embassy and obtain his biometric screening and passport. The cash would be used to bribe any officials, almost guaranteeing the process would succeed. Once all this was accomplished, Ya Marie would purchase the airfare, and Gaston would be here, in living color. We began to celebrate that month as if Gaston had already arrived.

Meanwhile, Ya Marie and I dedicated a few hours each night to prepare her for the US citizenship exam. As she sat at the edge of the bed with her eyes slightly closed, concentrating, I posed the questions listed on the practice test:

"What were the thirteen original colonies?"
"How many stripes are on the US flag?"
"How many stars are on the flag?"
"What do the stars symbolize?"
"Which was the 50th state to join the US?"
"Who was the first US president?"

We both became giddy as she correctly answered every question, in English, but with her cute, thick, francophone accent. Soon, she could take the exam and become a US citizen, at which point, it would become significantly easier for her children to emigrate from the DRC. It was only a matter of time, and the cloud of darkness would be lifted; Ya Marie would finally be reunited with all her children.

Then tragedy struck, and it landed deeply. She received word from Gaston, as always through the Bembas, that his documents, everything, were stolen and lost forever. There was no way to recover the thousands of dollars or the documentation that were devoted to delivering her son to the US. We didn't have extra cash lying around to start the process again. After that day, I lost all faith in humanity, especially the Bembas, as I believe they took advantage of our naiveté.

"You know what's also weird? Zalika's forty-four. I think that was the age my mom was when she died."

The more we talked, the more bizarre and unbelievable the trip seemed.

"How are you feeling? I'm so sorry that my dad keeps putting us in situations where we have to eat at their house."

"It's cool. The food at Sad Stepmom's house was good, and I think that Baby loves it. Hey, what was the name they kept calling Baby?"

"Mutoto. Like moo'toe'toe. It means baby, newborn, infant in Swahili."

"Mutoto," she said with pride, as if she had just been initiated.

The conversation moved ever so seamless from one topic to another. Celeste and I had never spoken like this. There were less jokes. We were both raw with emotion. As a very pregnant woman who could identify with the emotions and feelings that my mom must have experienced the many times she was pregnant and who was connected to my pain, I saw real tears in Celeste's eyes. For me, it was like discovering ancient text on my life. Even though we were in our pajamas and lying in our beds that faced each other, sleep was the last thing on our minds.

"What about dating?" she said. "Have you met anyone that you like?"

I didn't even know how to answer that question without falling into hysterics. How could I tell Celeste the truth, which was that I was so scared of being single forever? How could I tell her that I tried to date, but it just didn't seem to work out for me?

"I'm so complex, and I wish I could meet someone who got me. While I want to save the world, I also want to look fabulous and stay in the nicest hotels. Is that wrong?"

"Not at all," she said. "You just need to find your Ethan. Someone who can go into your dad's house and is gracious about the experience, but he can also take you to a five-star hotel. You will totally have that."

"Celeste, what kind of love is that?"

"Dude, it's the kind where you both have explosive diarrhea and afterwards he still loves you."

She talked about how she and Ethan had such bad diarrhea and were pushing each other off the toilet to go. Disgusting. It didn't sound romantic to me, but Celeste assured me that it was not the only mark of a solid relationship but one of a real traveler. I guess that's why I got excited when two hours into our conversation I got the runs.

"Congratulations!" she shouted from her bed after I shared my news from the toilet. "You're a real traveler!" Our conversation continued for at least four more hours and drew us closer. Celeste was no longer my friend, she was my sister. It was 6:00 a.m., which meant we stayed up all night talking! We were expected to meet my dad in just three hours. How did time escape us? In that moment, it all seemed deliriously funny.

III. AMEBIC DYSENTERY?

By the time we checked out of the Radisson Blu hotel three days after our arrival, my stomach was doing somersaults. My initiation into the World Traveler's Club didn't seem so cool with diarrhea on the loose. We were supposed to meet my dad at the bus station and depart for a seven-hour bus ride to Lusaka. This was Celeste's brilliant plan to take the bus so that we could see the scenery. It would also give my dad and I time to talk. How was I going to survive a lengthy bus ride? Under these circumstances, even a bug-infested outhouse looked appealing. The taxi took us to the market near rows of travel buses, looking very much like a Greyhound bus station. Celeste's belly seemed to swell with each day, and dare I say it, even her pace had slowed down significantly in the last two days.

"Taxi, miss lady," a swarm of cab drivers and bus drivers asked Celeste and me as we walked through the crowd in search of Dad.

"Oh, shut up!" I muttered under my breath, no longer impressed by polite overtures by strangers. The air in the open market was hot and thick, smelling of body odor, fried fish, and Fanta.

"We are looking for our dad," Celeste said, not realizing how funny she sounded. I took it as a compliment that she felt at home and had immersed herself in my culture. She was laser focused, and between her baby bump and her backpack, no one was going to get in her way.

"Dad! There he is!" She ran over to my dad and hugged him first. Okay, that part bothered me. He was my dad after all, so I get to hug him first. Dad was standing at the bus stop booth in a wide-brimmed hat made of faux alligator skin, a two-piece brown suit, a Hanes white tee, and sandals. He was a cross between a black Crocodile Dundee and world's corniest dad. How many bags was he holding? One, two, three . . . five! Where did he think we were headed, to America? Even by Zambian standards, Dad just looked out of place.

"My Doh'tas, how are you?"

Enough with the niceties; I was his daughter. My twenty plus years of not having a dad earned me the right to not have to share my father with anyone else at that moment. He must have sensed my jealousy, giving me a kiss on the cheek, which made me feel most important. The young men at the booth seemed surprised, as if only five minutes ago what appeared to be a senile, old man was a man with two American daughters, one of whom was white. After buying the tickets, my dad insisted on holding them as Celeste and I looked for a toilet.

"$2" the sign read to use a toilet that didn't flush in the closed market. If I didn't have the runs, I would have vomited from sheer disgust. I couldn't understand how Celeste could withstand all of it. The smells that came from the bathroom warranted a more crasser term for it, like latrine. There was no air conditioning nor windows, and the woman who collected our money was rationing out toilet paper. *Lady, I have the runs! I need more toilet paper!* When I was done, Celeste was ready with hand wipes and hand sanitizer for me.

The closed market was enormous and encased in aluminum, which only shielded us from the sun but made the air suffocating. Celeste and I couldn't walk more than two inches before a vendor tried to sell us fabric or miniature carvings. The combination of sweaty bodies somehow gave me the sensation to go to the bathroom again.

"Here take $4 so you can go as much as possible because we have a long ride ahead of us," Celeste said as she handed me coins.

How come I was just now noticing the signs for Ebola all around the market? It's as if someone put them up while I was on the toilet. Severe diarrhea, fever, muscle ache?

Crap!

I had all the symptoms, but I didn't have Ebola, I swear. Now Celeste and I were on a mission to remain discrete. "Oh God, if they think that you have Ebola, they won't let us on the bus," she chuckled as we walked through the marketplace. I didn't have the energy to laugh in that moment, but, yes, this would make great fodder for the stories that we shared when we got home.

When we went back outside to the bus stop, Dad was nowhere to be found. He had all our bus tickets and those five bags. "Maybe he ran off," Celeste joked, but I was worried about the same thing. The bus was leaving in fifteen minutes, and Dad was nowhere to be seen. Celeste was overheated but optimistic. "Let's wait for Mr. K.K. at the bench."

The bench sat directly across from the bus that we were supposed to get on. Now the fainting sensation started. I knew this feeling all too well. First numbness in my body and Celeste's voice sounded muffled. My hands grew clammy, and I felt the urge to vomit. My life flashed before my eyes. I would die of dysentery in Lusaka; my dad ran off with our tickets, scalped them; and my pregnant friend would be left to fend for herself in Zambia. I felt out of control like I once felt before.

By December 2006, the risk of Judge Colucci involving Attorney General Edward Gonzalez in my immigration case was diffused by the allegations surrounding him. Ultimately, Gonzalez ended up resigning from his post on August 27, 2007.

I was ordered to appear in the Buffalo court once again, my ninth hearing, in March 2007. Charlotte would accompany me this time; she would represent me whether Colucci agreed or not. Charlotte and I spent a few evenings and the prior weekend preparing my case, trying to clean up the mess that John created. Instead of meeting in her office, we met at her apartment, which housed almost five boxes worth of my files.

"Colucci needs to understand why you failed to mention your mother's abuse in your testimony many years ago. You suffered trauma. All your life with your mom, you feared her but in the year before her death she became vulnerable. You got to nurture her. You found a love, a bond. You had to now protect her, and that's what you did since then, and you buried the years of hurt and pain into your memory bank. But the final images of your mom to you were of her being weak, fragile, and vulnerable. These are the ones that stick with you and these are the ones you had to honor." It was incredible how Charlotte could read my mind. It was easy to confuse her for a therapist rather than a lawyer because of her level of compassion and sensitivity.

Reality quickly settled in the night before my hearing, which was when Charlotte and I arrived at the hotel in Downtown Buffalo. For the first time, Buffalo didn't feel like a prison, and I noticed all the trendy restaurants and bars in the neighborhood near the courthouse. Were these hotspots recent additions? How come I never noticed them? It dawned on me that I was happier, a feeling that was so foreign to me. Maybe the therapy was working.

"Charlotte, it's so bizarre, because I have never noticed this side of Buffalo before. I'm almost enjoying myself."

"You know, this always happens. Whenever I discover the magic in any bad situation, it always indicates that it is almost over. I bet this is probably the last time you will be coming to Buffalo, my dear."

Charlotte, who was ultra-femme, was excited to experience the magic of the Oscars with me. She bought me a present—a box of Belgian chocolates. "This is to celebrate you and your triumph, my dear. It's Neuhaus, the best chocolate from Belgium," Charlotte said as her creamy-white legs dangled off the side of the bed adjacent to mine, exposing her toenails. They resembled iridescent seashells. This was the first time I had seen her without makeup, not even lipstick. Her skin matched the whites of her eyes. Her bleach-blond hair dangled like straws down to her jawline. I wondered if all white people's hair looked like that after coming out of the shower. If I had it my way, we wouldn't have been sharing a hotel room in the middle of nowhere. In her mind, I had become like a daughter, but in my mind I still needed her to do her job. It was her idea as a way of trying to reduce the cost. Either way, I still didn't know how I could keep affording her on my budget. I wondered if she intended to charge me for the Neuhaus. Why couldn't she have just bought a Snickers bar instead?

"Martine, it's about to start. This is to celebrate your triumph, dear." She winked and then fixated her eyes on the television monitor. I wanted to believe her.

"Martine, sit down and drink all this water," Celeste motioned. I feigned a smile to not alarm her. Who admits to feeling like death when standing in a bus stop in a foreign country? There was no relief in sight. More was going to come out of one orifice of my body. I knew that one day this moment would be funny, but it wasn't at that time. Dad finally strolled back to where we were sitting as if he was on freaking tour of the zoo.

"Mr. K.K., she's really sick," Celeste said.

"What you say?"

"Dad, I feel sick," I uttered. "I have diarrhea." I had attempted to whisper as the tunnel vision effect overcame me.

"Mr. K.K., do you have something that she can take?"

It didn't occur to Celeste or me in that moment that I had a prescription for Ciperol. If it did, I must have been too literal in the directions that said only to take it in severe cases of diarrhea.

"Oh no. I am sorry," my dad said. It's like the knowledge of my being ill snapped him out of his happy-go-lucky place and brought him back into the world of dad. "Here, take this."

He opened one of his many bags and pulled out a bottle of pills. I was only instructed to take one. I looked at Celeste for approval.

"He's your dad so he's not going to give you something that will harm you."

I was sure he was my dad, and no, I doubted he would try to kill me. At least that's what we both wanted to believe.

I dragged myself onto the bus, which was state of the art with gently used seats. It was the exact opposite of the bathrooms in the market. Now whom to sit with? Did I sit with Dad and risk Celeste sitting with a random person, which I knew she wouldn't mind, or would it be Dad who would sit alone? It was like *Sophie's Choice*; I couldn't decide. Celeste decided for me and motioned to sit with her. We sat on the opposite isle and one seat behind Dad. Now that we were done with that challenge, the mother of all challenges lie ahead of me: a seven-hour bus ride in my condition. After my bathroom experience earlier, I refused to entertain the possibility of even asking if there was a toilet room on the bus. Maybe if I just lied back and fell asleep, I would be able to make it through the entire ride.

"How do you feel, my Doh'ta? Do you still feel very sick?" he asked with a look of concern, but it was hard to decipher against his toothy grin. The middle-aged, churchy-looking woman sitting to the right of my dad gave me a suspicious look, or maybe I just imagined it as suspicious because I was trying to hide the fact that I did not have Ebola.

"Oh God," I sank into my chair mortified by the stare from the strange woman.

"Oh my goodness, your dad is going to get us kicked off the bus," she whispered. "They'll think that you have Ebola." Her ability to whisper in an audible volume amazed me. This time we both laughed; the medicine must have started to kick in. I mentally checked off from my list of phobias the fear of travelling on an African bus: no smelly toilet on board to stink up the bus, no smelly people, and no air conditioning. Just as I was about to nod off to sleep and Celeste whipped out her natural childbirth book, the bus driver blared the music at almost full volume. *Fadda*

fadda . . . we love you God . . . Jesus is my glory, fadda fadda . . .
the Christian music station rang. Celeste and I looked at each
other and laughed.

The experience of going to the courthouse with Charlotte was
vastly different from that of John James and Owen Frost. She
was alert and prompt, as she practically carried my entire life
in her briefcase. Charlotte memorized my life story—the names
of every aunt, uncle, and cousin—and she dressed for success,
walking with sophistication and assuredness. I could learn a lot
from this woman. I noticed how the court clerk and the officers
looked at her; who did she think she was? Charlotte was a force
to be reckoned with. Judge Colucci tried to intimidate Charlotte.

We arrived at the Livingstone bus station, which didn't have an
open market, just a parking lot. We were greeted by another uncle
whom Dad never mentioned until we met him.

"This is your uncle. He is the cousin of your sister's brother."
What?

I was compelled to explain to my dad the anatomy of a family. This uncle had a similar temperament as my dad, very lighthearted. He and his wife owned a nice market that reminded me
of a New York City bodega in Livingstone with a freezer, electricity,
and a television. He seemed sophisticated, and I wanted my dad
to have his life, which seemed a lot easier than the one that he
currently had. Uncle was about my dad's age with a lighter complexion and a few less creases on his face. We walked through
the market, which was about four hundred square feet, to see if
there was anything that we wanted to buy. Was I supposed to buy
something from his store because he picked us up from the bus
station? Was this how the transaction worked? I didn't want him
charging my dad a million kwachas after I left. I shuddered when
my eyes came across more orange Fanta. No, I wasn't going to buy
anything from the store. I didn't ask Uncle to pick us up, Dad did.

Uncle dropped us off at Jollyboys Backpackers, a hostel, so
that he could go back and help his wife close the shop. I didn't
know what to expect for a backpacker's lodge, but the Jollyboys

hostel lived up to its pictures from the website. It was a bunch of cabins with patios decorated in mango trees and flowers with a check-in center, a communal kitchen, and a picnic area that served beer and meat for what seemed like all night long. I especially liked the canopied living room that had mounds of throw pillows decorated with Central-African fabric. A backpacker's lodge was a white people thing; Dad and I were the only two black people in the entire establishment.

I would much rather have been at the five-star Zambezi Sun, but Celeste was right, this hostel was nice and anything above this would have made my dad feel uncomfortable. Each lodge was named after a mammal. We were in the Buffalo Lodge, and Dad was three doors down from us in a nice lodge with air conditioning, a king-sized bed, and a private bathroom. Each wall in the rooms was a different hue of the rainbow. It was as if they couldn't decide what color to go with, so they decided to go with them all! Celeste and I also had our own private bathroom and double beds. I had always thought the mosquito netting over a bed was romantic, but I learned about its functionality now. It was time to unpack and get settled in. We were here for the next three nights.

As we walked down the side street to the neighboring supermarket, we received stares, smiles, and some people didn't seem to care about our dynamic trio; it was as if they were used to seeing a pregnant white woman, an old black man, and a black woman walking together all the time.

Although Lusaka was the capitol, Livingstone seemed to cater to a more Western crowd. The grocery store resembled a Wegman's or Safeway with an extensive produce section, meat section, and the like. I felt like I was in a regular store, which meant that I could shop! The feeling of being in familiar surroundings got me so excited that I was ready to buy everything on the shelves.

"Dad, get whatever beer you want, I'm treating," I said, not even looking at the prices. "What should we cook for dinner tonight?"

Somehow Celeste and I thought that fifty-cent ramen noodles with a side of steak would be the perfect meal. For one, ramen was easy to make, and it was almost like pasta, okay not really. But the point is we wanted to make something more common to what we would eat in America but also account for the time it would take to prepare it. The biggest challenge was finding the right utensils to cook with. Picture this: We were in an open kitchen that was not air-conditioned. It had fluorescent light shining down on us in a sharing space with backpackers from all over the globe. I waited for the cute Japanese woman to empty the pot so that I could use it for the ramen. It wasn't ideal, but I was excited to finally cook a meal for Dad, except that I had never cooked a steak before.

"I will take care of the steak if you will cook the ramen," I offered to Celeste. I couldn't make her do all the cooking; she had come all the way to Africa for me. There was just one problem. How do you cook steak?

I put some water in the pan and threw the steak on top, imagining the ten-minute steak dishes that I witnessed on Iron Chef. Did steak produce its own natural oils to fry with? How would I know when it was done? Was it safe to make steak in Africa medium-well? Crap, I forgot to get onions and tomatoes to marinate the steak in. Wasn't I supposed to sauté some onions on top or something? Mine was a complete disaster, and Celeste tried to salvage it by putting oil in a pan and frying it, which only made the meat tough as rubber. Who was going to eat this?

"We cannot throw it out," she said. "Think about how insulting it would be to your dad for us to waste good meat like this. I think he will still want to eat it, if not to show you how proud he is of you for making him dinner." She was right. In about five minutes, Dad would be down from his room, famished, and would wonder what happened to the piece of meat that we bought. And he would probably say it just like that: "The piece of meat that we bought?"

How did Celeste know all this stuff? I watched as Dad effortlessly cut into the steak and smothered some *peri peri* sauce to make it flavorful and ate each morsel like it was the most delicious thing his pallet ever came across. Celeste's ramen was more like overcooked lo mein, which I still devoured because I was famished.

I was so excited about the day ahead, that I couldn't even think about breakfast. Celeste and I both looked rough after several days of wearing the same clothes. How many ways could I possibly wear the same African-print scarf? I wore it as a bandana, a shawl, and a headwrap, and finally considered retiring it for the sake of the photos that would chronicle the trip. I gave up on wearing makeup, so there was no telling how I looked. The one mirror in our bathroom fogged up at the mere turn of the hot water in the shower and stayed fogged up for what seemed like centuries. God, I wished that we were in a fancy hotel right about now.

Celeste's bump was now a fully active baby who seemed to enjoy our African adventures secondhand. We were going on a safari! It was the culmination of the entire trip, and the memory that I would cherish forever—going on a safari with my father. I imagined telling my children about this adventure one day. I would finally create a memory with my dad that would make up for the years that we spent apart. All we had to do was take a boat across the Zambezi River to enter Botswana.

"Sir, we do not allow Congolese residents into Botswana right now," said the customs officer on the border of Botswana and Livingstone. She was tall and lithe and could have been a model in another life. "You would need to apply for a visa, and it takes a few days."

"Yes, ma'am," Dad said as he pulled out his wallet with a rolled piece of paper to present, "but I have lived in Zambia for over forty years, and I am a resident." Even when angered, my dad still maintained a calm sing-song to his voice, just like the very first time I spoke to him over the phone.

The customs office was a sizable brick building that sat on the edge of the highway; it looked minuscule against the vastness of the land around it. The lights were dimmed to cool the room, but the heat further circulated every corner of the room because of the ceiling fans. The interior of the building was occupied with lines of people looking for access into Botswana. Were they also going on a safari? Before my trip, I hadn't considered Botswana.

"Dad, what's wrong?" I asked, breathing a sigh of relief after getting my passport stamped.

Why were they giving him such a hard time? "Dad, what are they saying?" I asked him while ignoring the high-cheek-boned woman with microbraids who stood behind the counter looking very annoyed.

"They are saying," he started as he fumbled through the pieces of paper as if looking for a secret key. "They say I cannot go to Botswana."

The woman at the counter looked past us to assist the next person in line.

As the hearing commenced, Judge Colucci began: "In the matter of Martine Kalaw versus The Department of Homeland Security, I

ILLEGAL AMONG US

need more time to review the case. I'm considering taking it to the US attorney general for further review. Now, court is dismissed," he gave a smug look at Charlotte.

Judge Colucci never let her speak, and he dismissed court before she could utter a single phrase. How could this man be allowed to run a court of law? How dare he force us to travel from New York City, the time and expense notwithstanding, only to sit in the courtroom for five minutes so he can state that he needed more time? Why couldn't he have informed us in a written letter? He was relentless about taking my case to the US attorney general. I was not as outraged as Charlotte.

Charlotte felt disrespected and mocked. But he was the judge, and he had the power of authority. Any attempt to challenge him could lead to her disbarring, risk her reputation, or lose her credentials—even I could understand that. It was almost like he wanted to spite me more vigorously, after I found and hired a high-powered attorney from the Big Apple.

Charlotte later learned that Colucci used to preside over the Miami Immigration Court, but he was asked to leave because of his conduct. Instead of removing his title, they just "shuffled him off to Buffalo" where he could continue to abuse innocent people. What kind of dysfunctional system was this?

"No. That's not fair!" I exclaimed as Celeste and my dad motioned for me to go outside where the van was waiting to take safari participants to the boat docking station.

"Martine, it's gonna be okay, sweetie. Your dad's not going to be able to go with us. I think we should still do the safari because it's an experience that we have both been looking forward to."

What to do? I couldn't imagine going on a safari without my dad, but I wanted to have the experience and it would be unfair to deprive Celeste of this moment when she came all the way to Africa for me. Maybe it was the heat or the border patrols holding rifles and staring at the three of us that prompted my uncontrollable tears. Dad and Celeste created a fort around me to calm me down, because I was causing a scene.

"My Doh'ta," he said, holding my face, then hugged me. "You must not cry. Go to your adventures with Mama Celeste, and we will be together when you complete your safari."

It comforted me to hear my dad's consistent use of formal English even in times of crises. I imagined that was what it would have been like had I grown up with my dad. He would have hugged me after every fall and reminded me that he would always be there waiting for me. The thought only further saddened me as I cried for the little girl in me that missed out on all those moments with her dad. And now I was going to miss out on this one.

"Martini, it's going to be okay," Celeste said. "Look, your dad seems to know everyone here and your cousin can drive him back to Jollyboys. One of my cousins, whom I confirmed was really a cousin, worked in the copper mines, whose trucks and equipment were not too far from the customs office.

"Yes, okay. Yes, you can pick me up okay?"

Dad was already making plans with Uncle to pick him up from the Zambia border after the steamboat deposited back on land.

"My Doh'ta, maybe you can give me some money for food until I see you tomorrow."

What was happening? Too much was happening at once, and I couldn't process it all. Was this a ploy to get money from me? How could it be a ploy if all he was asking was money for food for the evening? Since I couldn't think clearly, I looked to Celeste, who didn't seem concerned by my dad's request. Although I understood the exchange rate, I still didn't understand the value of the Zambian kwacha. Exactly how much would cover dinner at a restaurant? What if there was medical emergency? Would a twenty-dollar US bill suffice? It must have worked because as soon as I discreetly handed it to him, he grinned and scurried Celeste and I along. For the first time in what might have been forty years, my dad was living the bachelor life. He had a plush home to go to, no responsibilities, no kids, and what was probably the equivalent of $150 in his pocket. Still, I missed him.

"Martini, your dad is going to have a great time. He is like a kid in a candy store."

I looked back one more time, and he was standing next to the solider with a giant rifle, waving back at us with the biggest grin I have ever seen. Maybe she was right.

"You can call me Captain," the motorboat's driver, navigator, and tour guide introduced himself when we got on the boat. His skin was as dark as mine but glistened under the sunlight. His eyes were piercing, as if he were always on the watch for danger. The Zambezi River was magical by itself, but driving down it with the narration from Captain and seeing the wildlife was unforgettable.

"Look at the hippos!"

These aquatic animals were deceptively huge, and one could only tell when the sunlight hit the water, revealing their true length and weight. They were beasts with bulging eyes, dancing ears, and large nostrils that also served as sprinklers.

"Martine, do you see the alligator?"

"That is a crocodile," Captain corrected with a smile.

I liked the way he made the final syllables of his words linger. It was the way he placed the emphasis on the word croc'o'dile, which made it sound like the most exotic creature in this water jungle.

"Africa does not have alligators."

Sheer excitement about how close to danger I was shot through my spine. The crocodiles were all teeth, and they didn't swim but floated in the African waters, remaining inconspicuous until they could attack. All you saw were there beautiful scales. Sure, I had seen crocodiles before, but something about them being African, where they are untouched by man's influences, made them seem that much more powerful and lethal.

Captain was knowledgeable about every animal in sight and enjoyed rediscovering nature through our eyes. He maintained a good control of the boat's steering wheel all the while.

Celeste and I made our way to the upstairs section of the boat to capture every detail on camera. All around us was water, land, sky, and animals, and all evidence pointed to a perfect synchronicity between each element. Why couldn't my dad have been here?

After what seemed like hours on water, we were back on land at a rest stop in Botswana before our jeep safari. I needed to reach my dad on the phone to ensure that he was okay and to tell him that we decided not to do an overnight camping safari. Instead, we would come back to Jollyboys. But what if I couldn't reach him and he left Jollyboys to sleep at a different hotel? Then we would be separated, and I feared both losing my dad and separating myself from him.

"Allo, my Doh'ta, is that you?" Dad asked after what seemed like my hundredth attempt to contact him. The reception was terrible particularly because we were using Skype to dial out. I felt my heart doing somersaults when I heard his voice.

"Dad, Celeste and I will come back tonight. We will—"

"Allo, my Doh'ta. What you say?" It was a combination of his poor listening skills and the reception that made the conversation impossible.

"Dad, I said that Celeste—" We either got disconnected or he purposely hung up. After a few more futile attempts, I realized that my dad was probably enjoying himself more than I was.

"Celeste, I'm so ready to see lions!" As far as I was concerned, a jeep safari was the only kind of safari that was out there.

"Sir, will we see lions?" I asked the tour guide as I anxiously waited for his response.

Celeste and I sat in the backseat of the jeep, and I assumed the window seat while she inched closer to the middle of the seat. These minor subtleties reminded me that this woman was pregnant and had to protect what was growing inside of her. A hint of guilt crept up, but it was overpowered by my strong desire to see a lion. I was sure my spirit animal was a wild cat, and I strongly suspected that it was a lion. Where were the lions, though? As we drove through the wildlife park and quieted our voices as the jeep snuck up on the animals, I grew increasingly anxious about seeing a lion. Yes, the impalas were cute, but how many impalas could one see on one safari?

"Shhhh . . .," the tour guide motioned to everyone. *What? Is it a lion?* While it wasn't a lion, just as spectacular was an elegant giraffe casually munching on leaves from a tree about ten feet away from us.

"Woah," I muttered under my breath. I never realized how incredibly special giraffes were with their patterned orange bodies that varied from one animal to the next.

Driving a few inches further we were accompanied by a heard of elephants, including two baby elephants. I had seen elephants in the zoo before, but experiencing them firsthand was like having wings to fly rather than being on an airplane. They were much larger than the jeep, and one kick to the jeep could probably send us flying.

"Sir, where are the lions?" I finally gathered the nerve to ask again, hoping not to downplay his efforts to make our safari unforgettable.

"No lions today. Sometimes they are sleeping, or they blend into the landscape."

"What about the other big five? What about the rhino?" Unfortunately, rhinos were nowhere to be found because of poachers. I was less disappointed about not seeing rhinos, but I was hoping that somehow, we could see a lion in its natural element.

"Dad, we're back," I exclaimed as soon as I saw him sitting at a picnic table in the lounge with a beer. He was deeply engrossed in his soccer game, basking in his newly found freedom. How many years had he spent toiling and scraping to feed his two wives and twelve kids while wondering when, if ever, he would find his missing daughter? With me back in his life, somehow the world no longer rested on his shoulders.

"What are you doing here, my Doh'tas?" he said, almost puzzled to see us. It's as if we interrupted him from his vacation. I guess Celeste was right in telling me not to worry.

Now that I had proof that Dad was okay, I was determined to get my unforgettable, clichéd African adventure. No way was I leaving Africa without it.

V. THE LION WALK

He was the equivalent of Henry Cele from *Shaka Zulu*. His skin was the color of tar lathered in Vaseline and then heated up by the blazing sun. His cheekbones were the Matterhorn sprinkled with charcoal, sitting on the sides of his face. His face was like a sculpture, chiseled by Michelangelo himself. He spoke with a deep and authoritative voice. I wondered if he was single as I sat across from him and pretended to listen to his instructions about walking with the lions. I was too busy trying to figure out how I could casually mention that I was single before my dad and Celeste returned from their tour with the caracals. We all agreed that they wouldn't walk with the lions because one being very pregnant and one being old.

"You resemble the older gentleman so much."

I was so proud to look like my dad, as if it was further approval from the world that he was my father, and I was right in trusting that he was.

"He's my dad!" I exclaimed.

I was eager to tell him the story in hopes that it would somehow lead to my being very single and looking for love now that I found my father.

"Really?" he asked, leaning forward as he sat on the wicker sofa that was so apropos for Africa.

"Yeah," I said, my heart inflating like a balloon. "This is the first time that I'm meeting him. I was born in Lusaka, but I left the continent when I was four years old and that was the last time I saw my dad. In fact, I thought that he was dead all these years, and last year he found me through LinkedIn. So here I am." I didn't pause or breathe while pouring my heart out to a stranger who probably had no interest in hearing all this detail.

His eyes bulged out, allowing them to increase exponentially in size. "That's amazing," he said. "So you mean to tell me that you grew up by yourself in America while your dad was in Africa all these years?"

It was only a few weeks after Charlotte and I came from my hearing in Buffalo, New York, where Judge Colucci went on another tirade. His threats about involving the US attorney general in his efforts to deport me kept me up in the wee hours of the night. Not to mention, Charlotte's plan of creating a DREAM Act, Dream Team, fell flat. I think that the other attorneys and their clients were focused on the matter at hand, which was securing their own statuses. Meanwhile, what would I do? Was it just a matter of time before this stateless, illegal immigrant found herself in a detention facility?

The questions continued expressing genuine interest. We were interrupted by the front desk, who indicated that the other party that was going on a lion walk was ready, and we could proceed.

An English couple and a guy, all white, were part of the lion entourage. I didn't notice the woman until Shaka Zulu proceeded to prepare us for the lion. She dug her nails into her husband's arms and buried her head in his back. This British lady was definitely going to get eaten by the lion.

"If you are scared, then you should not walk because the lion can sense fear and equates that with weakness. If you are weak, he will attack you."

Not me, I was so ready to meet the lion. I felt so calm and reassured remembering my father's words: "Nothing with happen to you. You do not need to worry, my Doh'ta."

I was too embarrassed to ask Shaka Zulu if my being on my period was dangerous; what if the lion could smell blood? Instead, I asked my personal Dalai Lama in almost a whisper. I wondered how much Celeste knew and how much she was making up just to reassure me.

"I don't think it's a big deal. Plus, you are wearing a tampon and not a pad."

"Dad, if I get eaten by a lion, then Celeste can be your new daughter," I joked.

But I had come all the way to Zambia, and I met my father, and I learned about my past and my mother's past. I acquired so much, and I felt an aura of protection engulfing me, which assured me beyond a shadow of doubt that nothing would harm me.

They were a brother-and-sister pair, and the male, with his regal mane, took my breath away. I surprised myself by how excited I was to come so close to death. Having my hand in his mane and then next to his mouth was exhilarating. I felt so connected to the lion. I had a deep connection to lions, because there was no other way to explain it. I wanted to make eye contact with him to fully connect with him, but a quick panic came over me, and I was reminded of what Shaka Zulu said: "Always stay at the same level as him, never higher. Otherwise he will see you as a threat and may attack." God, there were so many rules, I wondered if anyone ever confused them. Sure, there were four guides, but where were their guns just in case the lions did attack one of us? Somehow, I didn't think the sticks we carried were going to prevent a lion from chomping off my arm or leg.

"You are walking a lion!" Shaka shouted for the cameras as he recorded me holding onto the tail of the lion.

I felt a little weird holding onto the tail and then caressing it against my face. Was that weird? Was that appropriate? I just did as I was told. My attention span was heightened as we finished walking the lions, and I was headed off to the cheetah side of the park. If I thought lions were beautiful, then the cheetahs were breathtaking.

"This is Diana. She is the ambassador of all cheetahs in Zambia. So when you see photographs of cheetahs, it is Diana."

I felt so regal being around these spotted beauties. I lied down in the dirt where Sandy, the second cheetah was resting, and I felt so much at home. I thought about what a cliché I was being in this moment: an African girl hanging with wild animals like they were my best friends. It didn't matter though, they were so beautiful and soothing. It's like these cheetahs could feel my energy, and it brought them comfort. They both started to sleep.

"They feel comfortable around you. They don't normally sleep around strangers."

I felt honored by the thought of being the cheetah whisperer.

In the midst of my hopelessness in April 2007, the National Immigration Law Center (NILC), an immigrant organization based in DC, contacted me. "We would like to invite you to share your story in front of 110th Congress on behalf of the DREAM Act. We would need you to come to Washington DC, and you would sit among other panelists who also have compelling immigration stories to share. You would testify before the House Judiciary Committee's Subcommittee on Immigration, Citizenship, Refugees, Border Security and International Law. Please contact us immediately if you are interested."

Was I interested? At this point I had no other choice. Maybe my situation was futile, but I just needed America to know that I existed. I wanted the nation to learn about what was really going on to people like me in America. I never hurt anyone, I never lied, and I never stole anything from anyone. All I ever tried to do was survive and navigate the unfortunate life that I was dealt. There were probably others like me. Americans needed to know. I had to do it; if not for me, then for someone else who would benefit from the DREAM Act.

The events of the day could not get any more exciting, or so I thought. Unlike my dad, the man with little means, and Celeste, who believed in sharing every meal, I was eager to work off my appetite by ordering my own bowl of pasta and dessert. I wanted everyone to go crazy with the smorgasbord. Celeste gave me a slight nudge to remind me that even the move I made with ordering dinner would define my economic status in my dad's eyes. Even though they never say it, they always assume that Americans are rich. In their minds, we are all living the life of P. Diddy and Beyoncé. Even when we argue that we are paupers, the mere order of a $12 bowl of pasta to enjoy alone could send the wrong message.

Dammit!

I sulked within at the thought of not being able to go on a binge fest.

"My Doh'ta, why are you always sick? You are like your late mother, she was always sick," my dad said out of concern.

I assumed that my head hurt because I was dehydrated, but if untreated it would morph into a migraine, which would ruin the entire trip.

"Mr. K.K., do you have anything that she can take?" This seemed to be the common question for this trip. Dad was now my drug dealer.

I guess Celeste figured that we could be two for two since the diarrhea medication seemed to work well. My dad pulled out his little man purse and drew out a bottle with orange pills. Dr. Mason was the name on the bottle. He handed the entire bottle to me for later but advised me to only take two for now. There went nothing!

Ten minutes later the room started to spin slightly, and I felt a little loopy.

"I pink I know what . . ." I couldn't even get out a coherent sentence.

"Mr. K.K., what did you give her? What's in Dr. Mason? She can't even speak straight." Celeste laughed, and Dad innocently defended the powers of Dr. Mason.

"My Doh'ta, are you okay? But everyone take Dr. Mason. You can find it in every market."

Somehow knowing that you could buy it in any market did not give me any kind of reassurance. I knew that it wouldn't kill me, but it made me drowsy and obliterated my headache.

He was already waiting for me in his usual spot in front of his room at Jollyboys. He had a bag filled with the contents of his life. It was like a treasure chest that he was opening and unleashing memories. The night sky blanketed us, with just some brightness coming from the porch light. I was armed with mosquito repellent, which I lathered all over my body to the point where I could have been charged with mistaken identity with a lemon. I offered my dad mosquito bands, which I wore on each ankle and on each wrist. It didn't matter if I looked ridiculous at this point; I didn't want to catch malaria, and I wanted to be fully present to everything that my dad wanted to share with me.

"Here is my Zambia residence paper. If you ever want to come back here in the future and buy your own house or anything, you can show the officials this document, which is proof that your father was a resident of Zambia for more than forty years." It was a copy of a permanent resident card of my father as he looked today, minus maybe six or seven years. "And here are many photographs of my paintings." There were some negatives, some sketches of his paintings, some black-and-white and color photos of his paintings. Landscape, animals, religious relics. They were all so astonishing.

Some of his paintings were realism, some abstract, but all breathtaking. It was like discovering a pot of gold. Now I understood why the Indo-Zambian guy from our first night in Lusaka was so impressed with my father; the man created masterpieces. Was this the picture of the painting that was gifted to former President George W. Bush when he visited Zambia last year? My dad's pace picked up, and his breath was shortened as he talked about his art, it was his lifeline. How could I get some of his paintings back to America? Other people needed to see his talent.

"Dad, you did this?" I asked, making sure that my eyes were not tricking me under the moonlit night. It was very similar to something I would have seen in the Hindu temple that I visited with Priti.

"Yes," he replied while placing extra emphasis on the 'e.' "This is of the high Krishna that I painted for a Hindu temple. And this one was for the Greek Orthodox church, which exists in Europe."

I knew nothing about art, but I knew these paintings were good. To think that my dad's artwork was scattered all over the world and probably worth thousands, but he probably gratefully accepted five dollars for each piece, just so he could put food on the table, was excruciating. What happened to my dad was an illustration of what has happened to my Congolese community for decades; DR Congo has been raped and pillaged for its minerals. It's not just diamonds but also a rare mineral called coltan. Nearly ninety percent of the world's reserves comes from DR Congo, and this mineral is needed in every electronic device in order for it to function, including cell phones. Coltan is equivalent to "vibranium" from the movie, Black Panther. If DRC wasn't being robbed of coltan, then the country would be the closest thing to Wakanda. If only the rest of the world knew how a mere use of their cell phones had a direct impact on the suffering of DR Congo.

"Dad, do you know where your paintings ended up?"

How dare people take advantage of a poor African man? But then again, haven't I been guilty of bargaining and trying to get something from someone for less than its value? Isn't that what all people do? Then damn my dad for being so innocent. I was so angry with him. Forget Victoria Falls, this was his value. A self-taught painter who made his own canvases and painted by daylight because he didn't have electricity in his home.

The paintings were remarkable, and each one was better than the last. If these outdated, low-quality photographs of the paintings were breathtaking, then I could only imagine what the real paintings looked like. I could just picture what these owners of his paintings told people: "I bought this painting during my trip to Africa. This artist in Africa did such a great job and practically gave it to me for nothing." To think all this work would be reduced to him just being another African artist.

"And here is an article of the professor who came to Zambia and loved my artwork. She wanted to showcase it in the US galleries. Perhaps you can contact her." The magazine was dated 1977. He spoke about these encounters as if they happened a year ago. That must have been the lens through which he saw the house at John Howard, the mango tree, the birth ward where I was born, and even me. My presence created a nostalgia for my dad that warped his sense of time and reality. Would that be more harmful to him when I leave?

The mosquitos dare not bite us, but they were swarming around looking for unprotected flesh to enjoy. I wanted to see more of Dad's photos and to hear more about his children. I was not supposed to be his seventh child. But when he and Sad Stepmom lost a baby boy, she and my mom both became pregnant. My sister was child number six, and I was the seventh. This didn't matter, except while I'm not religious, I do think that the number seven is a very magical number. It gave me a lot of confidence to think that I was my dad's seventh child, and it was another miracle dictated by the heavens rather than the randomness of life.

I followed my dad to his room at Jollyboys and sat next to him, and he continued to go through more photos of his kids along with where they lived and how many kids they had. "I will write it down for you," he said as he began to craft a family tree. As he listed the names one by one and began to literally draw a tree, a surge of panic started in my stomach and manifested itself a burning in my throat.

"Dad, I can't. I cannot be responsible for all these people!"

All I could hear was Celeste's voice from one of our conversations. "Dude, they think that you are here to save them."

"Dad, I cannot save anyone but myself. I am struggling, too. Life is not easy for me, I hope you know that."

"Ms. Kalaw," Congressman Steve King of the House Subcommittee on Immigration began, "you know, there is a piece in your testimony, and I do not see it right in front of me, where you say that you went to the depths of human despair, and I see you here before us now, and I am wondering what that did for you. How did you respond when you were to the depths of human despair? How did you overcome that to be here today?"

It was May 18, 2007, and this poor, little, illegal immigrant woman had made it to Capitol Hill. I watched C-SPAN a few weeks leading up to this day to figure out what I would wear. Charlotte insisted that I wear a grey suit, because it would look good on television. Before the hearing began, the NILC advisors explained to me and the other panelists how to operate the technology. When a question was posed to us by one of the representatives, we needed to turn on the microphone by clicking the green button. When we were done speaking, we would click on the red button to turn off the mic. Did anyone know that under pressure I couldn't process directions? Surely I would confuse the two buttons.

My outburst came out of nowhere. It was unexpected, but it was bound to happen. There were practically a million people in this family tree. Was I expected to give money and to care for these people because they were my dad's children and grandchildren? I could only make out my dad's look of pity and confusion.

"No, my Doh'ta, that is not your duty. No one expects you to save the family. It is not your responsibility. You can just help when you can."

This final statement was vague and would ultimately blur the lines of what I owed my family and what they expected from me. But for the time being, this was comforting enough to stop my tears.

VI. EVERYTHING'S BLACK & WHITE

Thank God Celeste planned each day of our time in Livingstone; somehow, having activities created the right texture for conversations between Dad and me. But was I the only one who wasn't excited about hiking in the heat? It wasn't that hot, and Victoria Falls—called Mosi-oa-Tunya before a white man renamed it—was spectacular. The original name meant "The Smoke That Thunders." No wonder why it's one of the seven natural wonders of the world. But the falls were not as big as they could be because it was dry season. There was no way I could forget it because every three steps dad would remind us: "Awww. It is usually very, very beautiful. It is dry season." He felt the need to personally apologize for the lackluster performance of the falls. I could understand that because when you are talking to Americans about Africa, you want them to walk away impressed with new and modern images about the country, not just the stereotype of poor villages and starving children. It was also a source of pride for him; like a badge of the value of his homeland and, therefore, him. "I am so, so sorry, it is very, very boo-ti-ful."

"It's okay, Dad. Celeste, take a picture of me like this."

"Get close to the edge," Celeste beckoned as I saw my dad hesitate.

"Okay, now you."

The guard rails in some sections of the falls were nonexistent, and Dad seemed to think we were going to fall. "Please, Mama Mwanji. You are standing too close." His voice was so gentle and sweet even when he became stern. It was almost hard for me to imagine that this man could have battered my mother violently.

His worrying about my safety humanized him and framed the nature of every paternal relationship. At the end of the day, he was being a father who cared about his child's well-being. I relished every minute of the concern and attention.

"Well, it has been an interesting journey because . . ." This wasn't a trick question, and I knew the answer, but somehow the past seven years of my life seemed like a blur, almost as if they were vignettes of someone else's life. I was at a loss for words. Here I was, invited to be a panelist on Capitol Hill, to tell my story to the nation in an effort to save myself and potentially the masses by helping to promote the DREAM Act. Furthermore, this contender of the DREAM Act, a Republican from Iowa, asked me a basic question. The answer simply involved recounting the past seven years, yet I could not answer it. I felt all of their eyes on me, the entire 110th Congressional Subcommittee. I imagined the disappointment from Zoe Lofgren, from California, chairwoman of the Judiciary Subcommittee, who probably expected me to say something brilliant.

"Excuse me," King corrected. "The depths of human frailty."

"Yes, absolutely," I responded to Congressman King. My throat was dry and I considered sipping on the glass of water sitting in front of me but I didn't want the microphone to pick up my gulp. "At the same time—I think my counterparts can attest to this. At the same time, you are falling apart; you are in deportation proceedings and you do not know from day-to-day whether the immigration services will come to your home or not." But what did that mean?

Suddenly, I couldn't think of an example. I felt my palms sweat and all I could think about was the fact that there were reporters, C-SPAN cameras and the nation, expecting a profound answer. I had been ready for this question for most of my life, but no one ever asked so I stopped expecting it, and now here it was being shot out of a giant cannon. What I wanted to really say was that for practically a decade I imagined myself on the edge of a huge cliff about to jump off because I couldn't take it anymore. When it wasn't me attempting to take the plunge, I felt an invisible nudge trying to push me off the cliff. Life was that hard for that long. But could I actually say that in a hearing? Would that sound absurd?

"Did it make you stronger?" Representative King positioned.

"It did make me stronger. What I was basically trying to say was it is almost like living a double life essentially. You still have to try to survive. You still have to go on. There are no other choices. Your only choice is to, essentially, give up and be deported to a country you do not know." In that moment of panic, my thoughts appeared incoherent and I could not trust them. The weight of all undocumented immigrants was on me and this was the best that I could come up with?

Martine, tell him your story! Tell him everything. But that was it—that was all that I could muster. The pain was too deep, and I was afraid of exposing myself once again, to a room full of strangers. I knew that I had to tell my full story someday in response to Representative King and to the rest of the country. But I choked. It was as if someone had cut out my tongue or confiscated my voice. It wasn't fear more than it was the shock and confusion of it all and my not knowing how to summarize it.

As dad walked in his green ensemble of a soccer jersey, shorts, and brown sandals, I saw his boyish innocence. He was thin, excitable, and full of life as any teenage boy would be. If you saw him from the back, you would think he was twentysomething.

Celeste had her backpack so that she could carry her professional camera. Even though her belly was obvious, I had to keep reminding myself she was pregnant, especially after two hours of hiking over rocks and boulders at Mosi-oa-Tunya. I saw the two of them hopping about and maneuvering around the boulders like they were mere stones. The heat was killing me, and I was dying of thirst.

"Do you think she is okay?" I heard Celeste asking my dad as I trailed behind. *How embarrassing!* I was with a pregnant woman and a geriatric man, and *I* was the weakest link?

I was grateful when they both agreed to end the hike and get some lunch. That was more up my alley, and the fancier the better. At this point, I was tired of being in a hostel, no matter how decadent it was compared to others, and I was tired of starving myself. I was going to gorge out, and it didn't matter what anyone thought. And luckily, we discovered that the Zambezi Sun was right around the corner. It was the hotel I originally wanted us to stay at, but Celeste objected to. In the end, listening to her was the smartest thing to do.

It was straight out of a Jim Crowe movie with old, white faces with leathery bodies burned by the hot African sun. They sat at the poolside restaurant speaking in various English accents against the backdrop of a band of dark-skinned Africans playing bongos. The waitstaff, all dressed in floral tops and white pants, were an army of more black-skinned African men who kept their heads bowed and played their part as the black servant rather convincingly. It was as if the music stopped and all eyes were on us as we proceeded into the restaurant. There was a lack of subtlety in these parts as a waiter gave us a big grin and showed us to the table. I caught glances from the sides of my eyes and picked up looks that whispered: "How was a pregnant, white woman connected to a black African woman and old man?" The old woman with thick, red thighs and an Australian accent looked aghast, as if the three of us committed some heinous crime by being at the Zambezi Sun. Celeste must have noticed it at first, because she was like, "Ah, don't feel so comfortable here."

"Welcome to my world as a black woman in America," I thought and felt no sympathy for her just because everyone was staring at her, too. Instead, I insisted on living my fantasy of overeating in an upscale African restaurant even though the floral shirts and bongos screamed more Caribbean than African. Amidst all the whites, I could tell that we would be the last people to get served if we didn't push our way around. I felt very entitled with my American Express Gold card. Money was money, and I had just as much, if not more, than these racist assholes, so someone was going to serve me.

"Dad, if I could give you anything, what is it that you want?" I asked with sincerity over my burger and salad. If he said a house, I would find a way to get him one. If he said money, then I would find a way. I was feeling very generous in this minute and overwhelmed with emotion. It felt safe to ask this question now, because Celeste was there to act as a buffer to keep me from coalescing too much.

"I would like to sell my paintings." His response brought tears to my eyes, but I wouldn't show them. Here was a man who was a self-taught artist and had been waiting his entire life to showcase his work. He was held back by the choices he made in life, which could not afford him the option to travel and to pursue his talent. His artwork had been bypassed, or he had been taken advantage of by the occasional tourist who gave him $5 for a painting that would otherwise cost $700 and upwards. There was a time where I would be the one haggling with an old painter to purchase the painting at 25 percent of the price. But now that I saw my father's face and his journey at the other end of the deal, I felt guilt and pain. All he wanted was to be able to take care of his family like he once could. My father was looking for a way to be self-sufficient once again.

We discussed how we could sell his artwork in hotel shops like the Zambezi Sun. I would help him get back to the lodge in Namibia where his friend lived and hired him to go and paint.

"What material do you need to make more of your paintings, Dad?" Celeste asked him. The plan was to get him more oil paint and material for him to make his own canvases when we returned to Lusaka. I wanted to make this old man's dreams come true. He wasn't asking for much.

"Mr. K.K., you have blue eyes." Celeste motioned for me to look as the sunlight hit my dad's face to showcase greyish-blue eyes.

"Yes?" Dad said as if he had never noticed them himself.

"Dad, why do you have blue eyes?"

The waitstaff looked confused and impressed when I went up to the bar and put down my AMEX card to pay for dinner. The bartender and the waiter seemed both perplexed and proud that I was the owner of the Gold card. I knew that they didn't want us to leave. We were like a meteor that occurred once every couple of years. When else would they get to serve people who reminded them of themselves rather than a bunch of old, white, entitled Europeans?

"Let's get the fuuuuuuu outta here," Celeste whispered to us. Even though Dad didn't understand all Americanisms, he agreed it was time to leave Zambezi Sun. As we walked out, I was more grateful than ever to Celeste for talking me out of booking this place as our hotel.

As much as I tried to avoid it, my compatriots were eager to continue walking. "I can walk even 25 kilometers every day for exercise," my dad remarked. Knowing very little about the metric system, I couldn't even begin to guess what 25 kilometers meant, but I knew it was long. We travelled on a beautiful graveled road with grass, tall trees, and colors of various hues along the sides of the road.

We walked along the side of the road for what seemed to be about twenty minutes until we stumbled across the gates to the Royale Livingstone Hotel. I forgot all about this hotel, but I recalled seeing it online. It looked like colonial Africa with big, white mansions, huge lawns, and tamed monkeys placed to roam on the lawn, entertain guests, and act as a cliché for African hotel luxury. It was beautiful; in fact, it was straight out of a Hemingway novel. Unlike the cheesy Zambezi Sun, Royal Livingstone reeked of old money. The lobby of the main hotel was marble.

The bathrooms smelled of the freshest linen, and the napkins were expensive enough to feel like cloth against your skin. Chandeliers lined the corridors of the hotel. You could see *Mosi-oa-Tunya* from the lawn, which had gazebos and elegantly placed wooden swings. There was nothing modern or mediocre about this place. I imagined some porcelain-skinned white woman would come walking on the lawn in a white petticoat, a large, white umbrella, and her little black slave behind her. A repulsive sight. It was that eerily reminiscent of the eighteenth century, except that black people not only waited on clients, they also managed the hotel. That was the most delicious part. And there were more black people who frequented this hotel as guests.

"This is where I want to get married," I said aloud, already imagining my dad walking me down the aisle to some imaginary man who I was going to marry. There was no way I could capture the beauty of this place, not even a camera would suffice. So I knew I would have to come back.

"Sho'a, my Doh'ta," which was my dad's way of assuring me.

"This is so you, Martine. Mutoto and I would definitely come back for your wedding here."

Were they both placating me? Regardless, I believed them. Now the challenge was figuring out how I would get my entire African family here and have us look like we were not some village bumpkins.

The black woman in the gift shop didn't pay us much attention. She reminded me of some of those black saleswomen in those high-end Fifth Avenue boutiques who didn't give any attention to other blacks; as if she knew her "people" wouldn't buy anything. Whenever I experience this type of discrimination, I'm tempted to either buy a whole lot of nothings just to prove a point or to walk out of the store in disgust. In this case, I walked out of the gift shop and proceeded to wait for Dad and Celeste in the courtyard by the fountain.

That's when I saw the tiniest monkey on the lawn playing, and my initial instinct was to run after the baby and cradle him in my arms. He was so cute. Not just cute for being a baby and a tiny monkey, but he was legitimately cute like the giggle of a six-month-old baby. Momentarily, I imagined what it would be like if my life was like those aged movies of colonial Africa, but we would reverse the script so I was a rich African woman, with my pet monkey. Luckily, Celeste reminded me that stealing a baby monkey wouldn't fare well with mother monkey. It wasn't that I had never seen a monkey before or a zebra, but being in such proximity to them without being confined to a fence made it feel fantastical; almost as if they would start speaking to me in English.

As I stared at the zebra who walked past me on the trail, I started to question if I had in fact ever seen a zebra in real life. If I had, why didn't it ever occur to me how much they were like ponies, and the patterns on a zebra were unique to each zebra? The sole zebra found his compatriots, and it was three humans to three zebras. Celeste and I proceeded to take selfies while not getting too close to them.

"You can get closer," my dad motioned and smiled as he snapped photos of Celeste and me. He seemed more amused with the camera than the actual picture, so there was no telling if these pictures would come through.

"No, Dad, we are scared that they might kick us." I think this was my reminder that my dear friend was carrying a life inside her while risking her and the baby's health to accompany me on this trip. All this time, Celeste was taking care of me, but it was she who needed to be taken care of.

"They cannot harm you. They just want to protect the pregnant one. She is with baby like Mama Celeste." Up until then, I did not know my dad was a zebra expert. After walking through a forest for what seemed like ten minutes, we turned around and there were three zebras in the exact same formation. They stopped cold on their hooves staring at us, hoping that we didn't notice them. When we walked a little bit more and noticed them directly behind us, Celeste and I began to get antsy. What if these African zebras were going to attack us? What did zebras eat?

"Do not be scared, my Doh'tas," my dad's reassuring voice blazed through.

"But why do they keep following us, Dad? It's scaring me."

My dad's composure and reassuring smile was enough to calm us down.

"Because we are black and white like them," he said and laughed at his own joke. I had to admit, it was quite clever.

We found our way out of the forest and near the Zambia-Zimbabwe border. My only motivation for going into Zimbabwe was to get another stamp in my passport.

"I'm scared, Dad," I said as we walked out of the embassy.

There was a posse of baboons on the roof, perched like birds. As we proceeded to cross the bridge, a gang of them gave us the side eye. I had never encountered so many baboons at once. What if they attacked me? They scared me more than any lion or cheetah ever could. I couldn't trust such a hideous-looking creature. I couldn't even bare to look at the exposed and raw butt—disgusting! What if they stole my backpack like the tour guide from yesterday had warned? These baboons would fight a woman for the contents in her bag. I was obviously the weakest link in this trio, so I knew I would be the prime target. Celeste seemed unfazed.

"Aw, don't be scared, Martine. They won't do anything to you. I won't let them." What did she mean? There were more of them than us, and they resembled a gang waiting for us to make one wrong move.

"Eh? You are scared of the baboons?" my dad said. "Do not worry. Let me take your bag."

Even though he didn't have a trace of fat on his body, I felt incredibly safe in his presence. I guess all it took was reassurance from my father that I would be okay.

"Miss lady, do you want to bungee jump?" the vendor politely asked.

Heck no did I want to bungee jump in Africa! What idiot goes bungee jumping in a third-world country? That was white people stuff. No, I couldn't even watch this crap. The view into Zimbabwe was scenic. I wondered if Mugabe was still president? Wait, wasn't he the president that hated white people and didn't want them in Zimbabwe. Oh my goodness, Celeste was white, and we were walking into Zimbabwe. Was this safe? Should I say something, or would this alarm her?

"Here we are in Zimbabwe!"

"Martine, now you can tell people that you were in Zimbabwe," Celeste said as we all sat on tree stumps in a park. We had arrived, so now what? There wasn't a whole lot to do except admire the trees and the park. There wasn't enough time to go into the city. Even if there was, I would protest it because of Celeste being white.

"Should we head back to Jollyboys?" I offered.

"Americans!" shouted a teenage Zimbabwean guy who stood where the baboons were earlier.

How dare he? I felt like that comment was directed at me because of my accent, and I felt insulted in that moment. I was visibly Congolese looking, and where did this jerk come off accusing me of being an American?

"I'm Congolese. Not American!" I defended myself. I just wanted a country to embrace me as one of theirs. What was I saying, though? I was American and proud of it. I lived at the intersection of being American, Congolese, and Zambian. However, I felt like in Africa, I also had to reject my other identity to be seen as one of them. The sun was coming down, and it was time to leave the Zambia-Zimbabwe border. Dad phoned a cab driver, and I was shocked that Dad didn't introduce him as another uncle or cousin.

The cabbie spoke Bemba with my dad in the front while Celeste and I sat in the backseat. We headed from the Zambia-Zimbabwe border back to Livingstone, Zambia, to our hostel at Jollyboys. But before going back to the hostel, we decided to take a detour and look at some homes that were available for purchase. I was feeling generous and guilty at the same time and somewhere in between those two feelings I developed a notion that I could afford to buy my dad a house today!

"Why is he taking us here? We just said we wanted to see affordable and upper-middle-class villages in Livingstone," Celeste muttered to me in our code language.

Code language meant she was becoming irritable and was either hungry, tired, or needed some downtime. It meant I needed to reign it in. I was curious about what property looked like in Livingstone as it compared to Lusaka. Could I move my dad to Livingstone, which was more touristy so that he could sell his art? How much did it cost to buy a plot of land to build a small house with an indoor bathroom? Celeste and I explored the possibility, and we were looking for answers. But my dad and the cab driver got carried away and, somehow, we ended up in the Bel

Air of Zambia. The mansions were enormous and beautifully constructed in white. The homes were gated. I saw little rich Zambian kids in uniforms walking home from school. Here I was in Zambia, encountered by so much more wealth than I was accustomed to, even in New York City.

"Oh my goodness, Martine, this is so you." I loved that Celeste associated me with wealth and class. She was right, I could easily be the matriarch in one of these beautiful homes. Nevertheless, we were getting zapped into the aesthetics and missing the whole point of this ride.

"Dad, can we see some of the villages maybe?"

Livingstone seemed a lot more sophisticated than Lusaka. Even the villages had better quality homes. Instead of metal roofs, the shanties had more durable roofs that also made it seem slightly less poor. Just like how the inner cities in America are disguised by the beauty and splendor of the tourism industry, villages in Zambia were also masked by the falls, the large, white houses, and animals. But tucked away behind all of it was where the poverty seemed to dwell. This poverty was one or two grades above what my dad was living in Lusaka. I imagined my dad having the biggest house in the backdrop of Livingstone with running water in his home, perhaps three bedrooms, and one indoor bathroom. I would give him back what he lost when he left John Howard. His dignity.

CHAPTER 5

RED DIRT ROAD TO LOVE

*I never knew my mom really loved me until that very moment.
Finally, I was free as that dove.*

I. LOVE

"We don't want her thinking that your people are nobodies," Uncle, who picked us up from the bus station, commented when we arrived in Livingstone in our native Swahili, specifically for Celeste not to hear. Celeste was sitting right next to me in the backseat of Uncle's Honda. This was one of the few times when English was not used. How could she not know we were talking about her?

Uncle didn't want Celeste to be the next white savior that helped me get to Zambia and was contributing her dollars to making this trip possible. On the one hand, allowing Celeste to hold the purse strings took pressure off me so that my family could avoid asking me for money. On the other hand, it fed into every stereotype imaginable about Africa. Who knows how much Dad would later owe Uncle for taking us to dinner, but it was their way of asserting themselves as providers. To diffuse the situation, I allowed a quick "okay" to escape my lips.

Here we went again with food. I loved food from my country, but I was embarrassed that it was being forced down Celeste's throat. What if this foreign-looking and foreign-smelling food made her sick? What if she was thoroughly disgusted by all of it?

"You don't have to eat a lot," I began apologizing to her as we parked near the restaurant. It was a large restaurant with wooden benches outside, very typical of a restaurant in a hot climate. The music was stale and seemed to come from someplace off in a distance. Pots and pans clanked in the back, and women's voices trailed in and out. The restaurant had colorful, plastic lawn chairs from Walmart and tables with plastic tablecloths. It was one of those self-service type of places. Dad and Uncle found a seat for us. Dad became excited when he offered us food.

"You like *foofoo*, Mwanji!" What meant to be a thoughtful question sounded more like Dad placing an order for me out of excitement.

"Dad, a little bit!" I resorted to yelling at him, because that's the only way to get his attention.

"Dad, Celeste only wants a little bit, too." The pretty waitress who took our order didn't seem amused. She had been interrupted from her dinner to serve us, and here was my dad, running in circles trying to determine what to order.

"Mwanji, do you like mulenda?" Mulenda (pronounced moo'lend'ah') was Swahili for okra. Okra was a staple food in a lot of Congolese dishes. It is often sautéed with onion and tomato paste. If you can get past the slime, it's quite delicious. It had been a long time since I ate *foofoo* and *mulenda*. It wasn't since 1996 before my mom's death that I had a smorgasbord of good Congolese cooking.

"The doctor says that I have cancer," were the dagger-like words my mother had hurled at me. I was sitting at the kitchen table doing my homework when she walked in through the side door of our Columbus, Ohio, house. I was fourteen. Like clockwork, I started to cry the minute she said it. I had already lost my grandmother, grandfather, and stepfather from illnesses, and now it was happening all over again.

"See, I knew that you would get like this if I told you. I'm going to be fine." She was slightly annoyed with my crying. But she was not going to be okay; Lymphoma negatively impacts the entire immune system. In the beginning stages of her chemotherapy, Ya Marie fought off all weakness, clearly trying to prove that she was in control. She continued her compulsive episodes: cooking enough food for thirty people, rearranging the living room furniture while I was at school, walking back and forth to the grocery store, tailoring wedding dresses in our basement, and certainly drinking her wine. While she seemed fine at first, I was able to live in denial while focusing on freshman year of high school. My favorite class was Spanish, because our teacher taught the class to say, *"Pudiera sacar punta mi lapiz, por favor"* in our first day of class. All it meant was "Can I sharpen my pencil, please?" But it was in the romantic Spanish language.

A few months later from her original announcement, it seemed like the cancer and the chemo quickly won out. Soon, I had become her nursemaid. This created an odd paradox for me like "the gift" of Ya Marie's alcoholism. Lymphoma had made her harmless, and my heart softened—I wanted my mother to know that, in her moments of complete vulnerability, I loved her; all the physical and emotional pain that she inflicted on me no longer mattered. Every night I cooked dinner, using a cancer cookbook as my guide.

I wasn't a chef, though intended to do well, and Ya Marie would lash out at me with verbal cruelty and paranoia: "You serve me this shit like you are serving a dog! You would rather throw food at me like a dog than hand it to me like a human. It's like you don't want to touch me. You treat me like a leper."

The profanities that she hurled were heart-wrenching. Was Ya Marie blind to my efforts in trying to hold everything together? Seemingly overnight, my life as a fourteen-year-old catapulted into the daily regimen of a responsible adult. I had no time to think about it, or wallow in self-pity. I cleaned her vomit without hesitation, because I didn't want her to feel ashamed. She could hardly keep any food down. The only things that she craved were Kit Kats, Sprite, and Ensure milk. She would have two sticks of Kit Kat at a time with a quarter of a can of sprite and object to more food. We both fought to keep the weight on Ya Marie, but it was futile. Although she had no more weight to lose, she kept dropping on the scale. I helped her walk to the bathroom when she couldn't hold herself up anymore and held my tears back because I couldn't believe this was happening to my mother. I followed in her footsteps and walked a mile to the grocery store and back and stocked the fridge. I tended to the rose bushes that sat all around our house. The roses were so gorgeous in all the various hues that they bloomed around the house: blood red, bright orange, hot pink, white, and yellow. Along with caring for Mother, I had my daily homework requirements.

Additionally, I had to monitor my twelve-year-old cousin's homework. My cousin was living with us—my idea to inject another human presence into our home. I prepared all meals. I also managed the monthly bills, identifying to Ya Marie which had to be paid, writing out checks and sometimes forging her signature if she was too tired. Surprisingly, this process seemed more mechanical than grueling—someone had to do it.

"You know that your mother is going to die," were the solemn words whispered by the visiting beer-bellied priest in the white cloak and oversized crucifix. Apparently, the Catholic church offered drive-by services for individuals who were bed-ridden. My throat burned as I tried to hold back my anger while correcting this imbecilic.

"She will be fine," I rebutted.

We needed a miracle; if appealing to doctors and to religion proved futile, then we were going directly to God for answers. So began our nightly prayer rituals. After reading a psalm from the Bible, which was foreign to me and sounded like babble to Ya Marie, who was in too much pain to focus, we recited a few Hail Mary's, finally ending with "Our Father, who art in Heaven . . ." Holding onto Mama's light-blue rosary, sitting at the foot of her bed, I truly believed that God would come through. The harder we begged, the quicker the response time from Heaven. Sometimes Ya Marie felt moved to tell a fable, the same story, and I held onto her every word: "There was once a man named Job. He was a very good man. He obeyed God and his commandments. One day, God wanted to test Job's faith to see if Job believed in him . . ."

Ya Marie was the only person I had left to love; I would do anything to keep her with me, no matter how unbearable the verbal and physical abuse.

"Ya Marie, how do you feel today?" I'd ask her every day. She'd let out a sigh before responding, "I feel really good, Shesheme." She went to great lengths to spare me any anguish. Unfortunately, my rationalizations began to get the best of me to the point where I became delusional. If Ya Marie was going to die, then I was either going to die before her or alongside her. There was no point to living; one cannot survive without their mother. I thought about possibly starving myself to death, but instead attempted to swallow a bottle of aspirin.

I wondered how Celeste would fare with the slime from the okra. There was also fish and stew, which I figured she could handle with a little bit of *foofoo*.

The *foofoo*, okra, and fish came out, and it was double the amount of what Celeste or I could eat. "Mr. K.K., this is too much food. We don't want to waste it. I can only eat half of this," Celeste beckoned the waitress to cut the portion in half. Before any Fanta could be offered to us, Celeste remembered to ask for bottled water. Now the moment of truth came. A small tub of water was brought over to us to wash our hands before we ate. Because *foofoo* has the consistency of hard porridge, your hands have to be a little wet so that the *foofoo* doesn't stick to your hands as you're eating it. But the water we used to wash our hands could make us sick! I looked to Celeste for guidance. I watched in amazement as she dipped her hands in the water without flinching a muscle. How did she always know what to do? Did she realize what she was doing now? Had the heat gotten to her? Should I follow suit?

Alright, maybe Celeste had a trick up her sleeve. I stared at her as I dipped my hands in the cool water. I imagined the germs giving me more than just diarrhea this time, but dysentery or cholera. I had no idea what I would do. When the waitress walked away, Celeste whipped out hand sanitizer and squeezed some in my palms. *Thank goodness!* I was so preoccupied with washing my hands that I guess I hadn't noticed that Dad and Uncle disappeared. They were eating inside in the heat. They wanted to give Celeste and me privacy and perhaps create an ambiance. Maybe they needed time away from us, too.

II. YA MARIE

I sobbed inconsolably alone while my mom lie in her bedroom asleep from the painkillers. In July 1996, Trish and Forrest Morgan, Uncle Dan's sister and brother-in-law, offered to adopt me in the event of Ya Marie's death. Everyone, including Ya Marie, had enough sense not to position it to me that way. Instead, they presented it as an insurance policy. My mother approved of me living with anyone except her siblings, the Kalaws. "They're not good people. They abandoned us when Uncle Dan died and were waiting for us to fail. I will not give them that satisfaction. I don't trust that my family will treat you well and make sure that you finish school. I want you to go to college."

College was both of our dreams for me. Ya Marie didn't get farther than high school, so having her youngest child go to college was a source of pride for her. I didn't just want to go to any school. I had to go to Yale. Why Yale? It was where the famous black neurosurgeon Ben Carson went, and I wanted to be a brain surgeon just like him.

Trish and Forrest would suffice as parents; they were the fat married couple who let me eat pizza to my heart's content and watch movies like *Annie* until the wee hours of the morning. Trish and her attorney brought me to the downtown courthouse, where I filled out and signed mounds of documentation. The edict to "never sign anything until you read it first," was overpowered by my excitement to just get it done. Besides, I was fifteen and wouldn't have understood what I was signing if I tried. The final step was taking the documents home for Ya Marie to sign and then notarizing it to make it official. Then all hell broke loose. As misfortune would have it, Aunty Amelie and Aunt Frances's sixth sense kicked in: "Put your mother on the phone. Why is she trying to avoid us? If she doesn't return our call by the end of the week, we're driving out to Ohio." This threat was somewhat disingenuous as they had already planned a summer trip to visit. It would have been their very first time coming to Columbus since we moved here three years ago with Uncle Dan. Those bastards, they didn't even come to Uncle Dan's funeral. In fact, none of my mom's family showed up to her husband's funeral. A few days later, my two aunts arrived at our doorstep, intent on getting to the bottom of things.

"Why is your mother so ill?" Aunt Frances demanded after taking one look at her frail sister lying on her deathbed.

Suppressing my resentment for them and their tardiness by three years, I said meekly, "Her lymphoma cancer has gotten worse." Where were they all these months when she was sick? What kind of siblings were they? I wished they would leave us alone.

"Do you realize that she is going to die?" one questioned me, as the other paced the kitchen floor.

"I hope that I die before she leaves me," I responded spitefully, while Ya Marie's cough drowned out my desperate plea for help. They accompanied Ya Marie to chemotherapy the very next day, collected medical documentation from her doctors, and contacted our real estate broker. Aunty Amelie's wrath went into high gear upon learning about the guardianship papers. She dictated as I typed my mom's Last Will and Testament on my computer, which renounced Forrest and Trish Morgan's guardianship of me. Our home, once silent but for sobs and prayers, suddenly became a call center and a war zone.

A day later, more of the Kalaw clan showed up, this time with a U-Haul. I looked to Ya Marie to stop the madness, but she just lay in bed, slipping further into delirium. A few hours later, Trish, Forrest Morgan, and Anita, Uncle Dan's oldest sister, came to the house and demanded to know what was going on. The kitchen quickly became a verbal battlefield, with the line drawn between the Kalaws and the Coopers; accusations were launched like cannons. The voices were shrill, cold, vicious, and calculating. I stood in the hallway between the kitchen and my mom's bedroom, hoping that I could both shield my mom from the shouting and disappear into the walls somehow. Aunty Amelie—full of fighting words—was a force to be reckoned with; attacking people was her specialty.

"My family knows what you're up to. You just want custody of my niece so that you can collect her social security benefits!"

Anita shot back, "You call yourselves Louise's family but where were you all these years when she had nothing? None of you even came to her husband's funeral! It was our mother who took care of her and Martine in Columbus!"

After each insult, the tension in the room escalated.

Like an atomic bomb to my heart, Forrest proclaimed, "She's practically dead anyways!"

I wondered if Ya Marie heard this assault. They all seemed to forget that she was alive and breathing in the next room. The final venomous dart came from Aunty Amelie, who stood in the doorway in her elegant designer clothes.

As she leaned on her wooden cane and her face contorted into a predator about to attack, she screamed, "Your brother did this to my sister!"

The trauma continued for my mother and me, as we were suddenly being plucked from our unfortunate reality—uprooted from our Columbus home—to be transported to Maryland against our depleted will. Aunty Amelie, a registered nurse, insisted that we move in with her so she could care for her sister. We basically had no voice in the decision—Ya Marie was too weak to speak, and I was not asked my opinion in the matter.

At a severe ninety pounds, my mother could no longer walk, as her muscles had finally atrophied. It was unfortunately easy for Uncle Andre to carry Ya Marie out of the house. I watched through the window from the middle seat of the minivan as Uncle Andre cradled his eldest sister like a newborn baby—fearful of holding her bony body too tightly, yet afraid he may drop her. The scene spurred a thought from the darkest recesses of my heart: "Oh God," I finally confessed silently, "she is dying."

Aunty Amelie and Aunt Frances cushioned the van's entire rear section with the softest pillows and blankets to buffer Ya Marie's fragile frame from the bumps in the road. My uncle gently placed her as he would a baby into a basinet. She lay in a fetal position with her bones protruding from under that blue, cotton throw. As she lay helpless, I sat hopeless, wondering about my fifteen-year-old life. I would have assiduously guarded my belongings on that bleak August day in 1996, had I known that I would be forever separated from them. I watched my uncles hastily dump the contents of my life into a rental truck.

"Where did I pack Rachel?" My favorite doll was a gift from Ya Marie and Uncle Dan; I imagined it was at the bottom of a box buried under a pile of other boxes. Rachel was the first black doll I ever owned; prior to that, I was obsessed with ivory-skinned dolls, painted with Snow White ruby-red lips. I reminisced the passing of Mama, my maternal grandmother, and the early days living with my mother and her beau. "Why does she only carry that white doll with blue eyes?" I heard Uncle Dan ask, to which she replied unfazed, "I don't know."

But from that day forward, he insisted I only play with black dolls. Rachel seemed so real, with her mocha-colored, plastic skin, hazel eyes, deep dimples, and cotton body. "Your birth name is Rachel Kalaw," I said aloud as I kissed her forehead.

My mind reverted to present moment. The upheaval was overwhelming, as I yearned for Rachel to hold me together. It was a long drive from Ohio to Maryland, with my two aunts in the front and my mother laid out behind me. I muttered prayers—more like demands—while Congolese music played quietly.

"She can't leave me God; You can't take my mother away from me."

Yet I also sensed Ya Marie was moving on, her fight was over. Her spirit was gradually fading with every mile, and I imagined her whispering in my ear: "Go ahead, Shesheme. It's time for you to lead your own way. I'll always be right behind you." Gone were the days when Ya Marie would speak her broken English, and I would burst out laughing.

"Ya Marie, you're not supposed to pronounce 'all day' like 'holiday' because those mean two different things." But my correction would only create another blunder, as she would pronounce "holiday" like "holy day." I thought that if I never took my eyes off her, I could prevent my mother from leaving me. But when I looked back and noticed that she was fast asleep, I realized she was on her way to be with Mama in the afterlife.

Aunty Amelie's town house was August steamy warm, as there was little chance she would soothe us with the cooling expense of the air conditioner. The closets smelled like a fresh douse of fancy perfume.

Ya Marie and I moved into my cousin Emanuel's room; I took the bed in the far corner while Ya Marie was closest to the door. My aunts took Ya Marie to the doctor in readiness for hospital admission and to complete the transfer of records. It was the same hospital where Mama died; who could forget the name of Holy Cross? After giving Ya Marie a sponge bath and a sedative, my aunts gave me the third degree, void of any sensitivity.

"Martine, do you realize that your mother has full-blown AIDS?"

My mind raced as these words sliced right through me. *Oh my goodness, what do you mean she has AIDS? . . . How could she have AIDS? . . . I thought that she had lymphoma cancer . . . How did she get AIDS from cancer?*

"No," was all I could say as I burst into sobs.

Aunt Frances was more suspicious than sympathetic of my tears as she continued: "I just don't understand how you could not have known that your mother had AIDS. You have lived with her and you've been her personal caretaker. How could you not have known this? What's wrong with you?"

Aunty Amelie had obviously influenced my kindhearted aunt, who for many years I had wished was my real mother.

"Ya Marie never told me that she had . . . AIDS."

"Martine, you are a bright, young woman. How could you not have seen the signs?"

These insinuations from Aunt Frances who was my "favorite" aunt were like a flogging. My mind shuffled through the numerous dramas of the last three years, searching for clues. Ya Marie twice suffered from shingles that attacked her entire body—once before and then again after Uncle Dan's death. Was it possible that these "shingles" were signs of Kaposi Sarcoma (KS)? Or what about the short, little nurse who came to administer Ya Marie's medication twice a week? Why did she always close the door? One time she accidentally left it slightly ajar and I heard her mention AZT to my mother. But I thought I misheard her. Wasn't AZT the cocktail drug that was used to treat HIV patients? Is that why Ya Marie was paranoid about me being near her or touching her, in fear that I may catch the disease?

"You treat me like a leper," were her words.

How about when Uncle Dan died, and I overheard the doctor mention HIV? I overheard Ya Marie mention once that Uncle Dan had a history with drugs. Did that mean he used drugs or did he sell drugs? What kind of drugs though? Could that have been associated with him contracting HIV? Was it possible that he acquired HIV and passed it onto Ya Marie? "Your brother did this to my sister!" were the exact words from Aunty Amelie. Did Uncle Dan infect my mother? If this was the case, then I hate him! But Ya Marie was hospitalized for tuberculosis when we first came to the United States. Did she contract the virus through a blood transfusion? Or was it possible that she arrived into the United States already infected? If so, then she gave it to Uncle Dan. Who passed this disease onto whom? No answer provided solace. The Coopers must have known. Why else would they be so generous to me and my mom? Were they suffering from guilt? Did everyone know except me? It felt like I had been betrayed by all the adults in my life, including my own mother. My inner being was a complete mess.

At first, I became even more angry with Ya Marie—how dare she put me at risk without my knowledge or consent? Then I dug a little deeper and began to consider my mother's tragic life: a beautiful, vibrant woman who was beaten by her husbands, a survivor and mother who made it to America with hope and only one of her six children. She silently carried the deep shame inherent to AIDS; no wonder she used alcohol to drown her sorrow and pain. I became enveloped with a powerful compassion as, suddenly, her strength was honorable. I decided that I would act as if I never knew she had AIDS—my parting gift to her was to maintain her last shred of dignity. The next few days were spent seated on a wooden chair at Ya Marie's bedside. I had no interest in caring for my own well-being, like eating food, as sorrow consumed my entire body. I did not sleep, in fear that she would be gone when I awoke.

Ya Marie and I watched movies, the same two films: Mrs. Doubtfire and Forrest Gump. Ya Marie referred to the character, Forrest, as her friend; maybe it had something to do with their common love of chocolate. Perhaps it was also because Forrest lived as my mom had, chasing after those things in life that were fleeting. By three in the morning, Ya Marie, wide awake from the pain shooting through her body, would turn her heavy head to me and ask: "Shesheme, aren't you tired?"

I replied with a smile, "No, Ya Marie. I'm not tired."

The truth was that we were both exhausted. I never intended to leave Ya Marie's bedside; I would have to be forced to do so. A week later, the inevitable occurred, as my mother realized that her suffering was overwhelming me.

"Shesheme, I want you to go and live with your Aunt Frances. I trust her, and I know that she will take good care of you. Don't give her any problems."

I couldn't imagine being separated from Ya Marie, but I obliged because she asked me to go. This was the final conversation I had with my mother. Ya Marie's voice shook; she refused to look into my eyes so as to keep from breaking down. Aunt Frances stood behind me as if prepared to catch me if I fainted. My feet felt like they were glued to the floor, but my legs trembled uncontrollably. The more that I tried to hold back my tears, the more my throat burned. I wanted to beg to stay, to tell her that I loved her, but my throat closed, and my voice was locked behind its walls. The word *love* was so foreign to me.

I managed to let out a simple, "I won't," through intense sobbing. She shared her final words with me:

"And you just focus on school. No matter what, stay in school. Stay in school for as long as you can. School will save you," she said, beginning to sob.

The umbilical cord was cut; I was sent out into the world alone, and I was unprepared. Andover, Massachusetts, with its winding roads, miles of forests, and oversized mansions, was a different planet in comparison to my daily realities.

My new bedroom was small and had a tiny window that looked onto the porch and backyard. At night, I could lie in bed, see the blazing stars that lit up the night sky, and listen to the family German shepherd barking. Sydney and Bianca, my favorite cousins and best friends, were eager to have me live with them. I realized that a childhood prayer was being answered, and in the most unexpected way. For many years, I secretly wished that I was Aunt France's third daughter and that I could be sisters with my stunning half-Italian, half-African cousins. Had I known that it would be at the expense of my mom dying, I never would have made that wish. Finally, I felt a sense of relief, as this home wrapped me in a protective cocoon of loving support. But pangs of guilt also plagued me. How could I allow myself momentary happiness when my mom was dying? My adjustment to life in Andover began to take hold. By day three, my cousins coaxed me off the couch and onto the tennis courts. This was fun, as Jordan, my eldest cousin, tried to coach the girls: "Shesheme, focus on the 'V' symbol on the racquet center. Sydney, shift your weight from side to side. Bianca, you have to move your feet and run after the ball."

He was the brother that I always wanted—confident, handsome, with the physique of a professional basketball player. On that day, it was Jordan who gave me the final word about Ya Marie.

Within minutes of returning from our leisurely workout, he approached me from the kitchen, where he received the news from Aunt Frances. The pain on his face was all he needed to say. "Martine, I'm so very sorry," he whispered as tears streamed down his face. At that moment, I did not cry; my well was dry. The tears for my mother, which had been flowing for months, if not years, finally ceased.

Tsk tsk was the sound, accompanied by "poor thing," as close friends and relatives stared at me during the wake. "She's an orphan now without a mother or a father."

"She looks just like her mother. What a shame." Their whispers were laudable from across the room.

It sounded more like gossip than genuine concern for my well-being, and it caused frustration, rather than appreciation—where were they when Ya Marie was bedridden? As her body lay in the open casket, I tried to reflect on every conversation I ever had with Ya Marie. It was impossible to make sense of this woman—angry and loving, spellbound and fairylike, compassionate and terrorizing.

ILLEGAL AMONG US

I kept staring at her lifeless presence; annoyed by the lack of resemblance to the woman I knew to be my mother. Why did they make her look so dead? Why did they put so much makeup on her? She never wore foundation or powder because she had a natural glow that illuminated her beautiful mocha skin. Her once pouty lips were now glued together. At least they used her favorite wig and salmon-colored, silk suit—I was with her when she bought that suit—now it only blankets her bones. Aunty Amelie should have consulted with me. Ya Marie would've preferred to be buried in traditional Congolese clothes—her designs—like a blouse and matching wrap skirt and a head wrap made of *anglais* wax.

III. THE SEVENTH DAY

It was about 10:00 p.m., and we were in our usual spot on the porch. This was quickly becoming a ritual I wouldn't want to break for a few days. I didn't want to think about leaving my dad. I loved him so much, and I loved all the memories that I was creating with him.

"You know, I loved my late wife very much. And she loved me too-too much," was how his story started. Then he began sorting through his treasure chest. He was on a mission and had a lot to show me before we headed back to Lusaka the following day. He was like Charlie looking for Willy Wonka's golden ticket; there was more he needed for me to see. Never in my wildest dreams could I imagine what was in store for me.

"Dad, I forgive my mom, but she used to say awful things to me and beat me so bad. She had a bad temper. Is it true that she treated me the way you treated her?" There is no rulebook on how to ask your father if he battered your mom, but to ask. I knew the answer, but I wanted to hear him say it.

As a little girl, she was gangly and mahogany-skinned, forever pouting because she was irritated by most everything. The oldest of four sisters and one brother, Marie-Louise was in charge, and her parents let her reign over the younger kids. By the time she was sixteen, her striking beauty—the pout nestled beneath

Mount Kilimanjaro cheekbones, chocolate-brown eyes, jet-black hair that crowned her head like a lion's mane, and the signature baby-gap between her two front teeth—helped to finagle her way through any mishap. In her teenage years, Marie-Louise stood a leggy 5'7" and dazzled all onlookers, whether in a pair of bell-bottoms or a mini skirt and platform shoes. Marie-Louise's self-assured and rebellious nature was amplified by the fact that her father was one of the most powerful men in Lubumbashi, Zaire. Watch out world!

Marie-Louise ruled over her siblings with an iron fist, and her threats of beatings were taken very seriously. She demanded they buy all the chocolate needed to satisfy her addiction, and according to her sister, Amelie, ". . . if we refused to give her chocolate, she would beat the crap out of us." She also liked sneaking out of the house at night to go to local nightclubs with her posse of friends. If her sisters threatened to tell Mama or Baba, they would be swiftly beaten to a pulp. But Marie-Louise also had a super cool persona, evidenced by a most-famous night in Zairian history.

October 30, 1974, and "The Rumble in The Jungle" was coming to Kinshasa! This most momentous occasion would put Zaire on the world stage—Mohammed Ali and George Foreman doing battle for the heavyweight championship. Marie-Louise insisted that her brother, Samuel, accompany her to the fight. In later years, she often regaled.

"Everyone in the streets was screaming 'Ali! Ali!' He was like God. I had my best pair of bell-bottoms on and my afro was out to here. I looked good, and I made sure that Samuel was dressed to the nines. Everyone was drinking beer, and music was blasting; it was like one big party."

It was impossible not to have felt like you were right there with her at the fight.

I often ponder my mother's early years, and wonder: when did her vivacious and dynamic light for the world flicker out? Or was it snuffed out the day her first husband severed all relations with her four children. Alexandre was the man of her dreams; they met when she was still a budding teen. He was dark, handsome, with power, money, and prestige—any young African woman would fall for him. Alexandre was taken by her youth and beauty, and that's pretty much how their love affair began. The once-confident Marie-Louise questioned her worth when it came to winning the heart of this stranger—maybe she was too enraptured by the glamour of being his wife that she missed all the warning signs. It's like the beatings started right after she said, "I do." These lasted through four pregnancies; finally, Marie-Louise had to escape, because this man would fulfill his promise and kill her.

Nearly twenty years later when she and I lived in Columbus, Ohio, my mother received a letter, written in the King's French, from her oldest daughter, Mimi. In parts, it read:

How can a mother not want her own children? How could you just abandon us at such a young age? How could you hate your children enough to leave us, to never look back?

If it was physically possible, my mother's heart would've shattered into a million pieces at that precise moment. She realized her children did not know the truth—that it was their abusive father who took them away.

He stole my children from me, and I never saw them again. He forbid me to come near his children ever again, and he threatened to kill me. What could I do? He had all the power.

This final statement, "he had all the power" became the guiding mantra to how Marie-Louise viewed her world. She was victimized by many men, including my dad. These were the unfortunate circumstances into which I entered the world—my mother experiencing the repeating pattern of violent physical abuse by a man, who also screamed horrible diatribes at her while pregnant with his child.

"It is true, my Doh'ta," he said and sighed. "The times were very different back then. I have now learned that there is a better way to maintain a marriage." I couldn't bear to hear details of how my dad inflicted pain on Ya Marie. It was enough to learn that my dad beat my mother so badly that he left marks and bruises on her body. He served more lashings with his toxic words. If I learned all the gory details, I would grow to hate my dad. Somehow, I couldn't reconcile this sensitive and sweet old man with soft but bright eyes with the demon who terrorized my mom. But then again, I still couldn't grasp the fact that he had multiple wives, even though I had all the proof in the world.

It didn't suffice as an apology, but I could see that all his actions towards me since we met were his way of repenting. He was an old man now in his early seventies and was committed to making amends with his past. He also saw how his actions towards my mother damaged me, and as my dad he couldn't bear to know that I suffered because of him. I could see it in his eyes as he mentioned his "late wife" that he really loved her but not the way she deserved to be loved. What would Ya Marie have given to hear my father say this?

"Here. See this is the letter that you wrote to me when your late mother was alive," he said as his voice softened, trailing off. I couldn't believe it. He had held onto my letter for sixteen years. I remember writing it. It was after Uncle Dan passed away and we moved from Grandma Cooper's house to our own house; the house that was framed by rose bushes and a rose garden.

How could I forget that letter? I must have written it maybe a day or two after another one of Ya Marie's verbal assaults. I was seething with resentment towards my father when I wrote the letter. Albeit superficial, I wanted him to help my sister Zalika move to Zambia, and he obliged. Zalika had suffered enough in her short life. Ya Marie yearned to heal from the memories of the physical and emotional abuse that she lay upon her children, especially Zalika. She anguished over the thought that their lasting memory of her was of violence. She needed me to coax my dad into offering Zalika a better life to make up for how she mistreated her daughter many years ago.

It was 1993. During this same time, I was in ninth grade and had just moved from Maryland to Columbus, Ohio. Ya Marie, Uncle Dan, and I moved because he needed to be closer to his family while he underwent chemotherapy. It was my first time being with so many black American people.

I haven't quite figured out the word to describe me at thirteen. Was I a nerd or just a weirdo? Although I learned about it in school, puberty hadn't quite hit me yet so I wasn't physically that much different from the year prior, so the boys didn't care for me. Instead of wearing braids in my hair, Ya Marie let me go to a black hair salon where every Saturday my hair sizzled under a hot comb until it was bone straight. But then the hairdresser would put rollers in it and subject me to sit under the hair dryer for another forty-five minutes. Even though I blended in with my hairstyle, I couldn't get it right with my clothes. While all the kids in middle school wore name brands, I trailed behind with African print clothes or outfits from the Disney Store. I caught kids in the hallway pointing and laughing at me from the corner of my eye when I wore my brown, tribal-print jumper that Ya Marie sewed for me. I felt so African and not in a good way.

One day a classmate asked me: "Why do you talk white?" What an embarrassing question, so I acted like I didn't hear him. Did I talk white? All the kids in Maryland talked the same way I did, so I guess I never noticed. Since I continued to get A pluses on all my school assignments I figured that the way I spoke must have been okay. I think that's when "Martine the Brain" was coined and people considered me to be the smartest kid in the entire school, but that wasn't meant to be a compliment.

Running track was a sure way to become popular at Buckeye Middle School. I couldn't believe it when I made the varsity team. Now everyone would expect me to be good, and I couldn't deal with the pressure. Besides, competing made me anxious. I expected my legs to buckle from under me at the beginning of each race when the referee blew the whistle. I preferred being indoors conversing with adults, watching MTV music videos, or writing.

"And you, my Doh'ta. I missed you too much."

"But why then?" I implored. "Why didn't you look for me more, Dad?"

It would be the only way to justify all the skepticism that came my way from friends. "Why didn't your dad look for you sooner?" they asked. "Why didn't he try harder?" It was less about me knowing but more about my proving it to my friends that my dad was who he said he was and he did love me the way he said he loved me.

"You know, your late mother loved me too much. But your late grandmother, Mama Martha, would interfere in our marriage. Every time your mother and I fought, your Mama Martha would take your mother away and attack me. In the end, I said it was too much for me. I didn't want to deal with your mother's family."

I knew Mama was a strong woman, and I applauded her for taking care of my mother and intervening as any mother would do. Mama was soft-spoken but, somehow, I knew her tiny frame was not indicative of the fire she possessed. The anecdote just illustrated courage and love between a mother and a child. He took out a letter that might as well have been as sacred as the Bible. I could recognize that handwriting from anywhere. The letters were close together in tiny cursive lettering. However, the rounded letters like the "o" and "p" were plump and well nourished. The writing wasn't slanted like my skinny, right-slanted writing. And the ink on the page was blue. Not just any blue. It was the BiC blue. I could tell because of the skinniness of the lines. It was Ya Marie's handwriting.

"This is a letter that your late mother wrote to me when we were still dating. It is in French, Lingala, and Swahili. I have the original here, but I have a copy, which I have translated for you." His square glasses sat at the edge of his button nose, and he held the original letter in his right hand but read the translated version in his left hand, as he leaned towards me so that I could follow the words.

"My Dear Kayembe . . ." the letter began. She had poured her heart out as she asked him if he was still angry with her.

As if on cue, a white bird appeared from the thick, black night and made itself known to us by flying in front of us and creating the infinity symbol. Was I dreaming, or had I overdosed on Dr. Mason pills? Was it a dove? I hoped it was a dove, because how magical and unbelievable would this story be? It was definitely a white bird.

"Dad! Oh my goodness, Dad! Do you see that?"

He looked up for a millisecond just to confirm that what I saw was real and continued to read. "I know, my Doh'ta."

"But, Dad, can you believe it? It's a dove. It's a dove flying around and it's like midnight!"

I couldn't even focus on the words on the page, because I was trying to make sense of the current circumstance.

"I know. It is your mom. She is letting us know that she is with us." Was it his assurance that the bird symbolized my mom that ignited a fire in me? I felt like a lightening bug! I didn't even need his confirmation. All it took was one glance at that white bird, and I had no doubt that it was Ya Marie, my mom.

"Dad, maybe I should go get my camera. That way I can take a picture. Otherwise, no one will believe me." The bird moved too fast. What was my plan in taking a photograph of a bird in flight?

"Let her be free," he said. And he kept reading. She hoped that he wasn't angry with her because she thought about him every day is what the letter said. And she missed him and hoped that he would come back to Zaire for her. She made a mistake, she said. She hoped that he would forgive her.

"Dad, what mistake?"

"As I mentioned before. Your mum knew too many men. And after I first met her and said that I wanted to marry her and would come back to Zaire for her hand, I found out that she met your brother Gaston's father and became pregnant. Your brother's father was a very big thief and was eventually arrested and went to jail. Your mum wrote this letter because she was afraid that I would not want to love her anymore. Yes, I was very sad when I found out this news."

To my father and especially in those days, women who did this kind of thing were loose and oversexed. But in today's age, you were single until you were married.

She didn't just sign it "Love, Marie-Louise." Instead, she used the closing "with love" and signed it Tschilombe, her traditional non-Western name. A true symbol of her love for my father. It was the most vulnerable and exposed I had ever seen my mother. I watched his face as he read the letter; there was a deep love and connection. A fondness. It hit me then: I came from love. As if the scene had closed and the curtains had come down, the dove-like, white bird flew back into the night not leaving a trace of itself in sight. Celeste would never believe this.

No matter what, the bird was once here! She was here to confirm that I was created from love. Here I was all these years dealing with self-loathing. I believed that my life was a mistake. And this letter proved otherwise. It affirmed that not only was I conceived in an act of love, but my mother and father entered the institution of marriage in which they vowed to be together and to create a life with one another. I was intentional. My life was intentional. As bad as my life was, I was supposed to be in this world.

"I miss my late wife too, too much."

And I felt his heartache. There was so much he never got to tell her. This was his moment to also let her know how much she meant to him. I liked to think his life wasn't the same without the presence of my beloved mother.

"Sometimes I think that it was destiny for your mother and I to separate so you have this life that you have now. Everything happens for a reason."

To think that things could be written in destiny even thirty years in advance gave me goosebumps.

"Your mum did not want to divorce me. I wanted to divorce her, but she did not want to divorce me. But I told her I was tired of her family. So I asked her to leave my house and go back to her family. I told her to leave but not to take my child. That was the only thing I asked. Please do not take Mwanji. But I came home one day, and you were both gone."

That's how it happened? Ya Marie had the choice to leave me, and she opted to take me? It never occurred to me that's how the script was written. This version had an entire new meaning. It was one of sacrifice and love from a mother to a child and again from another mother to the other child. I directed the scene in my head. My dad probably woke up to go to work and Sad Stepmom, who probably wasn't sad at the time, gave my mom the green light that it was safe to take her suitcase from under the bed. Mama must have sent money to the neighbors to help Ya Marie get on the bus that would take her possibly one week to get to Zaire. Ya Marie most likely contemplated taking me, worried if my father caught her in this act of kidnapping his child he could kill her. But she probably decided in that moment that no more men were going to take anything more from her. And the neighbors could have snuck her out. Her best friend from the Zaire embassy probably helped to update her travel documents. In this case, it took an entire village. She was probably as frail and as thin as I had always remembered, fleeing from abuse. It would have been much easier to just leave me. But she took me. To spite my father, yes. But spite could not have been the only motivator to not only take me from my father but to also chose to bring me with her to America. Here was the proof that my mother loved me. The proof that I had searched for and agonized over for nearly two decades. I never knew my mom really loved me until that very moment. Finally, I was free as that dove-like, white bird.

CHAPTER 6

LUSAKA

How dare this outsider come in and treat me like
I was beneath her?

I. LUXURIOUS GUILT

We scoured through Uncle's store one last time before he dropped us off at the bus station. What would Ya Marie have worn? Dad helped with the search. The plan, thanks to Celeste's genius, was for my dad and I to find fabric that reminded us of my mom. Then I could take a piece of it to her grave when I returned to the States.

There it was. Two yards of an ornately patterned fabric that had various hues of blue, but the deep blue was most pronounced. Hadn't I even seen her wear this pattern before? It looked exactly like something she owned, which I admired her in.

"This one, right, Dad?" I didn't know what I would do with the rest of the fabric. Maybe I would wait until I had my own baby and make an outfit out of the same fabric. Who knew? But it felt symbolic to buy the fabric here, in her homeland, with my dad with me.

The bus ride felt longer going back. Dad was more subdued today in his white socks and sandals. I imagined that he had accomplished what he was set out to share with me these past few evenings. All five of his bags had been fully used. It must have been emotionally exhausting for him to not only relive these experiences but also to have to share them with his child, whose interpretations were subject to her own judgments.

There was nothing to overanalyze anymore. It was more a matter of processing everything that I learned about myself in the last three days and having it seep into my DNA. I wasn't a bastard child, my parents loved each other once, and they loved and fought for me. What more did I have to agonize over? And the dove; how could I ever do that story justice? I couldn't wait to go back home to New York and begin my life.

The US seemed so far away and eons ago, but there was so much I would do differently now that I learned my full identity. I was going to tell my story and share it with the world because people needed to hear it. I was going to reach out to Uncle Claude because he was always so kind to me and didn't deserve to be classified with the rest of the Kalaw family. I was going to walk with an air of someone who was created on purpose.

Noor was right when she said that this trip would be life-changing. I had no idea the extent to which it would be different.

I wasn't sure how we kept finding ourselves in cars of strange "uncles" and cousins when all I wanted was a taxi. After arriving back at the Lusaka bus station, Dad insisted that a family member pick us up. "Dad, who is he?" I couldn't believe Celeste was still willing to entertain this game, but I secretly loved how she called him Dad, too, because it just showed her comfort level.

"Huh? Oh. He is the cousin of your uncle's son, remember?" And with that certainty that we knew exactly who this person was, he arrived, and Dad hurried us into the car. This cousin of my uncle's son—whatever that meant—was of a muddy-brown complexion, thin, and short. He seemed to know me or of me, because he just started asking me about my trip as if we were picking up on a past conversation. His four-door Honda sedan was hot and sticky inside. The seats were worn down, probably from carpooling so many people each day. We arrived at a parking lot of a shopping mall, and Celeste hopped out of the car like a jackrabbit to find fresh yogurt. "I need dairy for Mutoto." She was so secure and confident about meandering on her own in Africa while I needed handholding even to the bathroom.

"Dad, what are we doing here?" I just wanted to check into a hotel, stuff my face, drink wine, and relax. I was tired of roughing it for the past three days, and I was looking for luxury accommodations. Dad assured me he would drop us off at the hotel once we got measured for our African outfits.

"Oh my goodness," I muttered under my breath so only Celeste could hear me. Her hair was back in a giant braid, and she looked exasperated. She didn't like any of the yogurt selections in the convenience store. I'm sure she just wanted to put her feet up. Now we were getting measured for clothes? This was wholly unnecessary. How much debt would this create for my dad? I didn't want people reaching out to him to collect tons of debt after we left. Guilt crept in. "Dad, you don't have to."

"You will see. Your uncle is a very nice seamstress. He will make you a very nice skirt and blouse for you to take back to America." There was no stopping him when he was set on an idea.

"We should just let him do it. This happens when I go to the Philippines as well. It's something for him to do for us that will make him happy." In the middle of a Zambian parking lot, uncle or cousin, or whomever he was, began to take measurements of me and then Celeste.

"You must look at the book and tell your uncle which design you want. Then he can make it for you tonight." The album was full of African designs that I was familiar with because my mom was a seamstress. Ya Marie could make the garments in the magazines come to life and look like haute couture. I immediately fell in love with a pencil skirt and matching top combination.

"Oh, Uncle, this one please!" I pointed as I let myself get carried away with my dad's plans.

"Maybe this one will be betta." Dad pointed to what appeared to be a frumpy, dowdy photo of a frock. Fine. Whatever. I just wanted to be done with this measurement process in ninety-degree weather in a parking lot after a seven-hour bus ride. I was slightly amused that Celeste and I were in this together, as Uncle had her wrap the tape measurer around her belly and read the dimensions. When would this charade be over with?

Finally, the measuring was done, and I braced myself for what this luxury hotel experience would be like. I booked Latitude 15 online after I saw the five-star rating. I could tell that this place was unique when we drove up the white, pebbled driveway and Dad and Uncle grew uncomfortably silent. The hotel was a two-story high villa framed with luscious greenery.

"Okay, Dad. We're going to go to bed because we're so tired. Can we meet tomorrow morning?" I said, feigning exhaustion. I just wanted to luxuriate without judgment.

"Okay, Mr. K.K. We'll see you tomorrow." Celeste must have been thinking the same thing. We jumped out of the car and grabbed our backpacks. If we beat him to doing so, then he wouldn't have to get out of the car.

"Thank you, Uncle."

"Yes, we have a reservation under Martine Kalaw," I said to the receptionist while looking back to make sure they had driven off. Concierge greeted us with flutes of the house freshly squeezed fruit juice. I loved being called madame. The combination of the white, marble floors and the mahogany upholstery made this hotel as elegant as it was chic.

"Oh my goodness! I'm so, so happy. It feels like home!" I exclaimed as I walked into our hotel room. Celeste plopped on her bed decorated in soft, white, cotton linen.

I absolutely needed this exact same bathroom in my home. The floors were made of granite. There was an open shower on one end of the bathroom and a deep bathtub on the other.

"Celeste, you will die when you see this tub!" I wanted to soak in the tub, but I was too excited to do much of anything. Our plans were lazy that night; dinner and then drinks with Sacha and her friends in the dining room, then just relax.

It bothered me that all service staff in Zambia assumed that Celeste was paying for everything. I mean, I needed my family to think that. But it was slightly disturbing that this stereotype was widely accepted even without us having to say anything. When the manager of the restaurant came by to see how we were enjoying the new hotel, her attention seemed to focus more on Celeste. I pegged the manager to be a white South African or a Brit. "And how are you enjoying the dinner?"

How were we enjoying the dinner? First off, we were sitting in a veranda that overlooked the square, where all four of the hotel's buildings connected. It was deep into the African night, and we were eating by moonlight. Celeste insisted on having a few sips of my wine and ended up pouring a quarter of my glass into her empty glass.

"A fourth of a glass of wine is totally okay. It's not like I'm going to drink the whole bottle." Her eyes did that sparkly thing that they did when she was extremely happy. Much of the lobby and the restaurant had open corridors, sliding-glass doors, and flowing, white curtains that danced with every warm breeze that brushed it. I thought this journey was about connecting with my father, and it turned out to be so much more. It was about Ya

Marie and her legacy. It was also about this amazing woman who sat across from me and her mutoto, who made the journey possible. And it had been about love all along.

The only way I would allow this night to end was for sunrise. After dinner, we made our way to the bar and lounge area of the hotel. The decorum was a collaboration between Ernest Hemingway and Ralph Lauren. Old maps, lamps, and magnifying glasses sat atop antique desks. The fireplace made it cozy, while the mirrors added sophistication. Both Celeste and I were tired and in desperate need of sleep. No one had any idea what we had just experienced in the last nine days. But we were expecting Sacha to stop by for a little bit. Then we had an early morning tomorrow; our last day with Mr. K.K. We were leaving the day after tomorrow. So, for tonight, we would have to keep going; it was the African way.

II. TUSKS

I knew I should have gotten up earlier to eat breakfast. Damn my laziness and love for sleeping. Sure, I loved to slumber for ten hours straight and justify by claiming emotional exhaustion, but this served me right. All Celeste kept talking about was how delicious the breakfast was. "And the eggs benedict," she elaborated. "And it was like the best coffee ever." I didn't even drink coffee, and I wanted some. Of all the times for my African family to arrive on time, it had to be the day I was planning to feast on a smorgasbord of a five-star hotel quality breakfast. And worse yet, they got out of the car and came into the hotel before we could control them. This was madness!

I knew it, my sister Fifi was up to this. It made sense that she was Scary Stepmom's daughter. Unlike my baby sister Imani who was wiry and cute and admired me, I could tell Fifi didn't want to just be like me but wanted to *be* me. I wasn't entirely sure if I could trust her even though I always wanted a sister. It appeared to me that even though she was raised in the village, she knew about the world and how good it could get. But she carried a profound ignorance with her.

Fifi was on the verge of getting her life in order and was in "computer school." What did that even mean? Was it programing and coding? Or was she doing more data entry work? Perhaps more in the realm of learning how to use basic Office products?

If you were a woman with children in Zambia, what were your chances of exceling in school and in your career? Apparently, Zambia has one of the highest birth and child death rates. What were all these children dying of? What did Fifi's son die of? Even though I was her sister, we were not close enough for me to ask the question. I didn't even feel comfortable acknowledging that I knew that her baby boy had just died. I couldn't relate to her life in any way.

When she gazed at me, what did she see? Maybe she pitied me for being single and without kids. Or perhaps she envied my freedom and my friends, like Celeste. While Fifi was pretty, she carried a certain vacancy in her eyes, whereas Imani carried hope in hers. Around her, I wanted to downplay my educational achievements, fearing I would come off as a braggart.

Fifi's eyes widened, and she nodded her head as she came over to give me a hug in the dining area where the waitress was about to take my order.

"Wait, I want breakfast too, hey."

That "hey" lingered, carrying a different connotation. That "hey" meant, "Look at this hotel. I knew that my sister was rich and wasn't telling us. She has a whole lot of money, and she should give me some. I will just spend, and she can afford to pay for it." If it was not for her backstory that Dad shared, I would have dismissed her from the get-go. She divorced her husband, and her baby boy died only one year ago.

I look as the waitstaff gave us side glances, as if mocking how out of place my dad seemed in this environment. Then I became ashamed. Guilt followed my shame of my dad. "We will stop serving breakfast in ten minutes," the waitress said, as if she knew I needed the help to get us out of the hotel.

"We can grab food later then. Let's get started with the day. Mr. K.K., where are we going?"

Dad had a host of plans but the first one was to get me copies of the photographs of his paintings I had asked for back in Livingstone. Dad had another cousin pick us up and drop us off at a bus station where we would take the local jitney to the print shop. I could smell the body odor before I even got on the jitney. How the heck could Celeste stand this? How was she handling being in the heat with all of us black people? Was it scary or weird for her? If it was, she hid it well. She plopped herself in the open seat in the back right next to Fifi, who probably wished Celeste was her sister more than me.

I guess I didn't expect to see a Korean-owned print shop in the middle of Lusaka. This wasn't even the nicer part of Lusaka. The area was more urban with one-story buildings that looked like vacant lots. There was one Korean woman and a single black staff member. It was an easy-enough process. I needed to make copies of Dad's photographs so I wouldn't have to take them back with me. I just needed proof of his artwork so I could help create a website for him to promote his artwork. Celeste made it sound easy, even though I had never created a website. There was one scanner in the 500-square-foot establishment.

"Dad, can you go ahead and start scanning these photos?" I said. "Meanwhile, I would find out the cost."

"Wait, first you said it was five kwachas and now you are saying it's ten kwachas per photo?" I asked the assistant who was just taking orders. Someone must have seen the album of photos that my dad had and figured this would be a quick way to make extra money. But a fool I was not.

"I want to speak with the owner. Is that her?"

I walked over to the checkout counter where the assistant had run back to explain my situation to the owner. "Control yourself, Martine," a cloud bubble appeared over my head as I attempted to slow down my breathing.

"Excuse me, I'm wondering how the price doubled." I looked back at Celeste and Fifi, who were sitting on a bench in the back of the print shop chatting but stopped to look over my way. The Korean woman must have been in her midforties. She wore a stoic expression. Although I addressed her directly, she spoke to the assistant to address me. It was as if she needed an interpreter, but we were all speaking English.

"Excuse me! Excuse me! I'm talking to you. You can just address me instead of treating me like I'm invisible!"

It was one thing to make me feel inferior and invisible in America where I was a triple minority. But I was in my homeland. In the country of my birth. Zambia was owned by black people. How dare this outsider come in and treat me like I was beneath her. She wouldn't even look at me, let alone speak to me. Did she think I was another one of her black African help? She had it terribly wrong. I was an educated American, and I would not let her treat me or my family like that. I wasn't thinking clearly at that point, because my anger had erupted like a cloudburst. I didn't even pick up on my own hypocrisy; the same way I deemed her an outsider was the same way people once saw me, an "illegal immigrant" in America. It was one thing for me to be triggered by her racist micro-aggressions, but it wasn't right for me to become territorial and exclusive.

"Dad, get your stuff! We are leaving. I will not tolerate this treatment. I would have made you a lot of money. But instead you decide to disrespect me. I'm going to make copies in America, where people don't lie."

I imagined that people with Tourette syndrome had a similar tendency to hurl profanities. It probably would have been better for me to hurl expletives. Instead, I was making stuff up like going to America where people didn't lie?

People looked at me with shock, dismay, or even confusion. Dad quickly collected his photos and followed my command. I felt a little insane. When a man who was making copies at a machine near my dad just stared at me, I became enraged: "And what are you looking at?" He quickly turned his head back to what he was doing, unsure of what my wrath would conjure up. Celeste and Fifi followed. From the corner of my eye, I saw Fifi smile. It was almost as if she wanted to stick her middle finger up at the owner and say something to the effect of: "And that's what happens when you mess with my sister."

It was very dramatic the way in which I stormed out of the building. Apparently, the Korean woman had followed my gaits in shock. Good! I wanted her to think twice about treating people that way.

The minute I was out in the open air I wanted to curl up and hide. *That was insane. Why did I do that?* Now my dad could never go back to that print shop. He would forever be known as the man with the neurotic daughter. Celeste reassured me though. "Dude, good for you for standing up for yourself. That was so wrong what she did." So much for me making a statement. We were still without copies of my dad's photos.

Another sister's husband, I had yet to meet that sister, would chauffeur us around for the rest of the day. It didn't take long for us to learn that he was a pastor. He was light skinned, thin, and wore his pants above his waist like Steve Urkle. The vibrato of his voice contradicted the authority that came from his words.

He spoke with much certainty, but his voice didn't carry a lot of authority on its own. I imagined that during his church services, he had to speak in a microphone to deepen his voice. I found him annoying and somewhat theatrical. Like when Fifi and Celeste and I were in the backseat and Dad and this pastor were in the front, Pastor started to prophesize. Celeste was right for calling him Rafiki from *The Lion King*. Sure, I could have gotten angry with her for associating every African with a character from a movie about animals, but I was subconsciously doing it, too. "You will have a boy!" he shouted in the car, just to ensure that Celeste knew the certainty of his conviction.

I guess in his congregation he was like God, and when he prophesized something people *ooh*ed and *aah*ed. In our case, I was wondering if Pastor Rafiki, which is what I called him in my head, was absolutely sure. "And you will get married this year!" he shouted looking at me. Was that part of his act? He couldn't just speak at a normal decibel, like the Wizard of Oz? It seemed to work when he mentioned my getting married, though. It was the thing I wanted more than anything else. In fact, when it came to determining when I would find love and get married, I made everyone a prophet. The car ride was at the very least entertaining.

We were going to the big shopping mall in Lusaka to eat some food, look for souvenirs, and hopefully find another print shop. We drove up to what was a giant mall that resembled what you would find in any suburb in the US. I was shocked as we drove into the multi-storied parking lot to find a spot. I was excited because this would validate my statement to Americans when I planned to say: "I was in Zambia. It's just like any city with highways and a shopping mall." Everyone always said that when they travelled to the third world but I wondered how many of those people visited a shopping mall, which was a true reflection of a country's modernity.

The crew found a lunch spot as I ran around the mall looking for an ATM. I needed to withdraw cash using my Bank of America Visa check card. But the first ten ATMs in the mall only took Mastercard. Was this a conspiracy to not give me money? But it was neat to walk from store to store and see how this mall compared to the ones in the States. The clothing stores looked different. The clothes looked like they were either manufactured in China or made in someone's home. There were tons of food courts that sold the typical fast food with a hint of African flare. For instance, a fried chicken place probably sold fried chicken with pepper. Before I could get too lost in the palatial place, I found an ATM that gave me enoug kwachas to last me my final day in Lusaka.

Walking through this mall to find stuff almost became comedic. First it was the ATM, and now it was a copy machine. We stopped in every store that resembled a print shop to see if we could find a copy machine, but we had no luck. "It's okay, Dad. I will just make copies of everything in the US."

"We can go to the market to find souvenirs for you. I have friends who can sell you good things for very cheap." I wanted the exact same wooden elephants that I saw in Botswana, but Dad insisted I not buy. "We can get better ones in Lusaka." Fine, I needed the elephants to be exactly the same if not better. There was so much to do in this one day. We needed to get Dad material for him to make his own canvases. We also wanted to get him paint. Celeste would also contribute to getting him oil paints. I felt like Daddy Warbucks, whipping out my AMEX card to make my dad's dreams come true. After each purchase, I qualified it by saying that our friends contributed a few dollars towards him getting material for his painting.

"But this is too expensive, my Doh'ta," Dad said as we walked around the fancy art shop and gallery. It was owned by a middle-aged British woman. I loved how the shop was situated on a plot of land decorated by trees and green grass. It was more than just a shop but rather a series of small buildings connected to each other. One was a shop and another was an art gallery of black artists.

"If you see Dad's paintings, you will see that he can do something even better than that," Fifi remarked as we looked up at an oil-on-canvas painting of a cheetah. Were Fifi and I just biased because he was our dad? I didn't know much about contemporary art. Celeste explained it as my dad having a naiveté with his art. I figured that was artist talk. What did that even mean?

"That's what makes it cool and unique." I didn't care if it was cool and unique. I wanted to protect my dad. I wanted to ensure that no one would make fun of him as the black village bumpkin when he presented a portfolio.

This was the kind of stereotypical, high-end place that catered to white people by exploiting black art. But this is what needed to happen for Dad to ensure he had a steady income. If they were going to exploit black artists, then it should be my father because he needed the money.

"Do you take new artists? Like how can one showcase art in your shop?" Celeste asked.

"They would simply bring their portfolio and have a website. Then if we like them, we would sell their art and we keep thirty percent."

A website and a portfolio? My dad didn't have either. In fact, how many of these black artists that they were exploiting had that? I thought that the third world made it easier to do this kind of work, but it was no different from the US. How could the average village person afford a domain name, a website, and to put together a portfolio. It was almost as if she were talking down to us, knowing that we could never achieve such measures. Her face changed when she calculated ninety US dollars for the painting, and I handed her my AMEX card.

It wasn't just a black-and-white thing, it was an economic phenomenon. The art gallery that we visited prior to this one was black owned. When I asked if my dad could showcase his artwork there, the black guy behind the desk was dismissive: "He would have to become a member and submit his art for the new showing." That was it. He didn't offer to give me a quote for membership and had no more to offer about the timeline to submit artwork. I wondered if it was my being black that warranted disrespect. I quickly learned that in Zambia, money talked louder than my skin color.

"What's the membership fee? I will go ahead and pay now," I said, just to prove a point. I relished in the shock factor that came with my paying. The man's eyes widened as he quoted what he thought would be a ridiculous amount of money. It came up to be about forty-five US dollars. From now on, these people would not look down on my father. They would know that he had a daughter in the US who was looking out for him. Just like that, Dad had paint supplies and a place to showcase his art. The last thing that needed to be done for him was to get him a passport and a bus ticket to go to Namibia to paint at the lodge. This would have to wait. It was time for us to get our souvenirs.

The minute Celeste announced that she needed to find a bathroom and I was left alone with Fifi in the clothing store, she batted her big eyes: "Sis, can you buy this for me? I need this blouse for work." Before I could even reply, Fifi dropped the black blouse in my cart along with my jersey and matching scarf and hat of the Zambia national soccer team, also known as Chipolopolo (pronounced Chee-polo-polo). It wasn't the price of the blouse that bothered me, but it was the principal. How dare this woman manipulate me in this way the minute my friend walks away? She must have been trying to read me all this time and realized that I was a softie. That Celeste was like my bodyguard. And she caught me off-guard, and I caved. That meant if she could do this once, she would do it again and tell the others. She acted entitled by being my sister. She was only my half-sister, and up until a week ago, I didn't even know that she existed. That's what I felt like saying to her, but instead I just paid for the shirt and gave it to her. *Doesn't she have to go to work soon? Why is she still with us?*

Thankfully, Fifi did leave after that incident to go to work, which left Celeste and I free of judgement to shop. Dad was so wrapped up in all the paint supplies that we bought him that he wouldn't keep tabs on everything we bought. Besides, we told him that we were buying things for everyone who contributed to the trip. It wasn't a lie. We were getting ourselves gifts for contributing to our journey to Zambia.

"Are you okay? Just hold your breath," Celeste said to me as we walked behind tents in the market to get to where Dad's friend was selling wooden statues. It smelled like sewage, and I got angry that I still had to put up with these smells. I didn't want to see this or be in this environment anymore. I just wanted my souvenirs and to head back to America. It was time.

"Dad, where are the elephants like you promised?" I asked as Dad's other friend showed us all the wooden animals that he was selling. I didn't walk through crap, literally, to not get these elephants. I didn't want a wooden lion or hippo. I wanted mahogany elephants like Dad promised.

"Dad, I don't want this. I just want the elephants." The polite African daughter went out the window, and I was now becoming the stereotypical, entitled American.

"Yes?" my dad asked while smiling. What the hell was he smiling about? I just told him that was not the elephant that I wanted. So he motioned for us to follow him to the next tent, as if the answer to humanity existed there. He was certain that my elephants would be in the next place. There were beautiful, mahogany, wooden elephants, but something was missing.

"Dad, where are the tusks?" *Dammit! I did not come all this way to buy elephants without tusks.* They needed tusks. "Dad, they don't have tusks. I need tusks."

"Sho', sho'," Dad tried to reassure me, but I saw no evidence of elephant tusks.

"Mr. K.K., can we get some with tusks?" Celeste asked, fearing that I would explode, especially after my episode in the print shop. She knew how much I wanted those elephants in Botswana because I kept talking to her about it. She also knew if I didn't get the elephants with tusks, the whole trip would be ruined. I was such a brat and felt bad about it, but also felt entitled to my tusks.

III. AN AFRICAN BLESSING

We sat inside Sad Stepmom's house waiting for the food to be served. Meanwhile, Dad insisted on fixing the zipper to my boot, which had broken a few hours prior. Was he a cobbler, too? I took off my shoe with skepticism as Dad pulled out needle and thread and got to work, with his glasses sitting at the tip of his nose. It was something he could do for me at no extra cost, but its real value was priceless. Whenever I wore my tan-colored boots, which I adored, I would have a story to tell about the journey they took walking with lions and cheetahs and then finally being repaired by my dad. *Voila!* The shoe was fixed, and it was good as new.

Dad insisted on a feast since this would be my last supper in Zambia. Of course, it would be African food, again. I would much rather be eating a plate of pasta at Latitude 15, but at this point, I only had to make a few more concessions and then I would be back to my normal routine in the US. Besides, it would make him happy. Zalika was there, sitting to the left of me on a stool. A million relatives—okay maybe not a million but it felt like it—were also crammed in the living room. The entire space was the size of a shed. We were sitting so close to each other that the room felt like a battleground between the stench of hot breath and aromas of spicy cuisine. To the right of me was Dad's easel and an unfinished painting. So this is where he got his inspiration to paint? There were no windows. The door across from us was the only access to sunlight. Sad Stepmom brought out the food on a platter and sat it on a table next to Celeste and me.

Yum! I licked my fingers as the gravy of the smoked fish and sautéed sauce trickled into the bed of my fingers. The fish was perfectly seasoned and skewered. I wasn't going to waste a single morsel. Ah, sweet savor! It was reminiscent of Ya Marie's cooking, which I missed. The food was delicious, and I no longer cared if I got diarrhea. I figured my stomach was strong enough by now. I was enraptured by the food eating, all the way down to the fish's scale, until I noticed Celeste and I were the only ones with plates in front of us. Everyone watched, smiled, and encouraged us to eat more. We were at Sad Stepmom's, and Zalika was also there, so I was pretty convinced that we weren't being poisoned.

"Dad, why aren't you guys eating?"

"We will eat after, my Doh'ta. We want you to eat well as this is your last night in Lusaka. You and Mama Celeste."

How would all these people ration what was left of the food?

"Dad, I'm full now," I said.

"Sho'. Let us pray then," Dad announced as the entire house became quiet and everyone bowed their heads on cue. "Heavenly Father, thank you for bringing Mama Mwanji and Mama Celeste here."

These prayer sessions seemed to always catch me off guard. Once he finished this prayer, it was time for my blessing. The moment I was hoping for but wasn't sure would happen! My youngest brother Maxwell, who lived in Cape Town, got me excited about this blessing months ago. "When dad visited me in South Africa, he gave me a blessing. He does this for all his kids, so I'm sure you will get a blessing, too, man." He made it sound like I would forever be protected in some bubble after my dad's blessing. When? What would it be like? I had so many questions for Maxwell, but he told me to just leave it up to dad. Then I wondered what would happen if I didn't get Dad's blessing. Did that mean he didn't value me as much as his other kids? I was relieved that I was not being left out of this movement. I had no idea what the process entailed, though.

"And now for your blessing, if you can give a small donation," he said as he held out his hand like a beggar. Everything and everyone in the room screeched and went into mannequin poses and all eyes were on me. A donation? Wait a minute, Maxwell never mentioned a donation. Was the donation part edited in after my dad saw me shop? My brain short-circuited as I was trying to determine if my dad was taking advantage of me. Why should

I have to give a donation for a blessing that was offered to me, which I didn't ask for? Was I being taken for a fool by the whole family? Hadn't I just given dad a ton of money in Zambia to buy art supplies? I had also given him a lot of cash to buy food. So how much should I give? Everyone was looking at me. If I gave too much then everyone would think I was rich. If I gave too little, then maybe they would ask for more. I didn't know what to do. I didn't want to pull out my wallet in front of everyone. I hadn't quite figured out this kwacha conversion. I was stalling.

"A donation? Okay. Celeste, how much should I give?" I asked, hesitating and forgetting that everyone else in the room could both hear me and speak English.

"Just give a twenty-dollar bill," she said, unsure, too. We were both dumbfounded.

"Thank you, my Doh'ta. Let us go outside for the blessing."

Celeste was only one step behind me, making sure nothing bad happened to me. Dad motioned for me to stand about ten feet from the house. He took a stick and drew a large circle in the dirt and motioned for me to step inside the circle.

"From this day forward, by the God of my ancestors, no one will ever harm you," Dad prayed. "You will have a power that will protect you from negativity and evil."

Why was he speaking like that? Now he started to sound like Pastor Rafiki. Should I have been laughing or crying from relief that I received the widely talked about blessing from my father? I guess I expected it to be flashier, like a David Blaine special. I know I watched too many movies, but where were the drums and where was the knife to puncture my flesh and to draw blood as a sacrifice? This was a lackluster performance.

"Mr. K.K., did you get that from *The Lion King*?" Celeste asked after the five-minute ceremony concluded. After the blessing, I was waiting for the euphoria, like a dope fiend after a hit. I expected to feel like *Crouching Tiger, Hidden Dragon*, or Neo from *The Matrix*, something. Nothing.

There was a spectacle for everything when it came to my dad. He ordered everyone to go back in the house to wait for our African clothes to be revealed. Dad built so much excitement around it that you would have thought we were getting a fitting for the Red Carpet.

Uncle was on his way with me and Celeste's garments. Meanwhile, I stood outside for a few moments with Sad Stepmom, who didn't seem so sad today. She looked like a little girl when she smiled, and I could see how Dad could have fallen for her all those years ago.

"Your dad was so sad until you arrived," she said. "It's like he has hope and energy again. You know for months he was not working. We were barely able to eat. I had to bargain here and there, and we had to put whatever change we had together." *Uh oh.*

I felt a request for money coming. I should have known. It was always about money. "So when you go back, please don't forget us. Please even send me a few dollars so I can feed the family." Celeste was right, they saw me as their Savior. It was too late to disappoint, so I agreed.

"Of course, I will," I said reluctantly. "You and my mom were very close, and I know she liked you very much. Therefore, you are the closest thing that I have to a mom. I will take care of you."

I half believed what I was saying but most of it came from my excitement about my escape in less than twenty-four hours. There was so much pressure to save the family, to give money. I wanted out, and tomorrow my wish would be granted. But weren't they the least bit ashamed of themselves? They were asking a stranger for money. Someone they didn't know. They knew, I'm sure, that I struggled in the US, but they didn't care because I didn't seem to be struggling now.

Thankfully, Uncle arrived with the frocks, which encouraged Sad Stepmom and me to join the others in the house. Celeste's looked cute, but mine looked like a colored rice sack. "Go try it on," Sad Stepmom and my sister Zalika exclaimed. Since Celeste had a thin enough layer on, she was able to put it on over her regular clothes. "Wow!" everyone exclaimed. Now it was my turn, and I had to change my clothes. "You can change in the bedroom," Sad Stepmom said.

The bedroom, which was also the kitchen, was a tiny hole on the right side of the house. It had a small crockpot and a pile of dishes on a table. And the beds were just a pile of blankets. I knew that this should have been commonplace to me by now, but I still wondered: Where was the sink to wash dishes? I stood frozen, unable to finish getting dressed. And how about a mattress? They had to at least have a mattress. Surely, I wasn't expecting Jollyboys accommodations, but everyone needs a mattress. My dad slept on the floor? This was a more devastating blow than the outhouse. Sleeping, the thing that brought me the most peace even in my worst of times, could not be enjoyed by my dad and his family. They slept in discomfort and on the floor, for goodness sakes! My seventy-something-year-old father had been sleeping on a cold, concrete floor for at least the last twenty years of his life. Discovering this site ate at my soul in the same manner as when I watched my mother being carried like a baby in her brother's arms. This level of impoverishment was palpable and left me with a sense of guilt. And here I was complaining about a donation for a blessing. Should I have given them more? Even though the clothes would appear bulky, I just decided to wear the new garment on top of my old clothes so I wouldn't have to come back to the bedroom to change. I never wanted to think about those blankets and that floor again.

It was like my dad spoke to Mother Nature and requested that we leave with a thundering applause. A torrential rainstorm came down. It was a rain I had never seen before; the raindrops looked like liquid daggers coming from the sky. There was lightening and then a thud. The rain landed on the tin roof, which created a clinking noise, like the whole country of Zambia was clinking their water glasses with a fork. "Please don't let me be stuck in this place. I just want to go home," I said to myself, feeling more claustrophobic as the door was slammed shut in the house, leaving the room airless and without light. The storm went as quickly as it came. Thank God! I wanted to leave, in that moment.

The skies cleared, and the sun blazed even stronger than before the storm. Dad ran outside to hear the commotion with Celeste in toe. I didn't dare move. Fear crippled me in my seat. "Oh my gosh, Martine," Celeste exclaimed halfway out the door. "The neighbor's tree was struck by lightning and fell. Thank goodness it didn't fall on the house." I couldn't look at the natural disaster, because it was too close to home both literally and figuratively.

It was finally time to leave. I couldn't bear to look at Zalika's face. It was probably the last time I would see her. I didn't plan on coming back, and the reality was that I wasn't going to be able to bring her to America. Once again, she was left behind. That must have killed her to have been left behind by our mom and now again by me. But how could I save everyone? I wasn't headed onto

CHAPTER 7

DEPARTURE

I held the key to my own worth authorization,
not Judge Colucci, nor the BIA, nor anyone else.

I. DAD

The Lusaka airport was subdued for the journey back. I wanted Dad to leave now but he insisted on seeing us off to the terminal. The longer he hung around, the more my stomach sank. He was making it impossible to say good-bye. Who knew I would quickly become attached to this old man?

"Okay, Dad," I said. "Here is a bag of things that you can give to Imani, and there are a few things to give to Fifi. Please give the envelope to Zalika." The envelope contained cubic zirconia studs. It was kind of ironic to exchange cubic zirconia in the place of diamonds in the continent that mined some of the world's most illustrious diamonds. But even if they only cost $50, she could probably sell them for more. Or she could give them to her pretty daughter, my niece. Imani was fashion conscious like me, so I left her the pair of sunglasses that I came with. I left Fifi with a few things for her daughter. The goal was to go back with very little and to give as much as I could, thereby relieving myself of guilt. I had about one hundred kwachas left, which I still couldn't figure out how it equated into dollars, but I gave it to my dad. "Here, Dad, take this." I inconspicuously handed him the money when Celeste wasn't looking. My dad was grateful whether I gave him one kwacha or a thousand, so I couldn't gauge the value of what I gave.

"Thank you, Mwanji. I love you."

"Dad, how are you getting home? Are you going to be okay taking the bus? You can use the money that I gave you to take a taxi." I knew that he wouldn't do that. I just needed a distraction to keep from crying. Out of thirty-three years of my life, I only had my dad for eleven days. I wasn't ready to give him up. And when would I see him again? What if I never see him again? "Okay, I love you, too, Dad," I broke down. Celeste tried to console me by making a joke.

"Okay, Mr. K.K. We will miss you," she said.

I saw my dad's eyes twinkle with a glint of water. If I witnessed my dad's tears, the compassion that it would draw out of me might cause me to turn over my life savings to him or something. It was time to go. Good-bye, Lusaka. Good-bye, Dad, I spoke softly into my heart.

"Let me take a picture of you," Celeste commanded as we were walking to the plane.

I was at a loss of words and was afraid that if I went to speak, I would burst into sobs. Every human emotion possible surfaced in these last eleven days, and they had all resurfaced incoherently in the final moments with my dad. There was anger that the time was so short, but also relief to go back to my comfort zone. Even in such an emotionally intense moment, he was still so excitable, and that made me want to laugh. Most of all, I felt an immense gratitude towards him, for giving me my identity back.

II. THE MINDY PROJECT

Celeste and I were zombies by the time we arrived at my apartment at 9:00 a.m. on a weekday. Life was going on around us per usual, meanwhile, I was just coming out of the biggest discovery of my entire life. It's interesting how we operate on different spectrums of life from person to person at the very same moment. If only my doorman or the clerk in the bodega understood the magnitude of what just happened to me! I was like an archeologist who had just discovered the oldest bones of mankind or something. It was November, and the Harlem air was cooler and crisper than what we were accustomed to in Zambia. How one came back to normal life after those eleven days, we kept asking each other. A good place to start was to perhaps go to the closest replica of Africa. We walked over to a Senegalese bistro almost three blocks from where I lived. The waitstaff were all Africans. I wanted to brag that I just got back from Africa, which finally qualified me as a true African. The waiter who took our order seemed to disappear for hours. Celeste and I laughed, taking comfort in the familiar.

"Celeste, you look so cute in my Paddington coat." Who knew if it was actually called that, but I bought the coat because it reminded me of Paddington Bear. We sat across from each other and reflected on the funniest moments about the trip. Most of it was too heavy to tackle right away.

"I'm trying to even figure out how to explain these eleven days to Ethan. They were gnarly. I don't even have the words."

Our time in Africa was life affirming. All these years I used my mother and her role in my life as the scapegoat for all my struggles and emotional handicaps: she failed to nurture me as a child; lied about her health condition; never thoroughly applied for my permanent US residency, and her death was my own death knell in terms of my immigration status. As long as I maintained such a mentality, I held onto my past demons and felt fully justified in doing so.

To truly walk in Ya Marie's shoes, I could not perceive her through the lens of my experience as her daughter. I started by objectively understanding her long-suffering journey through life. Suddenly, this monster of a woman became a delicate and wounded soul—fallible, just like me. She showed me love the best and only way she knew how, which appeared to be limited, because her own life experience involved deep-seeded pain rather than generous servings of love and kindness. But Zambia altered my perspective. My mom's love for me was as deep and rich as the red African soil and so was my dad's. They both wanted me. This was the freedom that I had been seeking all along that no citizenship could provide.

I wondered how much time my dad put into planning the unveiling of each facet of my life. He delivered each news to me with care and compassion. I reflected on the kind of strength that is required of an aging man to admit his shortcomings to his child. Now I understand why he couldn't have said all of this over the phone in our conversations.

I didn't just come out of these eleven days with a father and a mother, but I had more family than I could have hoped for.

"And I don't even know what to do next. Like how do I help my dad? Do I start sending him money?"

"I say wait. You can give him like a little bit every few months. Did I tell you the story about my mom and her family in the Philippines? She literally sent them every dollar she made in the US and went practically broke. When she needed help after she and my dad divorced, there was no one who offered to help her." I agreed with Celeste's point. I didn't owe anyone anything.

Celeste's flight back to Tahoe wasn't until the next morning. We had an entire afternoon and evening ahead of us. We wanted to vegetate because all the emotions from our trip started to come full force, like bullets at a shooting range. How would we process it all?

There was only one real way to do nothing. We sat on my roommate's plush, leather sofa and decided to zone out by watching television. We did not move. Not for hours. I recently learned how to use the Google Chrome feature on my phone.

"Hey, what about this show? It's called *The Mindy Project*? I have heard that it's good." There we were, two women bonded by almost two decades of friendship, a new dad, Africa, an unborn baby, and twenty-four episodes of *The Mindy Project*.

III. FREEDOM

Thank God, Uncle Andre agreed to take me to my mom's grave. Uncle Claude and him were the only two Kalaws that I trusted and whom I felt didn't resent me. Cemeteries made me nervous, not because of all the dead bodies, but because it was impossible to locate a grave. When I called the cemetery earlier in the week to find out where my mom's grave was, the woman on the other line said, "Yes, Louise Kalaw Cooper. She is in lot D," as if she were a car in a parking garage. What did lot D mean? There were over a million graves in lot D. Uncle Andre drove based on muscle memory. I sat in the passenger seat with two-dozen red roses in my lap, holding my breath. What if we didn't find her grave? This whole thing would be a disaster. How could Uncle Andre remember?

"It's over dere I tink," he said with a francophone accent that I sort of wanted to imitate because it kind of sounded cool.

"Okay, let's keep looking. I know it's close to here," he said as I started to panic. It was two days after Thanksgiving, Saturday, November 29, 2014, only one week after coming back from Zambia. The ground had hardened from the freezing temperature. The grass had bald patches from being dehydrated and cold. "Here it is." It was only a few yards away from where we were standing, but there was no way in hell that I would have found this on my own. I suddenly became nervous, because I wondered if Ya Marie would understand me. Her English was very basic when she died, and my Swahili was okay but not good enough to carry a conversation and say everything that I wanted.

"What language should I speak in, Andre?"

"She's with God, so she'll understand any language," Uncle Andre said. "I'mma go over dere to your grandpa's grave. Just come over when you're ready. Take your time. Dere's no rush."

Suddenly, I was shy. This place looked so foreign to me. To think that I had once been here to bury her. But that was August 1996. It was the last time I was here. I wasn't ready to return before this point.

"Ya Marie, *merci*," was how I began the conversation, by thanking her in French. It was how I ended many of our dinners where I thanked her for cooking the meal. It was part of my tradition. But this time I wasn't thanking her out of habit. I was indebted to her for everything she sacrificed to bring me to this moment. I cursed her and hated her for so long and all the while, she loved me. I still didn't understand how she endured so much trauma and pain without falling apart. She managed to pass that trait onto me.

I could never explain how I made it this far in my life. But I knew that it started with the single act of my mom choosing to bring me, her baby, with her. So I fell on my knees and thanked her over and over. And I told her about the journey to Zambia, Zalika, and Dad. She and my dad didn't love me the way I wanted them to, but they both loved me the best way they knew how. I forgave them both. "I have no more questions. I am complete, Ya Marie. But please, don't ever let go of me. I need you. I will always need you." I left her with the roses and a piece of the fabric that I picked out for her from Zambia. There was no white, dove-like bird flying around the cemetery, but I felt my mom's energy, and I saw her smile. I felt her love.

IV. LET IT BE GREEN

May 4, 2007, started out as a typical morning with a phone call from Charlotte. I would let it go straight to voice mail this time since I was running late for work. But as soon as the message was left and the phone started blinking, I felt a strong urge to listen to Charlotte's message. I had to brace myself. What asinine thing did Judge Colucci do now? Here we went: "Martine, I hope that you're sitting down for this. Are you sitting down?" she asked in the message as if it was a live conversation. I sat at the edge of my bathtub, in my house slippers, my hair curler sitting on the ledge of my toilet heating up, my blouse not fully buttoned, and my toothbrush in hand. "I have in my hand a letter from the BIA." What was with all the pauses? Could she speak faster? I had to get to work. "They declined Colucci's order. They refused to review the case any further, and they remanded the case back to Colucci to finalize and close. They are making Colucci issue you a green card! He has no recourse this time. Martine? Martine? This is unbelievable! This almost never happens with the BIA. They never look at the file this closely. They read your story, Martine. Attached to this top sheet is an eight-page letter from the BIA. They recapped your story in their own words. They read your story, Martine. This is a miracle! My dear, we won! Call me back."

"Oh, wow," were the only words I could formulate, but not even aloud, only in my head. It didn't matter. There was no one in site except my own reflection in the mirror. I didn't know what to say to her. Congratulations? The battle had been so long and endless that I almost forgot what I was fighting for. I lost sight of this day. And here it came, so unexpectedly, while I was half naked and brushing my teeth. I looked at the girl in the mirror, and she stared back, bewildered, befuddled. I fell to the floor and wept. They were tears of self-pity and joy. But I wouldn't believe it until I saw it. What if this was another cruel joke?

The BIA did in fact study my case, particularly since it passed through their files for the second time. They acknowledged all the poverty, turmoil, and abuse that I had endured and vindicated me. This body, made up of fifteen judges, had a reputation of not reviewing cases because of overload. Statistically, the probability of getting a case approved by the BIA was small, especially due to the backlog after 9/11. Their review and decision should not have been a shock to me because it was their judicial duty; but in that moment, I recognized it for the miracle that it was. I liked to think that I had won my case by sheer luck, persistence, and a strong support team. But there was no prescription that I could write to others to guarantee the same outcome.

All the years of pain, tears, and torture culminated to this one moment, in this one tiny envelope. It was just me again in another moment of glory. I sat on my bed with the unopened envelope in my hand waiting for something more climactic, like a dove suddenly flying into my room, hovering over my victorious head. I had placed so much importance on this document as my ticket to freedom, so this moment had to be monumental. So what if it was still two days away until Independence Day? July 2nd was technically the day that the *Declaration of Independence* was ratified by the US Congress. In essence, July 2, 2007, was my independence day.

This moment was surreal. In any second now, I would see and feel my permanent resident card. Oh my goodness! My hands were shaking as I held the envelope in my right hand to read the sender's address: United States Citizenship and Immigration Service (USCIS). I was like Charlie from *Charlie and the Chocolate Factory*, and I had the golden ticket in this envelope! I ripped open the envelope with the same force and might as the tearing down of the Berlin Wall. *Oh, please let it be green!* I needed the satisfaction of knowing that this document I had been chasing for almost a decade was real and was as grand as what I set it up to be. A flimsy piece of plastic sat in the envelope with my name, alien registration number, and "Permanent Resident" written on it. Great, I was still considered an alien. I should have been relieved and overjoyed, but a wave of exasperation and disappointment hit me. So this manufactured piece of shit is what I based my freedom on? This simple card determined my worth?

"Tini!" my friend Noah exclaimed on the other line three minutes later. "Did you get your green card?"

"Yes, I did," I said while trying to sound more excited than I was.

"That's so amazing! Is it green?"

"No, it's not." After a long silence, I clarified, "It's actually cream colored."

I had put so much of my life and my energy into chasing a figment of my imagination. This green card wasn't what was going to free me. Even with this card I was still without a nationality, I was still stateless. As a result, I could not obtain a passport to travel outside of the United States. I did not hold all the rights and privileges of being an American yet, like voting. I would have to wait another five years, until 2012, to be eligible to apply for US naturalization.

It was time for the greatest challenge of all, which was to break down the mental prison I was locked into from years of abuse, neglect, and denial. I held the key to my own worth authorization, not Judge Colucci, nor the BIA, nor anyone else.

EPILOGUE

"**T**he President of the United States resides in the White House."
Phew! Five years after getting my green card, I was finally eligible to apply for US citizenship. It wasn't that I impressed myself by getting the correct answer during my interview; the acknowledgement that I was getting closer to becoming a US citizen, yet one thing stood in the way, was the real issue. The immigration officer interviewing me asked me to read a sentence off a piece of paper to test my English ability. This was insulting at this point, I thought. I don't mean to brag—but I'm one of the most articulate English speakers out there! Why even bother testing my reading and writing abilities? But I relished every step along the way. Anything to keep from the dreaded final question: "Where is your passport?"

My heart dropped. This was it. It was over. I might as well just walk out that door and forget citizenship. This was the pinnacle of my immigration dreams, and I was so close. Maybe I could get used to being a permanent resident for the rest of my life. Just because I didn't have a passport didn't mean that I could never travel, at all. I could apply for a temporary travel document. I didn't need to see the world. Besides, traveling was expensive. And voting? Well, even US citizens didn't always perform their optional duty of voting. Maybe it wasn't the end of the world. Who was I kidding? It felt like the end of my world. I had been holding onto this daydream of becoming an American, and yet it alluded me. All these years of struggle and then hopefulness after getting my green card but it was for naught. It wasn't about becoming a US citizen to gain permission to feel or be American. I was American regardless of what anyone said or thought about me. It was simply a matter of affording the privileges that a stateless immigrant like me could never have with just a permanent US resident status but no passport.

"I don't have one. My lawyer couldn't be here today, but she wanted me to provide you with this document. I don't have residency from my birth country of Zambia. We have made countless attempts to obtain citizenship but according to their constitution, I'm not eligible. We . . ." I continued to say more, to defend myself, but he looked away and proceeded to look through files and clicked his skinny fingers on the keyboard. He must have tuned me out because he didn't even encourage me to keep speaking. I wanted to explain to him my seven-year ordeal and beg him to take pity on me. Right now, he was my final arbiter. Couldn't he see that I was a good person? I just wanted to be given a chance. Please, mister?

"You have had quite the journey," he said, solemnly. It was a slight but grand gesture. He tilted his head to one side as if he were taking me in. It was almost like he wanted to capture the before and after image of me.

"Yes, I have," I replied. Where were these tears coming from? Go away tears! This was not the time. I couldn't cry in my interview. Besides, I wasn't wearing waterproof mascara. I just wasn't expecting that level of compassion and affirmation from a stranger. All he had to do was take one look at my case summary, and he was able to commiserate with me. But I was still shaking. His compassion didn't mean anything if it didn't end in my becoming a US citizen. My leg felt like it was going into spasms, so I double-crossed my legs to contain it. He took a stamp and lifted it up. Was he approving my application or denying it? I couldn't tell. My fate lay in a stamp. This was unbearable. *Stamp!* He lifted the application and handed it to me: "You have been approved," he said, with a stern face while he smiled with his eyes.

My eyes lit up like night beams, and I shot up in my chair. I dared not question him before he changed his mind. "Thank you so, so much!" I wanted to hug him, toss him in the air, kiss him on the cheeks. What gesture would be appropriate to thank someone for saving his or her life?

My Swearing in Ceremony or my Oath was scheduled for Friday, August 12, 2012. At first, it was scheduled in Brooklyn, but they rerouted it to Lower Manhattan. I wanted to be patriotic, so I wore a blue, polka-dot jumper. Three of my friends were kind enough to get up at God knows what time to get to my swearing-in ceremony, which started at 8:30 a.m. The first two hours were protocol. There were at least sixty of us. We were seated in rows with a wobbly stage, a podium, and a projector screen in front.

"Please stand when we call your country of origin," a woman spoke into the mic. She never introduced herself, but I guessed that she was the Master of Ceremony. There were no assigned seats, so I appreciated the randomness of whom I sat next to. There were quite a handful of Italians in the room, Sri Lankans, and someone from Azerbaijan. As boring as the entire procession was, this symbolism as all of us coming from all ends of the earth and uniting as Americans was touching.

"And now, a message from The President of the United States of America." The Master of Ceremony made it sound like President Obama was going to walk out on stage. Well, was he? I sat at the edge of my seat. Wouldn't this make for a memorable swearing in? But instead, the lights were dimmed, and Obama appeared on the screen with a message of hope and fulfilling the American promise.

"And now, we would like for you to pick up the American flags that were under your seat and wave them as we solute America." They were miniature, plastic American flags with a plastic handle. They must have been left-over stock from the Dollar Tree after the 4th of July or something. "Please sing along with the words," she commanded.

> "If tomorrow all the things were gone
> I'd worked for all my life
> And I had to start again
> With just my children and my wife . . ."

"Sing louder," the maestro said through the mike. She must've been the hall monitor in grade school because of how insistent she was on us following the rules. I heard a few giggles from the woman who was sitting right behind me. Yes, that was the woman from Italy. She was chatting through the entire ceremony. I liked her just by taking one look at her. She didn't take life too seriously.

> "I'd thank my lucky stars
> To be living here today
> Cause the flag still stands for freedom
> And they can't take that away . . ."

"Make sure you're waving your flags like this," she instructed, as if this wasn't something a trained monkey could do.

> "And I'm proud to be an American
> Where at least I know I'm free . . ."

"Sing louder," Hall Monitor urged. That's when Italian woman let out the loudest burst of laughter, and she didn't stop just there. After every lyric she laughed louder. Then the whole row behind her picked up on her laughter and continued. I was trying so hard to concentrate. This was so exiting, so funny, so stupid. It was impossible to contain it any longer. The laughter was like a contagion that attacked instantly. I let out the loudest and most powerful belly laugh. I was finally releasing all the tension, the residue of trauma and the agony. The entire room of sixty newly naturalized Americans fell into a cacophony of laughter. Clearly, I wasn't the only one who needed to release and laugh the pain away.

With my newfound US citizenship, I was forced to let go of my lifelong, self-identifying story and create a new one; the Martine that I had allowed myself to become was a victim and now I lacked the all-encompassing obstacle(s) that defined me. Tragically, I relied so heavily on my pitiful story because it authenticated and affirmed my humanness. After my journey to Zambia, I was validated by knowing that I was loved.

Zambia forced me to excavate and accept my past—including all aspects of my relationship with my mother—on my own terms. By allowing the immigration system to define for me the errors that she made and translate those determinations into the sentiments I held towards her, I was giving all the power to that construct, rather than taking full ownership of it. Worse yet, I was reducing my mother to a list of transgressions, collected to fit the parameters of a legal statute. By relying on this framework, I was depriving both my mother and myself of our humanity.

All these years, I had been in search of inner peace by looking outside of myself; I thought the US citizenship would provide the elixir to my angst-filled soul. But to create this desired sense of freedom, I needed to forgive myself and others, let go of the past, and truly recognize that I had a responsibility in all that occurred. Only in this way could I then grab hold of my personal power and move through the fear. Yes, by raising my voice and speaking my truth I was finally able, along with my posse of warriors, to navigate through my immigration battle and conquer it. With this realization, I now have the body armor to go back into the fire and to pull others out.

Current immigration policy and processes are fundamentally flawed from a legal and administrative standpoint. The current administration continues to revoke existing relief programs for immigrants such as Temporary Protected Status (TPS) and Deferred Action for Childhood Arrivals (DACA). TPS was initially created during the era of George H. W. Bush to grant people the ability to resettle in the US due to ongoing conflict or natural disasters that took place in their own countries. Many of the 300,000 TPS holders have been in the US for almost twenty years and have homes, families, and jobs in the US. DACA offers qualified undocumented immigrants who entered the US as children (DREAMers) temporary lawful status. However, as these programs are revoked, we run the risk of the undocumented immigrant number increasing and, therefore, a greater likelihood for increased deportations, detainment, or individuals who fall into the immigration court system.

There is a significant backlog of cases in immigration courts and immigration judges (IJs) have quotas. While some IJs have bad reputations like Judge Colucci, there are others who intend to fairly review cases. However, with the pressure that they receive from the Attorney General to expedite the review of cases, they are left with little power to be fair. This will ultimately create a preponderance of cases like mine where the judge was quick to deport me, and I had to keep appealing over the course of seven years. I don't wish this fate on anyone. I intend to do something about it.

While I embark on this conversation of making immigration courts independent from the Justice Department, I also agree that some aspects of immigration processes have to be personalized and specific to the individual.

My immigration approach was multi-layered and attacked the issue from all angles. One day I would like to create a nonprofit organization that offers to the undocumented access to four services I received to acquire my freedom: financial investment for my education, a reputable immigration attorney, a mental health practitioner with an expertise in immigration-related cases, and an immigration consultant.

Education was the very thing that gave me access to a community that supported me along my undocumented immigrant journey. It exercised my critical thinking skills, illustrated that I had good moral character, and provided me with the academic pedigree that I needed to establish my career. It all started with Judge Wells's decision to invest in my private school education. If more investors knew the potential contribution that undocumented immigrant youth have to our future economy, perhaps they would be willing to invest in their higher education.

It was not enough to rely on a pro bono immigration attorney—disgruntled, underpaid, and overloaded—to give my case the proper attention it needed. This was the greatest lesson from the old adage—you get what you pay for. Although I could barely afford Charlotte England's fees, the work and effort she put into my case exceeded the cost.

My psychologist understood the context of my immigration situation and the shameful feelings that went along with being an illegal alien, which made a world of difference in maintaining my sometimes-frail sanity. During our sessions, I never had to waste time explaining the nuances of immigration law, which allowed us to spend more time treating the symptoms. The treatment I received from Dr. Saltz was incomparable to that of my previous counselors and psychiatrists because she understood the immigration phenomenon.

Finally, having a technical assistant like Heather, Elizabeth Giles, Giselle, or Dionne to act as my companion at the hearings and to help me fill out time-sensitive paperwork was invaluable. All this work provided the healing that was necessary to break through the mental prison that I created. I was able to finally see myself according to my own terms. Today, it's with great pride that I reclaim my full identity: I'm an illegal immigrant. I'm an undocumented immigrant. I'm a nonimmigrant late overstay. I'm a woman without a country, and before that, I was a girl without a country. I'm an orphan. I'm a survivor—a self-made woman. I plead guilty and proud of it. I am Congolese and Zambian, but mostly Congolese. I am African, and I am American. Throughout my entire journey, somebody loved me before I even knew how to love myself.

THANK YOU

Thank you to everyone who believed in my story before it was published. We did it!

Afriyie Fruster, Alba Reyes, Alexandra Knights, Amanda Mayhew, Amit Janco, Amy Anderson, Ana Nuchowich, Ana Kalline Jeronimo Silva, Anastasiya Blyukher, Andrea Schwartz, Andres McAlister, Andrew Ulon, Anna-Marie Woodard, Annie Temmink, Anzor Khipashvili, Arly Tuysuzian, Bahar Alagheband, Behnaz Gohari, Ben Rubinger, Bendita Malakia, Bill Allard, Brian Giacomello, Brittany Cowan, Calin Trenkov-Wermuth, Candida Reid, Carine Camara, Carol Fitzpatrick, Caroline Cavanaugh, Chandra Claypool, Chandra Talpade, Mohanty, Cheryl Lassota, Chris Burkett, Diana Thomas, David Wright, Davina Prabhu, Denise Gibbon, Denise Badila, Divya Rane, Donna Buckley, Eyasu McCall, Edvige Barrie, Emily Mintz, Erick Nunez, Esha Tewari, Farah Tayfour, Florencia Iriondo, Gale Green, Gene Kalaw, Glenn Jean, Grant Wasch, Gretchen Gilliland, Group Four Design Studio, Manuel Zavala, Gypsy Lorenzo, Heather Kinsman, Herry Pierre-louis, Ingrid Aielli, Isabel Ezrati, Iyore Adonri, James Lane, Jane Zemba, Javed Rezayee, Jay Swett, Jemima Mann Baha, Jennifer Gandia, Jessie Resnick, Joanna Moskwa, Jocelyn Jandovitz, Jon Bellona, Jon Hysell, Jonathan Rick, Josh Rubinger, Juanita Laurel, Karen LaChiana, Karen Sanjines, Kate Hutchinson, Katherine, Johnson, Kathy Monroe, Katie Roland, Kevin Gibson, Kimberley Smith, Kiranjot Kaur, Kris Watson, Kristen Love, Kunwei Lin, Lakuan Smith, Lauren Marquis, Leang Chung, Lee Constantine, Leila Kalousek, Leila Mesdaghi, Leila Sarvghadi, Li Rosario, Lidtz Jean-Philippe, Lili Trenkova, Lisa Genovese, Liyat Haile, Lorena Requejo, Lucas

Mentasti, Luciana Maxim, Luka Prodanovic, Manal Ataya, Marians Mendoza, Maurice Owen-Michaane, Meghan Genovese, Melisa Soto, Melissa Michaane, Meredith Bonham Michael Quinn, Michelle Kurian, Michelle Chaitman-Lynch, Michelle Nakash, Michelle Martin, Milan Prodanovic, Minnedore Green, Molly-Jane Rubinger, Monica Ramos, Monica White, Monique Tucker, Muland Kalaw, Nancy Waldman, Ndaya K, Obio Ntia, Oscar Zumaran, Owen Davies, Paola Budinas, Philippe Dejean, Phyllis Breland, Raina Bartlett, Randi Vallone, Raymon Walker, Rebecca Fabricant, Renee Hoskin, Romain Fravien, Ronya Foy Connor, Roshan Bharwaney, Rosita Pardo, Said Sabir, Sallie Rush, Sara Cohen, Sara Edeiken, Sarah Wolff, Selena Coppock, Sharon Topi, Sheena Gordon, Sherieka Smallwood, Shoko Carpenter, Sooji Im, Stefania Yanachkov, Stephanie Chun, Sunjay Dixit, Sylvia Alvarenga, Tajuana Cheatham, Taryn Hill, Tawanda Abdelmouti, Tenise Barker, Tracy Schmidt, Tracy Cooper, Varun Gudiseva, Weiwen Nie, Wendy Johnson, Yuliya Rimsky, and Yvette Miller.

ABOUT THE AUTHOR

Martine Kalaw is an author, speaker, and spokeswoman on current immigration laws and reform. Martine was a *Huffington Post* contributor on the topic of immigration. She is a graduate of Hamilton College and Syracuse University's Maxwell School with a master's in public administration and immigration law. She is an organizational development consultant with over eight years of designing professional/management training and building learning and development strategies for Fortune 500 companies and technology start-ups on a global level. While she currently lives in Washington, DC, she considers New York City her first home. Now that Martine is a US passport holder, she's an avid world traveler.

CPSIA information can be obtained
at www.ICGtesting.com
Printed in the USA
FSHW020307230119
55189FS